THE
NEW ROYAL
FAMILY

ROBERT JOBSON

THE
NEW ROYAL
FAMILY

Prince George, William and Kate,
The Next Generation

WITH EXCLUSIVE PICTURES BY ARTHUR EDWARDS MBE

JOHN BLAKE

Published by John Blake Publishing Ltd,
3 Bramber Court, 2 Bramber Road,
London W14 9PB, England

www.johnblakepublishing.co.uk

www.facebook.com/johnblakebooks ⬛
twitter.com/jblakebooks ⬛

First published in hardback in 2013
This revised and updated paperback edition published in 2014

ISBN: 978-1-78219-759-1

British Library Cataloguing-in-Publication Data:

A catalogue record for this book is available from the British Library.

Design by www.envydesign.co.uk

Printed in Great Britain by CPI Group (UK) Ltd

5 7 9 10 8 6 4

Papers used by John Blake Publishing are natural, recyclable products made from wood grown in sustainable forests. The manufacturing processes conform to the environmental regulations of the country of origin.

Every attempt has been made to contact the relevant copyright-holders, but some were unobtainable. We would be grateful if the appropriate people could contact us.

ACKNOWLEDGEMENTS

The birth of any baby is always special, a moment of undiluted joy and celebration. But the birth of a future sovereign is extra special – an historic point in time for Britain and the rest of the Commonwealth to savour. This birth marks a new beginning for a *New Royal Family*. Born into a multi-media age, Prince George will have to adapt to a fast-changing world – perhaps like no other future monarch – and one day reign over a new, more streamlined, modern monarchy, not to mention an increasingly diverse population. This book celebrates this highly significant moment in our history and attempts to shed light on the story behind the headlines.

I am delighted that my good friend and mentor Arthur Edwards MBE agreed to illustrate this book. His photographs are as brilliant as his career as the leading royal photographer of his generation. His decision to generously donate his fee to the charity Kids Company will help others, while his photographs that adorn this publication will, I am sure, give the reader great pleasure. He took all these photographs as an accredited photographer for the bestselling *Sun* newspaper. He has always enjoyed a good working relationship with members of the Royal Family, which shows in the iconic pictures he takes. We first worked together in 1991 when I started my career reporting royalty; I have always valued his wise counsel and honest friendship.

This book could not have been written and turned around at such rapid speed without the sheer hard work of my editor Chris Mitchell and the rest of the team at John Blake Publishing. Thanks, too, to my publisher John Blake for believing in the project and giving the go ahead for our fourth book together. Thanks also to Rosie Virgo for her unstinting support and to Toby Buchan, who edited my *Diana: Closely Guarded Secret*.

I am greatly indebted to many others, some I happily acknowledge here, others, for obvious reasons, remain unnamed. With that in mind, I would like to thank the press teams at Kensington Palace, Clarence House and Buckingham Palace, especially Dr Ed Perkins, Nick Loughran, Patrick Harrison, Ailsa Anderson LVO and James Roscoe. I would like to thank '*The Happy Elephants*' too – they know who they are.

I would also like to thank my colleagues at the *London Evening Standard*, particularly my friend Ian Walker, Deputy Editor, whom I have worked with for more than two decades, and my editor Sarah Sands. I would also like to thank Managing Editor Doug Wills. I would also like to thank my friend Ken Wharfe MVO, who has always supported me amid the slings and arrows. Lastly, I would like to thank my family for their love and for always being there through thick and thin.

ROBERT JOBSON
August 2013; May 2014

CONTENTS

PREFACE

William and Kate's baby, Prince George Alexander Louis, will be the first truly modern British monarch – descended from coalminers as well as kings. One day, this child will lead a very different monarchy; one that is more streamlined, inclusive and more cost effective. In this modern global media world, this child will be watched like no other; something George's parents will be acutely mindful of. If this child was simply the heir to the throne, that would be enough to retain the interest of the watching world, but that is not all George is. For the first time in history, this first baby would have become sovereign irrespective of its sex. It will also be the first for 300 years – since the reigns of the sisters Queen Anne and Queen Mary II – to have a commoner, not aristocrat or royal, as its mother.

Despite this, being Prince William and Kate's first child, he will, of course, be born into a world of vast wealth, ancient ancestry, palaces and royal titles. Privileged and princely, their baby will be the most famous in the world. The parents, and many others, will do their best to stifle the inevitable media frenzy, insisting the baby is just like any other. But the truth is this child will be special. Very special.

The scrapping of the ancient primogeniture laws – signed off by the Queen in Perth ahead of the Commonwealth Heads of Government Meeting (CHOGM) in 2011, before being passed in both Chambers of Parliament in the UK – signalled, too, a new dawn for the Royal Family. It is an important moment because it shows the House of Windsor is prepared to progress with the times. It certainly has its fair share of ancient traditions but it is an institution that embraces the times it serves.

The constitutional wheels of change were set in motion with the Succession to the Crown Bill, introduced into Parliament by the MP Keith Vaz. Importantly, the Bill had the Queen's support. When it passed, which it did when it received the Royal Assent on 25 April 2013, it meant that if the Duke and Duchess of Cambridge's first-born had been a girl, then she would automatically be Queen Regnant after the reign of 'King' William, her father, irrespective of whether her parents produce a younger brother later.

Through this Bill, the ancient laws of primogeniture – 1,000 years of history with royal male precedence – were scrapped before William and Kate's baby was born, perhaps for the avoidance of any doubt. Some, including Prince Charles, did raise concerns that the Bill in its entirety had not been given due consideration. Had all the 'i's been dotted and t's been crossed' was his main concern; it was nothing to do with him supporting an outdated law. The change in the royal succession rules brought this modern monarchy into the 21st century, ending sex discrimination in an instant. There can be no doubt that, to be relevant, this unelected institution simply has to be popular, and to do this it has to be seen to adapt to the times it serves.

William and Kate are 'absolutely determined' to raise their baby their way. Neither will allow the child to be weighed down by royal tradition or expectation, despite the pressure of birthright. Kate, who has refused to hire an army of servants up until now, is said to be reluctant to allow an army of old-school nannies to take charge when they take up residence at the palatial Apartment 1A at Kensington Palace, after an expensive renovation. However, it is expected that the pressures of her workload and public duties will mean she will have to have at least one nanny to support her. But, after all, that is no different to many middle-class working mothers who often do employ nannies. Kate's mother Carole, who she often turns to for advice, will, of course, also be there for support in the early days, and beyond. There has even been talk from Kate's indiscreet uncle that she will effectively move in for the first few months.

William and Kate will not want their baby – who, as a boy, will inherit a £700 million Duchy of Cornwall trust fund – wrapped in cotton wool and mollycoddled. Instead, they hope the child born to reign will be free to express individuality. For William – the last royal baby born to reign before his own child – it was a markedly different affair to his own father's childhood. Despite his extraordinary birthright, his mother had insisted her baby would be raised her way. 'Kate is just as determined as Diana was,' one source close to her told me. Princess Diana famously battled like a tigress to avoid the constraints of royal life being thrust upon William and Harry too early, because she feared it would stifle their carefree development as children. Her stance – at the time at first opposed by traditionalist Prince Charles – helped shape William into the balanced young man he is today.

Diana had a clear idea of how she wanted her sons raised. She axed their first nanny, Barbara Barnes, for protesting too vigorously that 'the Princes need to be treated differently'. The Princess was having none of it. She wanted her boys to be as balanced and 'normal' as possible, almost in spite of their extraordinary birthright. Her second nanny, Olga Powell, deferred to Diana on everything; there could be only one boss in the nursery. That said, Diana was known to allow either the nanny or the bodyguard to discipline her royal children if they stepped out of line as Ken Wharfe, William's former Scotland Yard personal protection officer, recalled: 'I remember on a number of occasions both William and Harry getting a smack if they were naughty. Another of their nannies, Jessie, knew exactly how to keep Harry under control. A large woman, she used to pin Harry to the wall with her stomach until he calmed down. They were given a sound grounding from royal staff, and both boys soon learned that, despite their royal rank, there was a pecking order, and they had to do what they were told. I am sure William and Kate will pass this on.'

Ever since, William, perhaps as a direct response to his mother's almost obsessive craving for normality, has longed to be known as 'just William'. He has said on many occasions that he does not want to be addressed as 'Sir' or 'Your Royal Highness'. Now that William is about to become a father himself with an 'ordinary' girl raised in a traditional middle-class English family, he, and his wife Kate, will face the same dilemma of how to raise their children.

All the signs show that William wants to follow his late mother's lead. He will want to be a modern, hands-on father – spending time in the nursery, for example, and being there whenever possible for bedtime. He and Kate have even chosen Kensington Palace – the scene of so many happy childhood memories for him and his brother Harry – as the place to raise their family. Restoration of Princess Margaret's old, very grand apartments are due for completion in autumn 2013, when the young family will take up residence. But no matter how hard they try to raise their first-born to be as ordinary as possible, they will inevitably be fighting an uphill battle.

So what sort of childhood can this 'special one' expect? Ken Wharfe knows better than most, as the avuncular ex-cop hand-picked to head up the princes' protection often stepped into the 'parental' role. He was fun and exciting, just what the royal boys wanted. He told me, 'This baby will have an amazing childhood, of that I am sure. But it will be different, of course. For one thing, he or she will have to get used to having an armed Scotland Yard personal protection officer watching over them night and day.'

Ken believes Prince William's own childhood is the blue-print he and Kate will base their own family life on. He said, 'William and Harry were such fun-loving children. They loved to play-fight and when they hit each other they meant it. Sometimes when I tried to break up the fights I was on the receiving end of their punches, they'll vouch for that. They pulled no punches when they did, I can tell you. They would fight dirty, too, thinking nothing of punching you where it really hurts. But Diana encouraged it. She thought it was good for them to just be boys.'

Ken recalled that, while some royal family members treated William differently from Harry, it did not bother the prince, which is something William and Kate's first baby may have to deal with too. Harry would often joke that if William did not want to be king he would happily step into his shoes. But it is fair to say that at first William was reluctant to think about the enormity of his future role. 'I remember William would often say to his mother that when he grew up he would become a policeman so he could protect Diana. Harry would often butt in and say, "Don't be stupid, William. When you grow up you're going to be the king, that is all there is to it.'"

But they had a ball. Ken joined them on trips to fun fairs, burger bars and go-kart racing. Once, he recalled how they tore up Prince Charles's beloved garden at Highgrove House when they turned it into a racetrack. 'I don't think Prince Charles was too impressed when he saw the mess they had made to his garden. He came up to me and remarked, "I suppose you're the new Bernie Ecclestone."'

Diana was adamant and strong in rejecting the interfering from outside influences. 'A child's stability arises mainly from the affection received from their parents, and there is no substitute for affection,' she said when describing how she would always make sure that William and Harry came first. Kate and William have similar values. There will be areas, though, where the baby's childhood will almost certainly follow a traditional path; education, for example. Previous heirs to the throne – like the Queen – never went to school and were taught by a governess. Prince George is set for a private school education at a top public school before going on to university like his parents.

Kate, who comes from a normal, if wealthy, middle-class family will, like Diana, do it her way. One source close to her said, 'Catherine is an extremely strong woman. Family, a close family, is extremely important to her. It has been her bedrock and I feel sure she will want the same safe environment for her children.'

Privately educated, Kate enjoyed an idyllic time with her siblings Pippa, 20 months her junior, and James, born in 1987. She loved dressing up, going to Brownies and starring in school plays. She was sporty, accomplished at tennis and hockey, and lived in a comfortable house in the Berkshire countryside. When asked about having a family during her engagement interview,

Kate made it clear she wants a large family. 'It is very important to me,' she said.

Although primarily based in London, William and Kate will look to take their family out to the countryside very often, as both of them have fond memories of their own childhood country pursuits. One former royal staff member recalls how William and Harry loved riding. On one occasion, William roared with laughter as his brother got into trouble on Will's old Shetland pony. From the moment he rode it, the pony seemed to take on its new owner's wilful personality and started doing exactly as it pleased. It refused to be led or ridden as the mood took it, and it seized every opportunity to bolt off with Harry in the saddle, run for anything from a quarter to half a mile, find the nearest stream and dump Harry in it. The scene was straight out of a Thelwell book, with the minimum of a groom, protection officer and William all on foot, trying to catch up with, and hopefully catch, the beast. It is moments such as these – moments of easy fun and happiness – that the royal parents will hope they can give to their young family.

Any new royal baby will be given a good grounding, not just from the parents, but from the royal staff as well, while William and Kate are on official duties. The young Prince George will soon learn that, despite his royal rank, there is a need for both humility and normality. Both William and Harry are prime examples of how a successful childhood can result in fine young men, leaders of both the people around them and, one day, the country. A similar childhood will stand the future king in good stead for his future career.

CHAPTER 1

THE CHANGING OF THE GUARD

*'She'll want to hand over knowing she's done everything she possibly could
to help, and that she's got no regrets and no unfinished business; that she's done
everything she can for the country and that she's not let anyone down –
she minds an awful lot about that.'*

HRH PRINCE WILLIAM, DUKE OF CAMBRIDGE
TALKING ABOUT HM THE QUEEN

A white-haired, well-loved, elderly lady cautiously climbed the steps of St Paul's Cathedral, without her partner of 64 years at her side. For once, she appeared frail. As she slowly progressed – followed by her immediate family – that abiding air of implacable confidence seemed to escape her. It was an image that potentially had profound implications for the Royal Family. The date was 5 June 2012 and Her Majesty Queen Elizabeth II, Britain's oldest ever monarch, was there for the Diamond Jubilee Service of Thanksgiving, an event held in her honour. It had been an exhausting weekend of national holiday, complete with pomp, pageantry and tumultuous celebration. It had clearly taken its toll on her.

Outside, the loyal Union flag-waving well-wishers kept on coming. By dawn, thousands had already gathered at the nation's Cathedral to stand patiently behind steel police barriers. One woman said she had risen at 3.30 a.m. to travel to the historic event from her home in Essex. 'My children wanted to watch it on television, but I told them the atmosphere would be so different if we were there.' She was proved right. Like so many, she wanted to feel part of it. Inside, senior members of the Government, the Opposition and representatives from around the UK and the Commonwealth heard Dr Rowan Williams, the Archbishop of Canterbury, praise Her Majesty's 'lifelong dedication'.

The Queen, however, seemed distracted, even a little lost. She could be forgiven. For once, her husband and stalwart, Prince Philip, the man she publicly described as her 'strength and stay' ever since she met him as a giddy teenager, was not by her side. Instead, he was recovering in hospital a few miles away from a bladder infection. Her Majesty was understandably worried, but, characteristically, she uncomplainingly carried on.

Four days of Diamond Jubilee events eventually culminated in an appearance by the Queen on the Buckingham Palace balcony in front of huge, cheering crowds. There was also a fly-past by World War II aircraft, and the Royal Air Force Red Arrows capped it off perfectly. Significantly, however, this was not witnessed by the usual extended Royal Family appearing at their palace vantage point. This time, it was just the core family: *The New Royal Family*. She was joined by just five royals: the Prince of Wales, the Duchess of Cornwall, the Duke and Duchess of Cambridge and Prince Harry. It can have been nothing other than a conscious decision to do this and, clearly, this was, and is, the shape of things to come.

Prince Philip's absence that June day was a key catalyst for a major shake-up in thinking at the heart of the Royal Family. Senior palace insiders remarked privately that it had simply looked wrong for the then 86-year-old monarch to be entering St Paul's for a celebration of her own life with a complete absence of a male family member to support her. It is a role that Prince Charles might have been expected to take on, but his responsibilities to his wife created a delicate quandary for him.

It came at the end of a glorious weekend of celebrations. The Thames River Pageant, in freezing rain, had contributed to the Duke's condition as he had stood on the deck of the royal barge for the duration, refusing to sit in one of the rather grotesque gilded thrones provided. Of course, as he did not sit, nor did the Queen. Despite this, he had seemed like he was having the time of his life; resplendent in his Royal Navy uniform, he appeared on top form.

As the party had rolled on, news emerged that, on the advice of his doctors, the Duke would have to miss the Jubilee concert, organised by Take That singer Gary Barlow, and had even been hospitalised. I was working for the American broadcaster NBC that weekend, sharing a platform for a Jubilee Special with American broadcasters Matt Lauer and the charming Meredith Vieira. Among the media, there was a mood of genuine concern.

Fortunately, on cue, Prince Charles stepped up to the mark and left his mother visibly moved by his kind, warm and sometimes emotional speech in praise of her at the close of concert. The Prince's opening word – 'Mummy' – earned him rapturous cheers from the crowd. She beamed back, looking every inch the diamond Queen when she arrived on stage, adorned with Swarovski crystals, in a stunning cocktail dress of gold lame designed by Angela Kelly, under a dark cape, with sweeping trimmings of antique gold lace and deep olive.

Mother and son, accompanied by the Duchess of Cornwall, had minutes earlier made their way down to the stage encircling the Queen Victoria Memorial to a standing ovation. Celebrities including Kylie Minogue and Cheryl Cole jostled to stand as close to the royal party as possible. There was no jostling by the 'pop knights', Sir Paul McCartney, Sir Tom Jones and Sir Elton John, who had all been guaranteed prime positions close to the monarch. Charles warmed his audience up by making a joke about the terrible weather for Sunday's river pageant: 'If I may say so, thank God it turned out fine!' But it was when he made a poignant reference to the Duke of Edinburgh, in hospital just a few miles away, that Her Majesty's stiff upper lip for once appeared to weaken, if only for a moment. He went on, 'Your Majesty, millions, we are told, dream of having tea with you. Quite a lot nearly had a picnic with you in the garden of Buckingham Palace. The only sad thing about this evening is that my father could not be here with us because, unfortunately, he was taken unwell. But, ladies and gentlemen, if we shout loud enough he might just hear us in hospital and get better.'

Spontaneous cheers and applause followed. The prince spoke for everyone when he added, 'Your Majesty, a Diamond Jubilee is a unique and special event. Some of us have had the joy of celebrating three Jubilees with you. And I have the medals to prove it. And we are now celebrating the life and service of a very special person over the last 60 years. I was three when my grandfather George VI died and suddenly, unexpectedly, you and my father's lives were irrevocably changed when you were only 25. So as a nation this is our opportunity to thank you and my father for always being there for us. For inspiring us with your selfless duty and service, and for making us proud to be British.' Turning to his mother, he paid tribute to 'the life and service of a very special person'.

It was a brilliant performance. That gloss, that had so pleased the cheering masses, won all the plaudits in the newspapers the next day. In the palace corridors of power, however, the absence of the Duke of Edinburgh – the oldest spouse of a reigning British monarch – and his ill-health the next day had focused minds.

4

Philip is certainly blessed with a remarkably robust constitution. No chances are taken with his health. It was abundantly clear to everyone, including the Queen herself, that it was no longer reasonable to expect him to keep up the same pace as he approaches his century. There would inevitably be more occasions when the Duke will not be in his usual place a few paces behind his wife.

It will not be an easy transition, but, in the course of celebrating what a magnificent service the two had given to their country, it had become obvious to everyone that it was time to allow them to step back, if only slightly. Even Philip had said publicly in a BBC interview that 'he has done his bit'. That said, he bluntly refused to let his wife down and is notoriously reluctant to cut down on his busy schedule of private engagements. Indeed, if he had cut back as he suggested he would, there was no real evidence of it in the coming months.

However, another hospitalisation for Philip – and the Queen's concern about his workload – accelerated her plans for a subtle handing over of some responsibility to Prince Charles. Together with his wife – the now fully accepted Duchess of Cornwall – his brothers Andrew and Edward, and the next generation of William, Kate and Harry, he began to ease the pressure on the Queen and her dutiful husband by taking on more of the royal duties. There has been talk of Charles adopting a 'Shadow King' role – enabling his mother to spend more time with her husband privately.

'There is no question of Her Majesty abdicating her responsibilities,' one senior member of the Royal Household explained. 'It's more about sharing the workload and being more selective of the duties she undertakes. Her Majesty and the Duke of Edinburgh worked tirelessly throughout the Diamond Jubilee. Perhaps too much was expected of them.'

The aide went on, 'The Queen is remarkably fit, but she

appreciates that when she is on duty the Duke, as her liegeman, believes it is his duty to be at her side. The difficulty is persuading him that any of his sons can step in for him to accompany Her Majesty and that that would be acceptable. If the Duke does not agree to that, the only solution is for Her Majesty to do fewer engagements and for the younger members of the family to represent her at the others.'

The younger generation had already acquitted themselves well during the London Olympics of 2012, when they appeared in Team GB T-shirts to shout encouragement to our athletes. Now they would become far more visible. Despite his PR slip in Las Vegas, royal advisers believed Prince Harry, too, had a key role to play. His improving reputation would survive the exposure. Successful Jubilee visits to Jamaica and Brazil in 2012, followed by an equally positive USA tour in 2013, confirmed his star quality as a roving royal. He may be risqué but, like his late mother Diana, he certainly has the wow factor.

But the Queen's subtle move to take a step back in 2013 undoubtedly had deeper and more far-reaching consequences for Prince William – still serving as an RAF search and rescue pilot for the first half of 2013 – and his pregnant wife. It meant, too, he would have to rethink any ideas for a longer-term military career in order to instead become a full-time royal to fill the void. When Philip was taken ill and hospitalised again a few weeks later – forced to spend six days in Aberdeen Royal Infirmary while on his annual Balmoral holiday – the Queen took the opportunity to discuss how to handle this important reshaping of the monarchy with her heir Prince Charles.

'It is a delicate situation, and one of which the Prince of Wales in particular is mindful. He is ready to do whatever Her Majesty requires of him,' a member of the Royal Household told me at the time. 'The transition will be imperceptibly gradual, tightly managed and no doubt entirely orchestrated by the Queen herself – she knows that, even if they come across as a little dull, we like our Royal Family to appear calm, composed and in control at all times,' the aide went on.

Then came one of the most significant stories I have ever written during my decades as a chronicler of the House of Windsor. On Tuesday, 7 May 2013, I wrote in the *London Evening Standard* that this was not just talk. The Queen was backing it up with real action. A senior figure told me a few days earlier that the Queen was poised to quit long-haul overseas travel so that she can 'pace herself' for her future role as monarch. In a highly important move, the 87-year-old Sovereign announced she would miss her first CHOGM meeting for over 40 years in November, and send Prince Charles in her place.

Coming just weeks after the Queen was herself hospitalised, suffering from gastroenteritis, it showed Her Majesty's determination to manage her workload more appropriately going forward. If she was going to stay the course, and there is no suggestion that she is not, she had to pace herself. Her decision to send Prince Charles to Sri Lanka and represent her at the high-level meeting was also a decisive act of a canny Sovereign. From now on, Charles, supported by Camilla, would be expected to step in whenever the Queen needed him to represent her on future long-haul trips, just like he and other royals had done during the Diamond Jubilee year.

It would be the first time since 1971 that the Queen had not attended CHOGM, but my source was keen to stress that Her Majesty remained as committed as she had always been to her role as Head of the Commonwealth. One senior aide told me, 'We are simply looking at better pacing the Queen's activity.'

The Queen takes advice on Commonwealth matters from a

number of sources, including the Commonwealth Secretary General. But her decision not to attend the meeting in Sri Lanka was hers and hers alone, and was, of course, eminently sensible. Once again she demonstrated the foresight that has been the key feature of her long and successful reign. In a stroke, she had given the Prince of Wales – our longest-serving and best-prepared heir to the throne in history – the chance to show us his strengths on the world stage.

It seemed that not only had the Diamond Jubilee celebrations, when she had taken centre-stage, been a crowning moment, but also it might perhaps have been her final great public display of pomp and pageantry. She remains remarkably physically and mentally fit for a woman of her age. She rides her horses regularly, loves walking and reading. But it was time, it seemed, to give the next generation their chance, and, for Prince Charles, there was no better place to showcase his skills than at the Commonwealth meeting.

The Commonwealth has been one of the great successes of Her Majesty's reign. It is not an organisation on a mission – as Her Majesty has said. Instead, it offers its 2.1 billion people the unique opportunity to work together to achieve solutions to a wide range of problems. It is, she is proud to say, a major force for change. With a combination of quiet modesty, wisdom and experience, she has been central to holding the association together for 61 years and taking it forward. It is central to her role as a modern monarch and, close sources say, she believes it is at the heart of the new Royal Family. Yes, she wants Charles to take his position at its head, but she also believes the next generation of William, Kate and Harry has a vital role to play here too.

That said, with Prince Charles poised to take on a 'Shadow King' role in 2013 and beyond, it is for the younger generation to take up the torch, particularly when it comes to the

Commonwealth and international diplomacy, which after all is at the core of what modern monarchy is all about. In the Jubilee year, it had been a team effort – particularly when it came to representing the Queen abroad. The Duke and Duchess of Cambridge visited Malaysia, Singapore, the Solomon Islands and the tiny island of Tuvalu. Prince Harry, who was on his first solo trip on behalf of the Queen, went to Belize, Jamaica and the Bahamas. The extended Royal Family did their bit too. The Duke of York went to India, while the Princess Royal toured Mozambique and Zambia. Her Majesty's first cousin the Duke of Gloucester went to the British Virgin Islands and Malta, and the Duke of Kent took in the Falkland Islands and Uganda, while the Earl and Countess of Wessex journeyed to the Caribbean, visiting Antigua and Barbuda, Barbados, Grenada, Montserrat, St Kitts and Nevis, St Lucia, St Vincent and the Grenadines and Trinidad and Tobago, with an extra visit to Gibraltar.

Her Majesty, in organising who went where, was sending another clear message – the Commonwealth really mattered to her. Under her stewardship, the Commonwealth has grown into a voluntary association of 54 independent countries, spanning 6 continents – about 30 per cent of the world's population, with half under 25 years of age. She calls it the original worldwide web. The Royal Family's future long-term involvement with the Commonwealth in an official capacity is, therefore, a delicate subject. Some within the organisation have argued that one of the central reasons for the success of 'the family of nations' has been the personal involvement of the Queen. She has been, and continues to be, the talismanic figure at the heart of it all. She knows most of the nations' leaders personally, and many of them are now old friends.

There is no hard and fast rule stipulating that a British monarch should be Head of the Commonwealth. Therefore, there is no guarantee that Prince Charles or his heirs and successors, as the rules stand, will succeed Her Majesty in this crucial role. The Queen, after all, was invited by the then handful of Commonwealth states to follow her father at its head. It was India's new president, Pandit Jawaharlal Nehru, who took the lead, and the rest followed. But in 2013 some senior figures and officials in the organisation have publicly cast doubt on whether the Prince of Wales should succeed the Queen, arguing that the next head should be selected from one of the other member states if the Commonwealth is to shake off its colonial past. A decade ago, Nelson Mandela would have been a popular choice, but now there is no obvious choice as to who would be the best replacement to unite the somewhat disparate nations.

Modernisers also want to relocate the seat of the Commonwealth from Britain, where it is currently based in Queen Mary's old home, Marlborough House, in London, in order to avoid accusations that it is still mired in the days of the British Empire. Two suggestions for the relocation have been Delhi, in India, or Lagos, in Nigeria. Moreover, some have said that Charles, despite his tireless public service, does not command the same respect as the Queen. Privately, the Prince is known to be passionate about taking on the job – having visited more than 33 Commonwealth countries, he regards the position as a vital part of his and any future monarch's role.

With that in mind the Queen's decision to announce that she was effectively quitting long-haul travel and entrusting Prince Charles to represent her at CHOGM was a hugely significant move. It showed too that she wanted him to follow in her footsteps – something some member states are obviously not so keen on. Clearly, Her Majesty's action speaks louder than words. In sending Charles to represent her she does not agree. Typically, the Queen has taken a decisive step here, but said very little. There was no fuss.

However, the emergence of the glamorous Duke and Duchess of Cambridge on the world stage may have revived the monarchy's future in the Commonwealth. They are young, elegant and charming, and their popularity across the globe has injected a new appeal into the ageing monarchy. Time will tell whether it will be enough to maintain the British Royal Family's current role in the Commonwealth.

Prince William, as well as his father, is taking on more public roles in the royal back-up team as he learns the ropes of being a future king, while at the same time providing greater support for his grandmother. In January 2010, Prince William took his most significant step yet in his apprenticeship as future monarch, carrying out his first solo foreign tour in his official capacity as the Queen's representative. The tour to New Zealand and Australia was considered very successful, and Prince William, who was praised for flying business class on a scheduled flight rather than arriving on a private jet, was popular with both the public and the press. He spent three days in New Zealand, opening the newly built Supreme Court building in Wellington, playing rugby at the country's famous Eden Park and being feted as a chief by the Maori people. He flew on to Australia for two days, where he was warmly welcomed in Sydney and Melbourne, met Aboriginal people and heard stories about the recent bush fires.

Indeed, his first trip was such a success that he went back again the following year on a last-minute trip to meet victims of Australia's floods and New Zealand's earthquake and mining disasters. 'I felt so strongly about going down there,' the Prince said. 'If it was someone you knew or people you cared about, which I do, you'd want to be down there consoling them. They're a good bunch and they've had a horrendous time: Christchurch got destroyed.'

His visit was high-profile, of course, but the style was deliberately low-key, with a minimum of protocol, as he met and consoled many distraught people, shook hands, heard sad stories and passed on messages to and from the Queen. 'I wanted to let you know that you've not been forgotten about,' he told residents of the Australian town of Murrabit, which was flooded that January. 'Onwards and upwards, you've got a great community spirit.'

The Queen let him know she was delighted by his performance on the trip. 'The Queen sent me the most wonderful letter saying "Congratulations" and "Well done, you did well down there", which meant a lot to me,' the Prince said. 'It's funny, but, when you get a letter from her or a bit of praise, it goes a long, long way, more so than anyone else saying "well done" to you. It's mainly because there's such gravitas behind those words.'

Prince Charles, always a stickler for duty, is clearly ready to step up to his increased responsibility too. Although Charles has, of course, been representing the Royal Family around the world for a considerable period of time, he was certainly more statesmanlike on his recent trip to Australia and New Zealand, a trip that, for many, was seen as a barometer of whether Charles was ready for the change in his duties. His wife, Camilla, assisted him in this. When I met them both at a reception in Australia, both seemed more assured and more confident during their dealings with the media, with whom they have not always enjoyed an easy relationship.

I was at a reception at Government House in Wellington, New Zealand, that coincided with the Prince's 64th birthday on 14 November 2012. I had been there, too, at Buckingham Palace for his 50th birthday. But it was a very different prince from 14 years ago – less chippy and less defensive – who walked into the bright, airy room in New Zealand that day. I was reminded of the words of the classic Beatles song, which I believed would not have been lost on him as he walked into the packed room: 'When I get older, losing my hair...' so the song goes, 'Will you still need me, will you still feed me, when I'm 64?' Should New Zealanders, Australians, Canadians and, of course, the British still 'need him' when he eventually does become king, he will be the oldest heir to the throne to have ever taken the crown. Those close to him insist, though, that he is as ready as he has ever been to serve.

On this particular gruelling three-country tour – crisscrossing Australia and New Zealand after first taking in Papua New Guinea – the Prince appeared from my close vantage point to be more statesmanlike than I had ever seen him. Perhaps, with the recent ill-health of his father and the strain it has put on the Queen, he knew, far before the events of the summer of 2012, that he was now less of an heir and more a king-in-waiting.

His 64th birthday celebrations – as fate would have it, a date shared with Jerry Mateparae, New Zealand's governor general, and Bronagh Key, the wife of Prime Minister John Key, who were also at the party – came towards the end of the testing tour for the Prince and his second wife. For the Duchess of Cornwall, already 65, her first tour Down Under had been relentless, with thousands of handshakes to be had. It had taken its toll, but she showed clearly she had what it takes to be his consort, although, following their whistle-stop Diamond Jubilee tour to Canada, she made it clear she did not want another trip at that pace.

To the outsider, royal tours can appear glamorous 'jollies'. In reality, they are a slog for the principals, whether that be the Queen, Prince Charles or Princes William and Harry, as, day after day, they interact with the public and an unforgiving press, constantly having to be on their guard, but also maintaining a friendly interest in everything and everyone around them. For the support team, too, it can be relentless. Everyone, from the dressers, the private secretaries, the security team to the press officers (and, yes, even the accompanying media, myself among them), has to be booted and suited everywhere they go, which can be especially difficult when changing hotels daily.

And, of course, those under the most scrutiny are those at the top of the tree – the stars of the roadshow. Everything has to be just so at all times, and to have it all go like clockwork is no mean feat. What's more, it costs serious money – a tab picked up by the host government. This fact is not lost on the host media, who at times have been known to forget that the royals are not celebrities, but in fact their next king and queen. However, the number in the travelling court of 'King Charles' does occasionally raise eyebrows. More than two dozen are in the back-up team, if you include the Scotland Yard-funded personal protection officers. And that, of course, does not include the scores of local officials who often accompany the entourage.

Significantly, however, given that the couple represented the Queen for the Diamond Jubilee, Sir Christopher Geidt – her private secretary and a man with a track record in military intelligence as well as diplomacy – joined Charles's support team. The team itself was led by the Prince's outgoing private secretary Clive Alderton, who was on his last tour before taking up a post as ambassador to Morocco after seven years in the Royal Household. With him was his successor Simon Martin, a Foreign Office high-flyer. The wheels certainly seemed to me to be in motion for a subtle handover of power in the support staff.

Camilla's schedule, while strenuous, has now been structured to give her time to recover. On one occasion, for example, in Hobart, Tasmania, when the heavens opened, she left Prince Charles to go it alone. She instead has focused her schedule more on subjects dear to her heart. Osteoporosis, a disease that claimed the lives of her mother and grandmother, literacy, animal welfare and the armed forces have all, in turn, featured heavily on her schedule.

Despite this, at every turn, she has tried to help the media, knowingly turning to smile for the cameras at just the right moment, reminiscent of the way that Diana, Princess of Wales did, except more supportively of her husband. Perhaps the difference is that she understands it is not really about Camilla herself, more about trying to give everyone – including the travelling media – the chance to do their job. When the couple attended media receptions in Australia and New Zealand, they allowed the press to travel on their Air Force plane around New Zealand, giving us the chance to get a picture of what they do and how they interact. My impression was that together Charles and Camilla are a formidable team. They are clearly in love, and able to laugh out loud together. Crucially, they operate as one.

In that respect, having covered Charles and Diana's tour in the 1990s, it is clear to me that, in Camilla, Charles may have found his perfect partner. She may not have the glamour of Diana, but she knows what is needed of her, and, crucially, she does it. There is no doubt, too, that Charles is taking his duty seriously. Charming, intelligent and erudite, he is a veteran of hundreds of royal tours. On this one to Australia and New Zealand, where support for the republican cause has ebbed and flowed over the years, he stepped up to the plate. It was never going to be the easiest of tours – there was always the chance that the 'Diana issue' would arise – but together they made it look easy. The monarchy's position on the issue has always been consistent: 'We will serve the people of New Zealand and Australia for as long as they want us.'

And the overwhelming spirit of goodwill that the wedding of William and Kate created in New Zealand and Australia had undoubtedly given their cause a huge boost. However, there is no doubt that, even with this boost, this was a big test for Camilla, and one she passed with flying colours. Diana, a global icon, was loved abroad, and Charles took a lot of flak over his affair with Camilla. But my impression from my privileged vantage point was that people had moved on. The Diana question was no longer an issue either Down Under or at home. Yes, there has been the odd crank standing in the crowd with a picture, but the reaction to Charles and Camilla had been largely positive. There was only one slightly awkward moment, at the Cenotaph in Auckland on Remembrance Sunday, when Charles and Camilla sang the hymn 'I Vow to Thee My Country'. It was Diana's favourite at school and sung at both her wedding to Charles and her funeral.

The question I, and perhaps the Queen, too, from afar, wanted answered had been answered unequivocally. Would Charles and Camilla be accepted as king and queen in Australia and New Zealand? Molly Dobson, 89, who emigrated to New Zealand in 1926 with her parents, and met the Duchess at an osteoporosis engagement, was sure: 'Yes, I think Camilla will be queen and I think she will do a good job. Absolutely. Charles needs her.' Of that, there is no doubt. For me, this tour had been crucial. They, as a royal double-act, had been formidable, determined to do their duty and take their place in history. That cannot have been lost on Her Majesty back home.

The Queen herself has been an incredible and inspirational servant, an example to all who follow her. After more than 60 years at the helm of the monarchy, few can remember a time without Elizabeth II as Sovereign. There is a quiet, irrational belief among us all that the Queen will just go on and on indefinitely. But both she and her devoted consort, the Duke of Edinburgh, are realists. They have acknowledged that their advancing years will inevitably force them to slow down. There is no question whatsoever of her abdicating like the Dutch Queen

Beatrix, who stepped down in favour of her son in 2013. Clearly, however, as she approached her 90th year, the Queen had set the wheels in motion for the significant adjustments that needed to be made.

When I asked Prince Andrew if it wouldn't be better for the Queen to be free to retire, as she gets older, he smiled and said, 'But that's the nature of monarchy. It's as simple as that. I don't think it's even a thought.' The man who will one day follow in her footsteps, Prince William, agrees with his uncle. 'For the grand-children, it's a bit difficult for us to say "take it easy" when she's so much older than us, and has done so much more. We do hint at taking some things off her, but she won't have anything of it. She's so dedicated and really determined to finish everything she started.' He went on, 'She'll want to hand over knowing she's done everything she possibly could to help, and that she's got no regrets and no unfinished business; that she's done everything she can for the country and that she's not let anyone down – she minds an awful lot about that.'

However, a new Royal Family is taking the reins; and, although, for now, Prince Charles will take the lead, there can be no doubt about who the star couple will be. From now, the focus will be on William and Kate, who have become international stars in their own right. Their global popularity, seen during the extremely successful tours around the world they undertook as a recently married couple, had been demonstrated nowhere more clearly than the fantastic support that they received at their royal wedding.

CHAPTER 2

THE WEDDING OF THE CENTURY

'We're quite a reserved lot, the British. But when we go for it, we really go for it.'

PRIME MINISTER DAVID CAMERON ON
KATE AND WILLIAM'S WEDDING

William and Catherine's wedding day was the crowning moment of the first grand act in the theatre of royalty this century. It was pomp and pageantry at its finest; a resplendent symbol of British national pride and unity, played out on the perfect stage, Westminster Abbey. The Abbey has been the setting for 1,000 years of royal history and, perhaps, one moment more than any other showed what the monarchy has become and, possibly, what it will be.

Prince William, on the balcony, looked at his beautiful bride and asked, 'Are you ready? OK, let's…' He drew Catherine Elizabeth Middleton – the newly ennobled Her Royal Highness, the Duchess of Cambridge – close. They kissed, not once, but twice, to the delight of the million-strong crowd tightly packed along The Mall opposite Buckingham Palace. Minutes later, World War II fighter planes roared overhead in the fly-past. It was all timed to military precision.

The Buckingham Palace publicity machine could not have asked for anything better during the royal couple's first public appearance as man and wife. But this was not just a kiss for the cameras; this was true love, and everyone watching, including the estimated two billion glued to their televisions around the world, knew it.

I felt emotional; proud and emotional. Only the most cynical among us wouldn't. My ringside seat to history – commentating for the US network NBC – gave me a perfect viewpoint from the specially erected television studios at Canada Gate opposite the Palace. The kiss was a wonderful touch, an iconic moment in the history of this new modern monarchy, and everyone there could feel something special was beginning.

Earlier, with two barely audible words, 'I will', Catherine sent cheers ringing around the country, not to mention the far-flung parts of the world that still hold monarchy at their heart.

And, with that, the one-time commoner Catherine in an instant took the giant step into the magical world of royalty – destined now to be the future queen consort of 16 countries across the globe. Together, William and Catherine erased the sadness of our recent royal past and evoked memories of happier times, when we still believed in fairytale royal marriages.

It was one of the most anticipated and watched events in our long national history, and, indeed, perhaps in world history, given the reach of our truly global media. It finally eclipsed the terrible sadness of William's late mother Diana's funeral, which had played out on the same stage of the Abbey. At last, the Royal Family could move on from the tragic circumstances surrounding her death, and now, finally, the icon of Princess Diana is able to rest in peace.

This was, quite simply, a very good day for both royalists and for the House of Windsor, created by George V out of necessity nearly a century earlier. Catherine was the perfect new recruit to their clan. Boasting an ancestry of working miners, she oozed class and natural grace. She had, like a certain previous Princess, her new husband's late mother, natural nobility about her.

Both were utterly unflappable as they delivered their vows perfectly. And as William placed the band of Welsh gold on her finger, both William and Catherine steadied themselves for the next chapter in this long royal story.

The Queen concurred. 'It was amazing,' she said.

But what I, and others, watching from afar, liked were the lighter, more personal touches. 'Are you happy?' she asked her husband as she climbed into the 1902 open State Landau. 'It was amazing, amazing,' replied the Duke. 'I am so proud you're my wife.'

The most striking aspect of the whole occasion was the simplest of the lot: two people, so obviously at one with each other.

Tradition dictates that royal men receive a title on their wedding day – and often more than one. As well as a duchess, Catherine Middleton is also technically Princess William of Wales. According to protocol, she is not officially Princess Catherine, as she was not born a princess in her own right. Instead, she adopts her husband's first name.

But for William, a man with his finger on the pulse of his people, it was not about titles. This, for him, was their day and he was determined to keep it that way. On that day, this young couple – the royal faces of the Facebook generation – became the most famous people on the planet.

When William first set eyes on Kate at St Andrews University in September 2001, he said he instantly knew there was some-thing special about her. They became friends first – they shared the same course (history of art before William switched to geography) and resided in the same halls of residence, known as St Sallies. Catherine was once asked if she felt fortunate to date

Prince William. Quick as a flash, she replied with supreme self-confidence, 'He's lucky to be going out with me.' She ticked all the right boxes for a future queen consort, but was definitely no fawning subject desperate to marry into royalty.

Theirs is a true love match. The next day – the pomp and pageantry over – they dressed casually before flying off in a helicopter on the shortest of breaks. Their honeymoon was put on hold as William had to return to RAF duties as a search and rescue pilot just a few days later. The couple sent a message of thanks to the nation for their support on the 'most wonderful day of our lives' and the new Duchess of Cambridge said, with characteristic humility, of their glittering wedding, 'I am glad the weather held off. We had a great day.'

But just 24 hours later the newly ennobled Duke and Duchess of Cambridge were Mr and Mrs Ordinary again. The pair – who used to use the pseudonym Mr and Mrs Smith whenever they checked into a hotel as students – looked just like any other young couple going on a weekend away. On the day, maybe overwhelmed by the splendour and formality of the wedding, they seemed to forget to hold hands, or perhaps they chose not to. But, the next day, they walked hand-in-hand, smiling before boarding the helicopter. In an instant, they were gone, but the whirlwind of goodwill they had created was not forgotten.

Walter Bagehot, the brilliant Victorian journalist and constitutional expert, was right all those years ago – a princely marriage really does rivet mankind. For this was our, the people's, wedding too and we were all happy to be a part of it.

From now on, Catherine Elizabeth Middleton, or, as she will always be known to us, the people, Kate's world would never be the same again. Now a fully signed-up member of *The New Royal Family* she was, quite simply, the most famous woman, not to mention one of the most loved, in the world.

CHAPTER 3

SCHOOL DAYS

'Every boy in the school fancied her rotten.'

KATE MIDDLETON'S SCHOOL FRIEND
GEMMA WILLIAMSON

In the months after Princess Diana's death in 1997, Prince
William emerged from her shadow as a heartthrob for thousands
of girls. They tore down their Leonardo DiCaprio posters and
replaced them with images of the handsome, young, tragic Prince.
The impressionable Kate Middleton was one of those girls.

Thirty miles down the road from Eton College, in the
dormitory at Marlborough school that she shared with two other
girls, they had a picture of Prince William on the wall. Back then,
Kate was a giggly, hockey-obsessed pupil who took little interest
in the poorly concealed adolescent lust of the Marlborough boys.
Kate later claimed in her engagement interview that she actually
had a poster of a Levi model, not William. But one of her
roommates, Jessica Hay, told me after the announcement of the
engagement that it was true. 'We all fancied Prince William. He
was gorgeous. It's fair to say that it wasn't just Kate, but his picture
was on the wall.'

Kate arrived at Marlborough at the age of 14 from Downe House, an exclusive girls' boarding school a few miles away in Berkshire. It was midway through the academic year, which just added to the apprehension of joining new classmates at her fourth school in a decade. Dressed in her new uniform, a smart blue blazer and tartan skirt, the teenager was driven to the renowned public school by her parents. Her time at her previous school had not been a happy one and it showed in the pale, rather reedy figure she presented. There was talk of bullying and it had shattered her confidence. Her mother Carole knew she had to act, and, after perusing all the glossy brochures, she thought Marlborough College offered the solution. It would not be cheap, but Carole believed it would be money well spent.

Founded in 1843, and situated in one of the most attractive market towns in the country, Marlborough is a flourishing and co-educational, independent boarding school for pupils aged 13–18. It was used to educating the sons and daughters of the cream of society and old aristocratic families. Notable 'old Marlburians' included those with royal links. Lord Janvrin, the Queen's loyal former private secretary, Sir Anthony Blunt, the Queen's art historian and traitor communist spy, the poet laureate Sir John Betjeman and the Queen's biographer Professor Ben Pimlott. Others included her future husband's first cousin HRH Princess Eugenie of York as well as the courtier Sir Alan 'Tommy' Lascelles, private secretary to the Queen and her father George VI. Actors James Mason and James Robertson Justice and statesman Rab Butler are also on the illustrious list of old boys. Surely, a former pupil as a future queen caps the lot.

The school motto – *Deus Dat Incrementum*, 'God Giveth the Increase', taken from Corinthians I – helped to establish the school as the first choice of parents who are seeking for their children an excellent, modern education in a coeducational environment. It boasts a community where scholarship is cherished, creativity is celebrated, diversity is evidenced, and conversation – the means by which knowledge is elevated into wisdom – is paramount. Certainly, it came as a welcome change for Kate. At first, Kate was homesick and chose to keep her own company after dining at Norwood Hall. She was conscientious, studying hard – but it added to her sense of isolation. She lacked confidence and was perhaps a little overwhelmed.

Soon, though, she began to relax. Collecting the nickname 'Middlebum', she began to mingle and form firm friendships. A capable teenager, she played hockey for the school, was in the first pair at tennis and was an accomplished cross-country runner and netball player.

Jessica Hay, her best friend from those days, who shared a dormitory with her, recalls her as a girl with 'very high morals'. She is not alone in her opinion. Gemma Williamson, who along with Jessica and Kate made up a trio of firm friends during their schooldays, also remembers Kate as self-contained and modest in the true sense of the words. Towards the end of her schooling, she may have blossomed into a fun-loving and popular member of the school but, when she first pitched up at the gates of the £21,000-a-year establishment, she bore little resemblance to the striking young woman she would become.

Gemma explained, 'Catherine arrived suddenly in the middle of the year. Apparently, she had been bullied very badly in her previous school [Downe House] and she certainly looked thin and pale. She had very little confidence.' It can't have helped that, with typical teenage cruelty, boys from more senior years would rate new girls as they came into supper by holding up paper napkins with marks out of ten written on them; Kate scored only ones and twos. One summer later, her scores would leap. By the following year, her willowy figure had softened and filled out.

She was still lithe and sporty but the colour was back in her cheeks. She was, her friends recall, 'totally different'.

'Every boy in the school fancied her rotten,' Gemma claimed, an observation with which Jessica concurred. Nevertheless, Kate, who was put in the all-girl schoolhouse of Elmhurst, was never terribly interested in all this newfound attention. She had a couple of innocent kisses and harmless fumbles but those who knew her best knew that Kate was saving herself for someone special. As with any school populated by the privileged offspring of wealthy but often absent parents, Marlborough has its fair share of wild teenage behaviour. Drink is smuggled into dormitories, cigarettes secreted in blazer pockets and teenage flirtations turn awkward youths and prim girls into sexual adventurers – but not Kate. Her school pal Jessica said, 'She didn't have any serious boyfriends at school. She is very good-looking and a lot of boys liked her but it just used to go over her head. She didn't get involved in any drinking or smoking but was very sporty instead and very family-orientated.'

She went on, 'One of Catherine's best assets is that she has always been very sure of herself. She has never allowed herself to be influenced by others and there's no way that she would be involved in any of that. She still doesn't really drink and certainly doesn't smoke. You're much more likely to find her going for a long walk across the moors than going to a nightclub. We would sit around talking about all the boys at school we fancied but Catherine would always say, "I don't like any of them. They're all a bit of rough." Then, prophetically, she would joke, "There's no one quite like William." We always said that one day she would meet him and they would be together.'

Kate may have gossiped with her friends about the boys she fancied, but her attitude to sex was, by all accounts, very old-fashioned – especially at a school where, as Gemma says, 'Half the pupils were already having sex.'

Kate, however, wasn't alone in her dream of meeting and marrying William. There were tens of thousands of girls just like her. Besides, William had grown into a strapping figure of a young man. But this teenage girl believed fate was on her side. When the pair of them appeared in the same Marlborough newsletter – both pictured in back-page sports articles; she playing hockey, he polo – she believed their paths would cross. A school source said, 'She called it her "kismet" picture because she truly believed fate would bring them together. Some of the girls thought it was a dream, but who is deluded now? She's got her man, so maybe there was something in it.'

It was at this time that the young Kate had a teenage crush on the swashbuckling adventurer Willem Marx, who was 'ever so slightly' supposed to have broken her heart. The two were to remain friends, which got tongues wagging many years later when he accompanied her to a nightclub without her royal boyfriend in tow.

Accusations would follow that Carole would engineer Kate's choice of university with the express purpose of seeing her daughter beguile, then ensnare, a future king – a charge that was wholly inaccurate but one that stuck.

Like many teenagers on the cusp of adulthood and readying themselves for life as full-time students, William decided to take a gap year. In August 2000, while he learned of his A-level results, he was already in the jungles of Belize and preparing to embark on survival exercises with the Welsh Guards ahead of his travels to Chile. His gap year, or at least a large part of it, he spent in South America as a volunteer with Raleigh International; these jungle manoeuvres were part adventure, part necessity.

Kate too was preparing for her own gap-year experience. However, hers was a less rugged itinerary and one more in keeping with the history of art course at St Andrews on which she would soon enrol. Kate was planning to spend three months in Florence – the Renaissance capital, steeped in history, and promising months of relaxation and mind-broadening culture. In the corridors of the Uffizi and the cobbled streets of the city, she would see at first hand some of the treasures that, the following October, would exist for her only in the pages of her course textbooks. Her preparation focused on booking language lessons at the British Institute, organising accommodation, studying guidebooks to the city and excitedly poring over her travel plans with friends and family.

While St James's Palace was rather pompously 'pleased to announce' the Prince's A-level results (B in history of art, A in geography and a modest C in biology), the beautiful and carefree Kate was ripping open the results envelope at home in Berkshire. Secure in the knowledge that her university place was safe, she headed to Florence, while William, a month after his 18th birthday, flew to those humid jungles of Belize. He mucked in with the soldiers, slept in a hammock strung between trees, swapped his jeans and baseball cap for jungle combats and floppy hat and trainers for heavy army boots, and his daily food was no more or less than the troops' British Army rations.

While Kate sent postcards home and took snaps of her travels and the friends she made *en route*, William's 'postcards' home were rather more contrived. In October, November and December, he was photographed in a variety of staged PR opportunities. Using the tame Press Association, he was shown sharing a joke with ten-year-old Marcela Hernandez-Rios, while helping to teach English in the village of Tortel. There were photos, too, of him with little Alejandro Heredia, a six-year-old child who hitched a ride on William's broad shoulders at the nursery. And there were others of the future British king scrubbing toilets, carrying logs and hammering posts into the arid earth.

Kate's life was less strenuous. At this time, she was enjoying an adolescent relationship with a boy called Harry. She was also, inevitably, being relentlessly pursued by the Italian waiters at the fashionable Art Bar in Florence, known for its bohemian clientele and cocktails, and a place that quickly became a firm favourite for Kate and fellow romantics, drawn to the city for its art and atmosphere. Awkward teenagers and experienced Casanovas alike tried their best to chat up the stunning brunette with the dazzling smile, but it was always to no avail. 'She managed to give you the brush-off while still making you feel good about yourself,' recalled one failed suitor. Others were not always so considerate of her feelings. Harry, apparently, messed her around and the two parted, leaving Kate emotionally bruised, perhaps even a little heartbroken as only teenagers – heart-stung for the first time – can be.

Without Harry to distract her, Kate threw herself into her studies with enthusiasm. One of her reasons for travelling to Florence was to learn the language at the British Institute in the city. There she shared a top-floor flat with four other girls – within easy reach of the Duomo and other art treasures. She and her friends could spend hours wandering through the labyrinthine streets, gazing up in wonder at buildings so perfect it seemed impossible that they had stood just so since Roman times.

Evenings were spent in the Art Bar or another similarly lively place. Unlike some students, who indulged to excess, Kate would always stop after a few glasses of wine, a sign of remarkable self-control and a moral compass already set.

While others experimented with drugs, Kate passed them by and did not partake – but she was never judgemental, never prim, and never unpopular or ridiculed as a result. Quite the opposite: she charmed all she met. One fellow student and contemporary of Kate's said, 'The Italian barmen loved Kate. In addition, because they fancied her, the rest of the girls used to get free drinks. They were charmed by her beauty and English-rose appeal.' But they would have to make do with lusting from afar. Kate never gave the slightest encouragement to her Italian suitors. Perhaps she had her sights set on higher things than the slick charms of some Latin Lothario. Whatever the source of her disinterest, it was an abiding characteristic in those days – days when, unbeknown to both, she and William's first meeting was growing ever closer.

William had been expected to follow his father's example and attend Trinity College, Cambridge, but he had decided to eschew tradition and, instead, go to St Andrews, an ancient and well-respected establishment, but never before considered fit for a future king.

He had followed his gut instinct. He plumped for the small coastal town that would, he believed, allow him a level of privacy that a southern university might not. At the same time, Kate Middleton was anxiously awaiting news of whether her application to her university of choice had been successful. She was every bit as set on her course as William was on his, and it was a course that would lead to a chance meeting with a prince that she had for so long only dreamed of.

CHAPTER 4

TEEN ICON

*'My father always taught me to treat everybody as an equal.
I have always done and I am sure that William and Harry are the same.'*

<small>DIANA, PRINCESS OF WALES, INTERVIEWED IN LE MONDE, 1997</small>

There was no great ambition behind the trip. It was another family skiing holiday – some much-needed time for the Princes William and Harry to spend with their father just seven months after the appalling loss of their mother. Before the three Princes retreated to Whistler and the mountains of British Columbia to enjoy four days on the slopes, a stint of royal walkabouts had been pencilled in for the entourage on arrival in Canada.

Nobody, neither Prince Charles's closest advisers nor the following rat pack of royal journalists – including me – knew quite what the public would make of this beleaguered trio. Charles still had to contend with a great deal of blame and resentment from those among the public who ludicrously viewed him as somehow culpable for Princess Diana's death.

Meanwhile, the very mention of his grieving sons prompted outpourings of public sympathy and heavy doses of galling grief by proxy. William and Harry had been largely spared public scrutiny in the months since their mother's death. Nobody could forget their composure on the day of her funeral at Westminster Abbey on 6 September 1997, and during the very public mourning that preceded it when they had walked among weeping strangers and viewed the flowers and cards laid at the gates and along the paths and roads outside her west London home of Kensington Palace. William in particular had conducted himself resolutely in the face of almost incalculable adversity. He was much taller and seemingly much more mature than Harry, who, not yet 13, had appeared heartbreakingly young and vulnerable. It was easy to overlook the fact that William, too, was a boy who had lost his mother. Now, three months short of his 16th birthday, he was still camera-shy, by turns sullen, quick to blush and possessed of all the awkward self-awareness of teenage years.

When they touched down at Vancouver airport on 24 March 1998, the royal party did so with a great deal of apprehension and few expectations. This was, to all intents and purposes, a family holiday with a few public engagements thrown in for good measure – a sop for the devoted royalists and a scrap for the fascinated press. But within minutes of their arrival in the country's west coast capital something remarkable happened – something that would mark the trip out as a watershed for the teenage Prince William. From the instant he stepped out onto Canadian soil, a new phenomenon was born: 'Wills Mania'.

Crowds of frantic teenage girls, hundreds of whom had waited for hours to see their hero, went wild as they finally caught sight of him. They jostled against police barricades and wept, screamed and waved banners offering to prove to Wills in a variety of forthright fashions just how devoted to the young royal they really were. It was an astonishing spectacle. It would have fazed the most seasoned public figure. This was the sort of adoring hysteria associated with the Beatles in their heyday, when frenzied female fans screamed themselves into fainting fits and had to be pulled unconscious from the crowds.

This was unlike anything I had seen as a royal reporter. Even the fevered adoration of Diana had stopped short of this unashamed teenage lust. There were about 30 or so of us in the press contingent that had travelled to Canada – photographers, reporters and television crews alike. If truth be told, it caught us all on the hop, but it was a dream story. The copy just flowed. My erstwhile colleagues Richard Kay, Charles Rae and I rushed around gleaning quotes and scribbling notes and filing reams of information for our newspapers back home. We knew that we were literally witnessing the making of a royal icon. Not a replacement for Diana – nothing so brash or so mired in the recent past. This was something new. After months of navel gazing and gloom, this was something so spontaneously upbeat that you could not help but get carried along with this unexpected surge of enthusiasm.

It was not an entirely uncomplicated birth for the new royal hero. As the adrenalin pumped through our reporters' veins, it was easy to forget that William – this tall, athletically handsome young man – was still just a boy, a teenager having to deal with the weight of so much expectation. It would have been all too easy to dismiss his acute embarrassment were it not for the fact that William, revealing a determined streak of character, made sure that the press and his advisers were well aware of it.

At first, he did his best to hide his discomfort at the extreme adulation with which he was met. He hated every second of it, as we were soon to find out. As he arrived at what was supposed to be a private visit to the Pacific Space Centre in the heart of the town, row upon row of screaming girls – about five thousand – greeted William. The death of his mother had turned him into a somewhat romantic, tragic hero for many a dewy-eyed teen.

At first, both Harry and William seemed appalled by the phenomenon. Harry's nonplussed appearance was perhaps more to do with the fact that the girl fans were not screaming for him. William was just horrified at the heaving mass of adoration.

'Look at him! I've got posters of him all over my wall,' said one.

'They should declare it a national holiday, William Day,' screamed another.

The poor lad did not know which way to look. Eyes downcast, his bashful smile redolent of his late mother, William did his best and showed great resolve, rising to the occasion and spending ten minutes shaking hands with and accepting gifts from well-wishers. Not once did he allow his smile, however apologetic, to fade from his face.

One observer reported that he looked close to tears. I did not see that and I was pretty close to the action, but the young Prince's discomfort was obvious. He could not wait to get inside, and when he did, and only his father and the entourage were in earshot, all hell broke loose. William had had enough. He refused to go on. The task of talking William down from the ledge fell to his anxious father, who, with a grace and diplomacy of which many believe him incapable, coaxed the petulant teen back from the brink. While his newly installed PR man Mark Bolland hovered haplessly nearby, Charles had a heart-to-heart with William. Later, it fell to Bolland to try to negotiate a truce of sorts with the overheated press. There was precious little he could do to cool the ardour of a nation's teenage girls. The Royal Family, we were told, wanted our coverage to be 'calmer, cooler'.

Back in Britain, Bolland found unlikely allies in the form of various doom-mongering commentators reporting from the comfort of their desks thousands of miles away. Self-appointed guardians of the young Princes' welfare did their best to dampen down the frenzy we on the ground had reported. It was not a case of our whipping it up: the reaction was natural and real. Chief among the commentators was *Daily Express* columnist Mary Kenny, who argued that the boys were being exposed far too soon after their mother's death. She wrote, 'Diana was adored all over the world. And this is a halo effect that William and Harry will carry everywhere: that they were Diana's sons. But would Princess Diana, if she were alive today, want her elder son to start carrying out royal duties at such a tender age?'

The implication was that she would not. The finger of blame pointed at Charles, not for the first time, and also at his officials for exploiting Diana's sons. As would often happen in the years following Diana's death, Charles's critics would conveniently overlook the simple fact that, despite scurrilous untrue rumours relating to Harry's paternity, the boys were both his sons too, he loved them unconditionally and would do anything to protect them. Still, it was a difficult situation. How could the Princes visit a country of which, as a realm and part of the Commonwealth, William would one day be king and yet still hide away from an adoring public? Moreover, how could they even begin to control, never mind quash, such a spontaneous outpouring of affection for William? It was too big an ask: the genie was out of the bottle and not even an accomplished media fixer like Mark Bolland could put it back and seal up the stopper. Besides, the emergence of William as the new royal star was not without its benefits for the family – once he had embraced the situation.

With his initial nerves and truculence soothed, the actor in William emerged. Maybe, just maybe, he was beginning to enjoy this. As the British media headed off in chartered helicopters for the next photo call, on the ski slopes of the Canadian Rockies, William started to perform. When the three Princes were presented with bright-red 'Roots' branded caps – worn by the country's Winter Olympics team – William showed his youthful credentials and a grasp of the real world that his father never possessed. The caps are worn back to front but Charles inevitably put his on the wrong way round before William, laughingly, corrected him – upstaging his father in the process. William, prince of cool, was a media triumph.

It was very different from the first time I had sought any meaningful encounter with William at another royal skiing holiday, in 1995 in Klosters, Switzerland. William was 12 when I conducted his first, brief interview. A photo call had been staged for him, along with his brother and cousins, Princesses Beatrice and Eugenie, daughters of the Duke and Duchess of York. The idea had been hurriedly conceived and executed by Commander Richard Aylard RN, who, like so many courtiers before him and since, believed he knew how to handle the media to promote his boss – even though he famously issued a memo instructing no member of the Prince's household ever to talk to members of the press. Given their ages, the good commander had cleared all questions. I asked William, 'Who's the best skier?' He smiled. He was not going to admit that his little brother was better than he was.

'These two,' he said, gesturing at his cousins, 'are coming along really well.' It was a deft diplomatic touch for one so young, a mischievous batting back of my question. Yes, the whole encounter had been organised with military – or rather naval – attention to detail and William had known what questions were coming. However, one should not underestimate how nerve-racking a one-on-one encounter with the media can be. There, in that low-key interaction on the slopes, was a hint of the humour and self-possession that would unfurl in a week when he faced the press in Canada just three years later.

In the intervening years, William would go through many shifts of character. Contrary to popular belief that has Harry painted as the tearaway – frequenting lap-dancing bars, taking swings at photographers and generally ripping up the town – William is no goody two-shoes. His character is one forged in the fires of a youth at once troubled and blessed. He would hardly be human or, frankly, particularly interesting had he not kicked against the pricks occasionally. Certainly, he would not be the Prince he is today were it not for a mass of often conflicting influences and a healthy dose of childish rebellion and adolescent wildness. Today, William is a young man who often confounds the predictions of those who would like simply to slot him into a convenient category. He is by turns intensely sensitive – his mother often worried that he, like her, was *too* sensitive for the life that royalty demanded – and laddishly bullish. He is the baseball-cap-wearing prince who posed for official portraits sporting a hole in the elbow of his sweater, the future king who visited amusement parks as a child, who plays football, who is up to speed on contemporary culture and who enjoys a pint with his friends. But he is not, for all that, a man entirely of our time.

Home to William is still a variety of palaces and mansions where the walls are hung thick with exquisite works of art and where shooting-party weekends follow the seasons. This 'sensitive' young man loves the hunting-and-fishing lifestyle that seems a complete anachronism when set against the flipside of his character. He takes pride in bagging rabbits, grouse and stag. He plays polo, and a favoured 'pub' in younger years was Club H – a bar set up by William and Harry in the cellars of their father's Gloucestershire home, Highgrove.

For many years now, William has veered between the traditional and the unexpectedly modern in many aspects of his life, including his taste in women. He has been linked – often mischievously – to pop stars, supermodels and the daughters of foreign leaders. And, with a similar degree of regularity, flirtations have been spotted, and imagined, between William and the sort of ruddy-faced, jolly-hockey-sticks daughters of aristocracy and giddy 'it' girls who fall more naturally – in some cases literally – into his royal path. He is a mass of contradictions and even more appealing to the opposite sex for it.

William is a young man on the cusp of embracing public life and, hopefully, securing private happiness. He knows that his duty makes his life a sort of sacrifice to the state. He has shown that he has not completely submerged his personal needs and desires as a result. He is starting to find a personal equilibrium that long eluded both his mother and his father in their private and public lives, perhaps partly because, in the figure of Kate, he has found a girl who can make sense of his conflicting character traits and the opposing demands of his life as a modern prince. She keeps him in touch with a lifestyle from which, by virtue of his HRH status, he will always be one step removed. And, while newspaper reports may have started to portray Kate as the 'new Diana', much of Kate's appeal lies in how she differs from Princess Diana rather than how she resembles her. Yes, she may have injected a bit of youthful glamour and a dose of romance into the Royal Family once more. But, more importantly, in Kate William has found a sensible and attractive girl who, in emotional terms, demands very little of him. For a boy who has lived through the heat of the War of the Waleses, that must seem like bliss – not least because his mother leaned so heavily on her elder son in her own times of need, times when William was still just a little boy.

William and Harry were asleep when the first reports came through that something was wrong. At around 1 a.m., Prince Charles was woken and told by telephone that there had been a crash in the Alma tunnel in Paris. Dodi, he was informed, was dead. His ex-wife was injured. The Prince woke the Queen. Then moments later came the call with the terrible news that Diana was dead. The poor man, racked with guilt and grief, broke down and wept.

It must have been sheer agony. The Queen wisely advised against waking the boys. Let them sleep now, she counselled, knowing that sleep would not come easily over the following days and weeks, when they would long for its oblivion and nourishment. Instead, Charles paced the corridors as they slept. Overcome with fear at the prospect of telling his sons such devastating news, he went for a lonely walk on the moors. When he returned at 7 a.m., William was already awake. Charles, his eyes swollen and red from tears, walked into William's room and broke the awful news. They hugged each other like never before. Brave and sensitive, at the worst moment of William's life, he directed his thoughts to his younger brother, who was still asleep in the bedroom next door. The task of telling Harry was one that Charles and William undertook together. Gently, they explained that Diana had been injured and that the medical team had struggled and failed to save her. Now, embracing each other protectively, they wept uncontrollably as the sounds of raw pain echoed around the old house. Nothing would ever be the same for any of them.

In the sombre moments that followed his mother's death, William, who had lost so much, would show in the depths of his grief a strength of character and dignity that was quite simply regal. Charles would show a warmth of which his critics never believed him capable. Diana's brother, Earl Spencer, was certainly no fan. At her funeral in Westminster Abbey, he delivered a eulogy to his sister riddled with both covert and blatant criticisms of the Royal Family. He insisted that the boys would continue to be influenced by his sister Diana's 'blood family', and seemed to imply that it was her kin who stood the best chance of offering them a rounded upbringing, saving them from the grim clutches of an unadulterated and traditionally royal background.

The words irked and hurt Charles, maybe in part because they struck a chord. Had a traditional royal upbringing been such a success for him? Diana's visits to homeless centres, theme parks and fast-food restaurants seemed gimmicky and had made him cringe in the past. But Charles could see that her devotion and unconventional methods had paid off. William and Harry were well-rounded little chaps with a fresh and confident outlook – in spite of the turbulence of their parents' love lives and divorce.

It was up to Charles, he recognised, to ensure that they did not become weighed down with the responsibility and duty of their birthright. He cancelled all his immediate engagements. Diana's past accusations of his being an absent father echoed in his mind. If he had been a poor husband then, now that she was gone, he was not going to fail her again as guardian to the sons they both cherished. Charles threw himself into the role of devoted single dad. He took Harry with him on an official royal tour to South Africa, listened more to their views and began, tentatively, to embrace modern life. One minute he was posing with the Spice Girls, the next he was embracing children infected with AIDS. Out of adversity, Charles triumphed – and so did his sons.

Given William's uniquely close bond with his mother, those in her inner circle were astonished at how rapidly he seemed to recover. But then, William had shown his strength before, back when his mother needed him and used him as an emotional crutch. Now he showed that same generosity of spirit as he recognised that Harry and his father needed him. Harry was more of a worry. The gregarious, impish little boy all but disappeared; he retreated into himself, as he had done in the wake of his parents' divorce. But with time, with William and Charles and 'big sister' Tiggy, he gradually re-emerged. The tears still flowed in private moments but Diana was never coming back and life had to carry on.

The fact that the media could not do the same did upset them. Every time there was another instalment in the Diana saga and another front page of their mother was published, the seething grief with which they were learning to live surged forward with renewed intensity. They grew protective of their surviving parent and were genuinely hurt by what they saw as unfair criticism of him. A year after Diana's death, they decided to do something about it. They issued a touching personal statement calling for an end to the public mourning and what had been called the 'Diana Industry' – the commercial exploitation of the Princess of Wales. William in particular was angered by what he saw as blatant profiteering on his mother's name, such as her own Memorial Fund using her name on margarine tubs.

The two Princes insisted that their mother 'would want people to now move on – because she would have known that constant reminders of her death can create nothing but pain to those she left behind'. They were distressed by the continual references to their mother's death and the endless speculation and conspiracy theories this generated, many of which emanated from Mohamed Al Fayed. There was a tart response from Al Fayed's spokesman, saying he could not rest until he knew the full truth about how his son had died.

The boys issued their statement on the day that William returned to Eton and that his brother joined him there. It was William's idea but the appeal fell on deaf ears. They would have to live with the conspiracy theories for at least another decade. Still, William continued to flourish at Eton. His housemaster Dr Andrew Gailey, a respected constitutional historian and music lover from Northern Ireland, took the Prince under his wing educationally and emotionally and exerted an important and positive influence as William sought to rebuild his life. He worked hard. He proved himself to be the fastest junior swimmer at Eton in ten years and was made joint keeper of swimming – a grand title for what is in effect the school swimming captain. He was made secretary of the Agricultural Club and he received Eton's Sword of Honour – the school's highest award for a first-year cadet. This was the young man who stepped onto the tarmac in Canada and ignited 'Wills Mania'.

He was no longer a rebellious schoolboy, but he did not simply toe the line either. He was not afraid to buck a few trends. One courtier said, 'God help anyone who tells William what to do. He listens, but he won't be pushed around by the system.' Never was that more evident than when the issue was raised of where William would continue his education once his schooldays ended.

It had long been presumed that the Prince would follow in his father's footsteps by attending Trinity College, Cambridge. A committee of advisers had made this decision for Charles, but William was given more freedom, and he grabbed the opportunity with both hands. He would not follow the Oxbridge route mapped out for him. He would break with tradition and go, instead, to St Andrews.

CHAPTER 5

BEST DAYS OF
OUR LIVES

'I do all my own shopping. I go out, get takeaways, rent videos,
go to the cinema, just basically anything I want to really.'

PRINCE WILLIAM ON HIS UNIVERSITY LIFE

A round 3,000 onlookers lined the streets of the small, east-coast town of St Andrews, a place that revolves around the 'town and gown' divide in much the same way as Durham, Oxford and Cambridge. On the morning of 24 September 2001, all focus fell on the dark-green Vauxhall Omega as Prince Charles at the wheel attempted to negotiate the narrow, cobbled entrance to St Salvador's College.

A sharp wind blew across the famous Ancient and Royal golf course as Charles nosed the car in under the gothic clock tower. A group of curious students had gathered inside the ancient quadrangle, quietly holding anti-war placards aloft and shivering slightly in the crisp autumn morning. Their presence was predictable but peaceful, an opportunistic bid to piggyback on the publicity generated by the main attraction that day: the arrival of Prince William as he embarked on undergraduate life.

Dressed in jeans, trainers and a pastel sweater, the standard uniform for the modern student, 19-year-old William looked a little shaken by the size of the welcoming committee that had pitched up to mark the occasion. William composed himself quickly and fixed his trademark toothy grin. After stepping smartly from the car and adopting a suitably fixed smile, he strode, hand outstretched, towards the university principal, Dr Brian Lang. Lang stood ever so slightly in front of a host of other academic dignitaries, smiling rather too eagerly and keen to meet the VIP student who, despite his princely status, would be treated no differently from any other fresher.

This place of ancient learning would be William's academic home for the next four years. If he was nervous about what lay ahead of him, he did his best not to show it.

In the weeks prior to the Prince's arrival, Lang had sounded a note of caution. He implored the media to respect the wishes of the Prince and other students, and allow them to get on with their respective courses without constant intrusion and pestering. However, behind closed, oak-panelled doors, Lang must have quietly rejoiced at how good for business William's choice of alma mater was.

St Andrews was hardly an unknown backwater to start with. It is Scotland's oldest university. Steeped in history and myth, it dominates the small town and overlooks a sweep of sandy beach and world-famous, wind-buffeted golf courses. Applications for courses had risen by 44 per cent in the wake of William's decision to attend, and some fanciful reports claimed that female students had been ordering wedding dresses in anticipation of his arrival.

William looked every inch the student prince – but, as a student, he was determined not to stand out. It was a desire that partly lay behind his decision to study at St Andrews. It meant that the young Prince was particularly irritated by reports that his choice of St Andrews, where he was to study the history of art, geography and anthropology in his first year, had been opposed within the Royal Family. William instructed palace aides to deny rumours that the senior royals had really wanted him to attend one of the colleges at Oxford or Cambridge. The family, the officials insisted, were 'thrilled' by William's departure from tradition, not least because his choice underpinned the monarchy's firm ties with Scotland.

William took the time to explain his choice in an interview published the day before he matriculated. He had, he said, dismissed studying at the University of Edinburgh because the city was too big and busy. He maintained, 'I do love Scotland. There is plenty of space. I love the hills and the mountains and I thought St Andrews had a real community feel to it. I've never lived near the sea, so it will be very different. I just hope I can meet people I get on with. I don't care about their background.'

I am confident that the egalitarian-minded royal meant what he said, even though he had chosen a university with the highest percentage of privately educated undergraduates in the country.

However much William longed to slip quietly into student life, concessions were always going to be made for his status. He arrived a week late for a start, having decided to skip Freshers' Week, the notoriously hedonistic seven days traditionally set aside before term officially starts when new arrivals launch themselves into student life, minus the inconvenience of study. William missed out on the raucous behaviour associated with drunken fresher parties. It had the potential for media frenzy, he said. 'And that's not fair on the other students. Plus, I thought I would probably end up in a gutter completely wrecked and the people I met that week wouldn't end up being my friends anyway. It also meant having another week's holiday.'

It was a well-rehearsed script, cleared by the palace PR men, upbeat and positive. William made all the right noises but he touched too on the underlying and inevitable tension that would be a feature of his student life. For most students, the fun of Freshers' Week is offset by the sort of indignities best forgotten. If a few compromising pictures are taken or a few ill-advised liaisons forged, then the worst the fledgling intellectual might face is some common-room ribbing or the wrath of the dean. But how could the future king, however normal he wants to be, fall out of student bars and into student beds without generating the sort of moral outrage and public debate reserved for wayward cabinet ministers? Where other students worried what their peers might think, or sweated over whether or not college authorities might notify their parents, William had to concern himself seriously with what the nation might make of him should student high jinks get out of hand. He would have to be discreet and he would have to choose friends wisely.

William had already stated in his pre-university interview that he was confident in his own ability to gauge the sincerity of strangers. 'People who try to take advantage of me and get a piece of me I spot it quickly and soon go off them. I'm not stupid,' he said. No doubt he felt the same certainty when it came to women.

Before he met Kate, the girls he felt most comfortable with tended to fall into a particular and predictable type: tall, slim, leggy, blue-eyed blondes with trust funds more substantial than their frames and double-barrelled, sometimes triple-barrelled, surnames. They may not have presented him with any profound connection but they were fun, they were of his circle, they had the 'right' sort of background and they were there. Naturally, some speculation was patently nonsense. When he was 18, it was reported that William had been carrying out a flirtatious email relationship with American pop princess Britney Spears. Publicly, the suggestion was ridiculed; privately, William found it both hilarious and flattering.

By the time William was embarking on student life and preparing to embrace his increased freedom (however qualified it might remain), he was well aware of his powers over the female of the species. But equally, as a titled lady once linked to him informed me, he was tiring of the girls who were conventionally considered his type. She said, 'He was drawn to the riskier girls and he likes a challenge. But a lot of the aristocratic girls he has been linked with are too much trouble for him. It is interesting that he's settled for an ordinary middle-class girl. It's because she does not have the baggage some of these titled girls do: problems such as anorexia, drugs, drinking. He doesn't want all those problems.'

Still, William would have to negotiate some problems of his own before, as this source so succinctly put it, he would 'settle' for Kate.

In spite of the numerous girls to whom William had been linked before his arrival at St Andrews, none was deemed truly special. In his 21st-birthday interview, William insisted that he did not have a steady girlfriend, but said that if the right girl came along he would make his move. Echoing his father, William seemed to agonise over the impact dating a prince would have on these girls. 'There's been a lot of speculation about every single girl I'm with and it actually does quite irritate me after a while, more so because it's a complete pain for the girls,' he said. 'These poor girls, you know, who I've either just met and get photographed with, or they're friends of mine, suddenly get thrown into the limelight and their parents get rung up and so on. I think it's a little unfair on them really. I'm used to it because it happens quite a lot now. But it's very difficult for them and I don't like that at all.'

He was, as ever, careful not to be drawn on media speculation about specific girls: 'I don't have a steady girlfriend. If I fancy a girl and I really like her and she fancies me back, which is rare, I ask her out. But, at the same time, I don't want to put them in an awkward situation because a lot of people don't quite understand what comes with knowing me, for one; and, secondly, if they were my girlfriend, the excitement it would probably cause.'

Apart from any possible issues with girls, university life was undoubtedly a shock to the system for the young Prince. However much William had claimed to be looking forward to managing his own time 'in a relaxed atmosphere', it must have been daunting. Despite his egalitarian protestations and the levelling experience of his gap year, when he stayed at one of the royal houses William had enjoyed all the princely comforts. When in residence at Balmoral, Highgrove, Buckingham Palace, Windsor Castle, Sandringham or Clarence House, William is surrounded by order and opulence. He usually woke at 7.30 a.m., when a footman would come into his room carrying what is known as a calling tray, bearing a pot of coffee and a few biscuits. This would be placed on a table next to William's bed. He drank the coffee black with no sugar. The footman would then switch on the radio, which was usually tuned to BBC Radio 4 so that he could listen to the breaking news. Then the servant, not William, pulled back the curtains to let in the morning sun.

William usually got up straight away, had a shave and a shower and did his Canadian Air Force exercises – a strict 11-minute regime of stomach crunches, press-ups, stretches and running on the spot inherited from his father and grandfather Prince Philip and favoured by the young Prince because it was easy to do in his own room. By this stage, one of his valets would have laid out his smart clothes for the day but, instead of changing into them, he would pull on a jumper and jeans and head for a breakfast of cereal with cold milk and fresh fruit. As a rule, he eschewed the full English breakfast that would always be on offer.

Despite having had a taste of a less privileged existence at boarding school, nevertheless his accommodation must have seemed sparse to William when he arrived at his student room in St Andrews. He carried with him his own duvet, pillows, a television and a stereo as well as a trunk full of clothing, personal belongings and selected items from the formidable-looking recommended-reading list sent to students during the summer. The following day, he would collect his student identity card and get down to business with his first lecture, on Renaissance art.

William set about making his minimal room more homely, putting up pictures and unpacking books and files. Along the corridor, his Scotland Yard personal protection officer, a constant reminder of the privilege and threat of his status, was going through a similar routine. On another floor of the same halls of residence – mixed but split into male floors and female floors – a certain Kate Middleton had already said her goodbyes to her family and was going through the same angst and excitement as William as she started a new phase in her life. For William, the excitement was tempered by his awareness that his life was being scrutinised and governed by his family. While he may have looked forward to sowing a few wild oats, the Queen and Prince Philip and courtiers at the palace had long since kept files on the right kind of girls that might one day make a suitable bride for the future king. While the Queen and Philip were keen that William have fun and enjoy his bachelor student life, it is no secret that they favoured his settling down sooner rather than later.

From his very first term at St Andrews, Kate, hardly a true social match, was becoming part of a circle of friends tentatively established by William. Like William, Kate had taken a gap year and spent part of it abroad in Chile. From the outset, they found common ground. Like William, she was touched by shyness but found it no barrier to being popular. Like William, she loved sports. In addition to skiing and riding, she was an accomplished hockey and netball player at school and adored sailing. They had a fair number of things in common and they were both young, attractive people who, over a drink or coffee or the occasional bacon butty, would chat with increasing candour and intimacy about their respective lives.

William's greatest hope in those fragile early days of student life was that he would be allowed to enjoy it without the intrusion of the press. To that end, a deal had been made, an agreement between Prince Charles's office and the British media, whereby, in return for the occasional arranged photo call, in which the Prince would sometimes answer a few questions too, William would be left alone to work and play.

To a large extent, it was a deal that worked. Yes, there were paparazzi at St Andrews and, yes, the odd picture had been taken, but for the most part newspaper editors were not publishing them. It was a brittle truce, however, and one that the university rector, former *Sunday Times* editor Andrew Neil (the man who during his tenure at the respected broadsheet newspaper had serialised Andrew Morton's brilliant biography of Diana), always knew would be difficult to maintain. However, for the most part, it held firm, barring a few hiccups.

William's first few months were perceived to have gone relatively smoothly. The press deal was honoured and this meant that William was able to integrate into student life and let his hair down. He was still keen to establish a core group of trusted friends, people he could trust and who, once part of his clique, he would keep close to the point of exclusivity. He was still finding his way. One of the friends who helped him to do that was one Kate Middleton, who lived just a staircase away from his own modest room.

They lived in such close proximity in the halls of residence, known colloquially as St Sallies, that it was easy for Kate and William to see each other often and without having to make any elaborate arrangements. Their lives fell naturally into each other's rhythm. They would meet in the same bars and even played tennis together. Kate was an accomplished player, having represented her school in the sport. William would occasionally invite friends back to his room for a drink and Kate would invariably be among them. However, during his first term of university, William had a good reason not to notice Kate, at least romantically.

Within weeks of arriving, he met and struck up an intimate relationship with another beautiful brunette, Carly Massy-Birch. There was an instant mutual attraction. Her natural aloofness and charm intrigued the Prince. He pestered her and they dated for around two months. The couple agreed to cool things and split in the first term in October 2001. According to Mimi Massy-Birch, her mother, there is no rift between Carly and Kate. The pair – along with the Prince – were still friends. Before William and Kate were married, she said, 'In fact, all three of them are best friends. Carly has her own partner, with whom she is very much in love. She really wants Kate to marry Wills so that she can be sure of going to the wedding. If he falls for someone else, she's worried that she might miss out.'

For all the normality, after he and Carly parted, it added to William's feelings of insecurity. He was increasingly unhappy and unsettled. Perhaps uncertainty and a touch of homesickness and disenchantment were the flipside of normal student life, which he had failed to anticipate. In April 2002, the first reports began to emerge that all was not well with the Prince. He was apparently dissatisfied with his course and bored by his environs. He was seriously considering a change of scene. Perhaps Edinburgh University, with its city attractions and bustle, might have been a better move after all. The Scottish coastal town of St

Andrews, with little to offer but a couple of pubs, a bit of charm and wind-buffeted headlands, was not, it seemed, all he had hoped it might be.

By some reports, the Prince was miserable. Given the crisis that once surrounded his uncle Prince Edward when he decided to quit Royal Marines training after practically completing the gruelling course, just to make a point to his domineering father, this was a potential scandal the palace was anxious to head off at the pass. The press had pounced on Edward's failure to make the grade. With unforgiving ferocity, they called into question everything from his merit as a royal to his sexuality. Nobody wanted William exposed to that sort of mauling. Besides, princes – particularly ones destined to be king – don't quit. Not any more.

Doubts about William's decision to opt for St Andrews had surfaced in the press when he went home at Christmas after just one term. He was depressed, uneasy and felt he had made the wrong choice of college. He discussed the matter with his father, spelling out his desire to abandon the four-year course altogether. Charles was sympathetic at first but understandably alarmed. Palace officials revealed that Charles felt such concern for his son's unhappy start to student life that he asked his private office to devise a strategy that would enable William to withdraw from the university should it prove necessary.

The Prince's two most senior members of staff at the time, Sir Stephen Lamport and Mark Bolland, were horrified at the prospect. 'It would have been a personal disaster for William – he would have been seen as a quitter – and it would have been an even bigger disaster for the monarchy, particularly in Scotland,' a royal aide confided.

Eventually, Charles took a different tack and got tough. He strongly advised his son that most students take a while to settle in and urged him to 'stick with it'. Prince Philip was predictably rather more gruff and forthright. He told him in no uncertain terms, with one of his trademark phrases, just to 'get on with it'.

William's wobble and contemplation about quitting university life was also pinned on his association with a 'beautiful PR girl'. It emerged that he had enjoyed a four-month relationship with 21-year-old Arabella Musgrave before starting university and, although they had agreed to 'cool it' before he headed for university, he still held a candle for her. Moreover, while his friendship with Kate may have been deepening, after his brief intimacy with Carly had ended, it was still just that: friendship. Claims that William was still pining for Arabella were probably unfounded, but it is true that he did increase the number of weekend returns to Highgrove, hundreds of miles away from university.

But William had no choice. When he explained first-hand how he wrestled with the idea of quitting university, he said, 'I think the rumour that I was unhappy got slightly out of control. I don't think I was homesick. I was more daunted.' He conceded there had been a problem and that his father had been a big help. 'We chatted a lot and in the end we both realised – I definitely realised – that I had to come back,' he added. But being told to belt up and knuckle down was not likely to solve any deep-seated concerns. William did go back, but he was still toying with the idea of making his excuses and leaving.

Coincidentally, another first-year student was having wobbles and doubts, too. Kate was struggling with the transition from school to university. She had her tearful moments, telephone calls home and anxieties over work. It was something she and William shared as she became his confidante and he hers. Something was beginning to shift between the two. It was Kate who suggested that perhaps what William needed was not a change of scene but a change of course. It was Kate who really averted the crisis of his flunking-out of his first year at university, translating it instead into a perfectly acceptable decision to change from history of art to geography – a subject he had always expressed a particular interest in.

William had admitted before going to St Andrews that he was 'much more interested in doing something with the environment'. It was something his father had drummed into him at an early age and the connection was made. He switched courses and he immediately felt happier, as if a huge weight had been lifted from his shoulders. His social life began looking up, too. The reticent Prince, who had held back from joining the societies everybody thought he would, became a member of the Kate Kennedy all-male dining club. Kate became, in turn, a founding member of the female equivalent, the Lumsden Society. As part of a group of friends, they enjoyed meals in the local pizza restaurants and trips to Ma Belles, a favourite student bar in town, where they enjoyed a few drinks, but nothing excessive. William liked beer and wine, but his favourite tipple was a pint or two of cider. He rarely drank during the day, sticking to spring water, having ditched fizzy drinks such as Coke in his early teens. Life was fun for the young Prince, and Kate was, it seemed, a more central fixture in it.

Kate was also by now known in public and linked by friendship to the future king. In April 2002, pictures of Kate entered the public consciousness as the lithe brunette was seen strutting down a student catwalk for a charity fashion show watched by a clearly mesmerised William. She wore a black lace dress over a bandeau bra and black bikini bottoms. William had paid £200 for a front-row seat and he was not going to miss Kate's sexy-model show for the world. A fellow student tipped off the *Mail on Sunday* and on 7 April 2002 the story ran under the headline

WILLIAM AND HIS UNDIE-GRADUATE FRIEND KATE TO SHARE A STUDENT FLAT. Earlier that month, he had been on the cusp of quitting university; now, after a heart-to-heart with Kate, he was not only staying but he had also begun looking for a flat with Kate and two friends.

The student mole revealed, 'Kate was the real reason behind William's decision to go [to the fashion show]. She's one of a group of good mates he has who all hang out together and have helped him through the past few months. She's a nice girl and good fun. However, they're strictly friends; there's nothing more in it than that. Four of them are going to share a flat for the second year.' The *Daily Mail*, who referred to Kate and the Prince as 'firm friends', picked up the story. They had only scratched the surface. Until then, Kate had been an anonymous friend. Now she was well and truly on the public radar. So-called 'friends' were quick to contact the press in the hope of making a fast buck and pass on the details of Kate and William's friendship.

It was exactly what William had been hoping to avoid, but there was no stemming the flow of information. The press had promised to leave William alone. However, that only meant they would not publish anything unless it was arguably in the public interest and too good to pass up. Information about Kate was also, some argued, genuinely within the bounds of public interest. Besides, there was nothing negative in the reports. 'They get on really well. She's a very lovely girl but very unassuming. She's very bubbly but also discreet and loyal to William,' confided one friend. 'She treats him just like any other student. Many girls, especially the Americans, follow him round like sheep and he hates that. He just wants to live with people knowing he can be himself,' said another. He just wanted to live with Kate.

When William began looking to move from the university halls of residence into off-campus accommodation, observers were surprised that he and Kate, along with their pal Fergus Boyd, were considering properties in the town itself. For reasons of privacy, it had been assumed that William would look further afield – and when it came to it the student quartet did eventually move to a more remote residence – Balgove House – close to St Andrews golf course. It was still close enough to the town for the elite 'community' surrounding William to socialise but, significantly, it was far enough out of town to be away from prying eyes. There were a number of properties on the farm, known as Strathtyrum estate, just off the A91 three-quarters of a mile from the outskirts of the town. The property was owned by the cousin of Kate's closest university friend, Alice Warrender, a fellow history of art student, and daughter of the well-known artist Jonathan Warrender, descended on his father's side from an early-18th-century Lord Provost of Edinburgh. She was somebody Kate could always count on, and, along with her circle of pals, Bryony Daniels and Ginny Fraser, she had a good support network. She would soon need them.

The move to the farm marked a sea change in William's approach to life, which some ascribe simply to growing up but others put down to Kate's influence. However, while all seemed to be going swimmingly well for William and Kate, there was one small problem: Kate already had a boyfriend. While William stuck to his father's advice and was careful not to become involved romantically in the early days of his student life, Kate had fallen for a good-looking chap called Rupert Finch. He was her second serious boyfriend after she had ended her first real romance with Ian Henry. Rupert was darkly handsome, sharing the same patina of privilege and sporting good health with which Kate herself is blessed. He excelled at many sports, but cricket was his main game and he even led the university cricket team on a tour. He wanted to become a lawyer and had the brains and the charm to suggest that, if he did, he would be a successful one. He was, in many respects, a very good catch for Kate. More her speed, some might say, than the future king.

But, as her friendship with William blossomed, Kate must surely have felt torn. All those chats, those shared confidences, all that opening up to each other was bound to turn her head, and it did. Set against royalty, the future solicitor Finch did not stand a chance, especially as William had apparently been Kate's secret passion, albeit in the form of an adolescent crush, for years. As William and Kate began to be bolder towards each other, what had passed for friendship became obviously something more. Kate's youthful passion for Rupert began to dwindle. It might well have done anyway. After all, this relationship mushroomed in the early days of student life. It certainly could not, and did not, survive her moving into a house with William, however much they continued to insist that there was nothing going on between them. Finch confirmed his courteous credentials when questioned about his relationship with Kate by the respected *Mail on Sunday* journalist Laura Collins. He told her bluntly that his relationship with Kate and the circumstances under which it ended was not a subject he would discuss, saying, 'It's not something I'll ever talk about. It's between Kate and me and was a long time ago.'

Only Kate and William will truly know the moment when friendship turned to passion and the platonic sham ended in favour of a more honest intimacy.

Kate and William began cohabiting in their second year, living a normal student existence. 'I do all my own shopping. I go out, get takeaways, rent videos, go to the cinema, just basically anything I want to really,' William said, acknowledging that the deal struck with the media was working. Some evenings he would stay in and cook. Discussing his prowess in the kitchen, he said later, 'I've done a bit at university when I had to feed my flatmates, which was quite hard work because a couple of them ate quite a lot.'

The fact that William and Kate were living such a cosy existence inevitably led to increased speculation that they were intimate and not just good friends. One university contemporary told me, 'There was a bit of a buzz about them living together. But they were so careful in public you would never have guessed they were an item in the early days. They had the whole thing off pat. Obviously Fergus Boyd [their flatmate] knew, but at first they were seen as just mates.'

And perhaps they were, at least at the outset. In May 2003, Kate's father felt moved to make a good-natured rebuttal of a report that Kate was William's girlfriend. 'I spoke to Kate just a few days ago and can categorically confirm they are no more than just good friends. There are two boys and two girls sharing the flat at university. They are together all the time because they are the best of pals and, yes, cameramen are going to get photos of them together. But there's nothing more to it than that. We're very amused at the thought of being in-laws to Prince William, but I don't think it's going to happen.' Nevertheless, in spite of her father's fairly ironic denials, there was no mistaking just how integral a part of William's set Kate had become.

Whether Kate kept her father in the dark or whether it was just another smokescreen is unclear. Despite her father's strong denial, the media were convinced that they had the right girl. Barely a month after Michael Middleton's light-hearted statement, Kate turned 21, and her parents threw a party in the grounds of the family home. Old school friends turned out in force as well as her crowd from St Andrews. There was champagne and a sit-down dinner in a marquee with everybody dressed, on Kate's request, in 1920s fashion. In addition, there, slipping unannounced into the marquee, was William. He and

Kate exchanged knowing looks. William told her she looked stunning. She smiled her acknowledgement and they began talking and relaxing into each other's company. William left soon after dinner with the party still in full swing. Discretion has always been crucial to William and Kate's relationship.

However, perhaps Michael Middleton was telling the truth, because in the autumn of 2003 William was not behaving like a young man in a full-time relationship. When back in London, he became a regular at the hedonistic Purple nightclub, based in the grounds of Chelsea Football Club, a favourite with the local Sloanes and owned by Fulham businessman Brian Mason. The club, now closed, had been a haunt of Prince Harry, too. They were heady times. Buoyed by his newfound freedom and unrestricted emotionally, William was enjoying spreading his wings.

His exuberance, however, got him into trouble that summer and back onto the front pages. In June 2003, Prince Charles was forced to apologise on behalf of his elder son to an aristocrat who condemned William for 'driving like some yob in a beat-up car' during a weekend break from university. The 76-year-old Lord Bathurst prompted a security scare in a road-rage incident when he chased the Prince, who had overtaken him on a private road on the Earl's estate in Gloucestershire. It was an extraordinary drama, occurring just a month shy of William's 21st birthday, which again showed his readiness to take risks. It came after William had played a polo match at Cirencester with his father. Ignoring the unofficial speed limit on the estate, William was pursued by a furious Lord Bathurst's in his Land Rover, blasting his horn and flashing his lights at the Prince's vehicle. William's police bodyguards intervened. Despite the apology, the aristocrat blasted William's behaviour. He said, 'I don't care who it is, royalty or not – speeding is not allowed on my estate. The limit is twenty miles an hour. If I were to drive like that in Windsor

Park, I'd end up in the Tower. I thought he was some young yob in a beat-up car.' When he was unable to give the speeding Prince a telling-off, the Earl turned on the Prince's bodyguards, whom he described as 'looking like a pair of yobs'. Charles's officials played down the encounter as 'a very minor incident in which no one was injured'. However, it did demonstrate William's more reckless nature.

By the following August, Kate and William's romance had become well and truly public. Four months after the Christmas ball, in April 2004, the *Sun* published pictures of William and Kate on holiday in Klosters, the ski resort in the Swiss Alps, causing some undeserved backlash from Clarence House. The paper had already speculated about the nature of the relationship, reporting that it had flourished thanks to a series of trips to the Balmoral bolt-hole cottage Tom-Na-Gaidh, a getaway given by the Queen to William and Harry.

Privately, William, a young man now just shy of his 22nd birthday, had been proudly showing off Kate and introducing the stunning, dark-haired girl to various friends. Just over a week before the April trip to Klosters, he and Kate had travelled from St Andrews to join a group of his friends riding with the coincidentally named Middleton Hunt in North Yorkshire. Even there, they were at pains not to show the extent of their attachment to each other. One observer noted, 'They were not touchy-feely. They were really so very careful, and afterwards, when everyone else went for a meal, they'd disappeared.' It was no bad thing for Kate to be publicly associated with William. With her by his side, the sometimes irritable Prince was notably more at ease.

During that holiday in Klosters, Kate was one of the royal ski party of seven who had flown from Heathrow to Zurich airport. The group included Harry Legge-Bourke (younger brother to

William's unofficial nanny, Tiggy), Guy Pelly, William van Cutsem, son of Charles's old Norfolk landowning friend Hugh, and van Cutsem's girlfriend, Katie James.

Kate had already been a guest at Highgrove at least three times, as well as at Sandringham, the Queen's Norfolk estate. William had taken her for weekends to a Highlands bolt-hole, the cottage of Tom-Na-Gaidh, Birkhall, Ballater, on the eastern edge of the Balmoral estate, by the River Muick, given to him and Harry by the Queen and renovated at a cost of £150,000. It was inconceivable that she would escape notice. She was, after all, his first publicly acknowledged serious girlfriend. In Klosters, she was part of a lively, wealthy bunch that, every night after an energetic day on the slopes, set out to enjoy the après-ski. One evening, the now remarkably carefree William, with his girl by his side, took to the microphone for a rousing shot at the karaoke bar. Kate sat at a table with Charles, there with his old pals Charlie and Patty Palmer-Tomkinson. Laughing at William's attempts, totally at ease in such elevated company, Kate was a picture.

William did not attempt to deny that Kate was his girlfriend after the pictures appeared in the *Sun*. The issue now, one on which royal observers including myself were divided, was: just how important was Kate?

CHAPTER 6

TOO YOUNG
TO WED

'Look, I'm only 22, for God's sake. I'm too young to marry at my age.
I don't want to get married until I'm at least 28 or maybe 30.'

PRINCE WILLIAM'S COMMENT TO A REPORTER

It had been a long night in Casa Antica, a nightclub in the Swiss
Alps and a popular venue for the Klosters après-ski crowd. It
is one of Prince William's favourite hangouts. On the evening in
question, 30 March 2005, it was no surprise that he could be
found amid the smoke and throbbing music, holding court at a
table in a dimly lit and sectioned-off room at the back of the club.

Sitting next to a flushed Prince Harry, who was a little the
worse for wear himself, Prince William did something
completely out of character. He spotted a tabloid reporter in
conversation with his Scotland Yard bodyguards and
spontaneously invited him over for an impromptu chat. Duncan
Larcombe, a new royal reporter for the *Sun* and just a few years
his senior in age, had arrived at the club just after midnight on a
hunch that the Princes and their friends were there. He had
wisely made himself known to the protection team, some of
whom he had met while covering Harry's earlier holidays to

Africa with then girlfriend Chelsy Davy, offering to leave if they felt that his presence was a problem.

Fortuitously for the tabloid reporter, at that precise moment, Guy Pelly, William's eccentric but often hilarious friend, seen by many as his court jester, burst out of a side room wearing nothing but a pair of brown, silk boxer shorts. Inexplicably, he sat on the reporter's lap, perhaps assuming the journalist was a new royal protection officer (although quite why that would justify his behaviour is another matter), and began talking to the officers. Much to William's amusement, Pelly disappeared almost as quickly as he had arrived when one of the officers introduced the chap on whose lap he was sitting as 'the *Sun*'s new royal reporter'.

Perhaps sensing an embarrassing headline in the newspaper the next day, William indicated to the bodyguards that he would like a chat with the hack. Emboldened by drink, William decided to give him an interview. Apparently, at no stage did the Prince say his comments were off the record – although the next morning a flustered Paddy Harverson, Prince Charles's communication director and media minder for the boys on the ski trip, insisted that the conversation was private and not meant for publication. The editor of the *Sun*, Rebekah Wade, by now reading the copy back in the newspaper's headquarters in Wapping, East London, rightly stood her ground.

They discussed the latest picture taken of the Prince and Kate on the slopes. The previous year, the *Sun* was banned for reproducing such paparazzi pictures. This year, however, William was relaxed about the photographs, although he appeared genuinely surprised as to why there was such frenzied interest in them. The reporter suggested it was because there had been speculation that this relationship could lead to marriage, and that an engagement could be on the cards. Perhaps, gaining in confidence, the journalist did not expect a response, but it was certainly worth a punt. He had thrown the talk of marriage into the conversation, almost in jest, never seriously anticipating that William would take it on. The Prince's forthright remark gave him quite a story: 'Look, I'm only 22, for God's sake. I'm too young to marry at my age. I don't want to get married until I'm at least 28 or maybe 30.'

With those few words, William had given the *Sun* a notable exclusive. The next morning, over five pages and in what was billed as a world exclusive, the paper ran the details of the extraordinary moment in which the young Prince 'opened his heart' to one of its reporters.

Kate Middleton had been in the same room as he had chatted informally to the reporter, but at no stage had William thought of making an introduction. If Kate had serious feelings and hopes for her relationship with William at that point, such a public dismissal of the prospect of a proposal any time soon might naturally have upset her. After all, she was standing close to William when he uttered his surprisingly frank words.

William's candour, however, did little to dampen Kate's spirits, to her great credit. Far from appearing subdued, she joined wholeheartedly in the drunken rough and tumble of the evening. Good-natured horseplay ensued, resulting in the beaded bracelet that Prince Harry was wearing, a gift from girlfriend Chelsy, being grabbed and broken. As he scrabbled around the club floor trying to retrieve the beads, his whooping sibling, Kate and friends swooped on the intoxicated royal, threatening to pull down his trousers and underwear. Lost in peals of laughter, glowing and hot with the night's excesses, Kate was hardly the image of a girl who had just witnessed the man she loved inform a relative stranger that, romantically speaking, he was still up for grabs.

William is media-savvy. There were many in his circle of friends who suspected that the world exclusive, the denial of any serious thoughts of marriage blurted out so apparently carelessly, was, in fact, a smokescreen designed to cool the media frenzy about William's steady girlfriend.

Despite the sensational coverage given to the chat, this statement surprised no one among the royal press corps. He was simply trying to have it both ways. He saw what happened to his mother and what happened to his father. His father made a catastrophic mistake in letting the woman he loved, Camilla, slip through his fingers 30 years ago and was miserable for years. On the other hand, his mother married far too young, and he had not wanted to make the same mistake.

The Prince, echoing his father's view, often jokes with friends that the press 'never let the truth get in the way of a good story'. But William and his advisers know very well that in recent years the band of royal writers of which I was a part, known with a mixture of irritation and affection as 'the royal rat pack', got it right far too often for the Royal Family's liking. Fleet Street legends, such as James Whitaker and Richard Kay, have been working the royal beat and breaking stories with relentless accuracy for many years. This is no mean feat when their enquiries are often met with a stream of lies, half-truths and denials from palace officials and even from the mouths of members of the Royal Family themselves. Like his late mother, Princess Diana, and in spite of his relative youth, William knows how to play the media. Would it really be so surprising if, in an attempt to put the press off the scent and give his relationship with Kate time to develop, William had embarked on a little late-night subterfuge in the Swiss Alps when he poured scorn on talk of marriage?

One senior official on that same skiing holiday left me in no doubt about what the future held for the Prince and his girl. He revealed, 'The Prince knew exactly what he was doing; he would not open his heart about his private life to a reporter he barely knows, no matter how much drink had been taken, without thinking about it first. It was for show, a way of dampening down speculation about him and Kate, a way of protecting her from the press.'

Kate's obvious lack of concern as she partied with her boyfriend showed just how close the couple had become. She, like others who know William intimately, knew that whatever he said was with Kate's best interests – rather than the next morning's headlines – in mind. William has a protective instinct towards all of his friends when it comes to the press. He has inherited a style from his supremely loyal father. It is understandable, given his position and past. Emotionally scarred by the death of his beloved mother, he still believes, like Diana's embittered brother Earl Spencer, that the paparazzi had hounded the Princess to her death.

From that night on, Paddy Harverson placed himself in charge of William's press during his Klosters holiday. He took it upon himself to be William's chaperone, inhabiting a sort of awkward no-man's-land between laddish companion and maiden aunt on all the Princes' subsequent visits to nightclubs. As is so often the case, though, the spin doctor was resolutely slamming the stable door shut long after the horse had bolted.

Unbeknown to Harverson, undercover reporters had been working in the resort for more than a week, observing the young royals' drunken antics in all their glory, including Harry's bid to turn the tables on some members of the press by snatching up a camera and pursuing them as he snapped pictures and howled with laughter. The royals' relationship with the press – especially the tabloids – has always been a protracted game of cat-and-mouse. In addition, that particular royal 'stag' trip, as it was dubbed, was the last holiday Charles and his sons would enjoy before his wedding to Camilla in April 2005.

Within days, I heard a markedly different story from a reliable – perhaps in this instance *more* reliable – source than the Prince himself. A senior royal courtier let slip during conversation that the relationship between William and Kate was very serious and developing at a fast pace. It rang true with me, even at such an early stage.

'The relationship is very much ongoing. Just because the two of them choose to keep things private and play their cards close to their chest does not mean it is waning. Far from it: in fact it is quite the opposite,' a senior contact told me.

Given the seniority of the source, I did not hesitate to rush this story into print. The following morning, the *Evening Standard* splash (newspaper jargon for a front-page story) carried the banner headline SERIOUSLY IN LOVE, Beneath were the words: 'Wills and Kate romance moving at a rapid pace, say royal sources'. A photograph of a smiling William looking lovingly into his girlfriend's eyes accompanied the report. The look of love certainly seemed to me to betray something of the besotted Prince's true emotions, even if his own words had not.

CHAPTER 7

ROYAL MARRIAGE BUSINESS

'Marry Prince William? I'd love that.
Who wouldn't want to be a princess?'

BRITNEY SPEARS

B y the summer of 2006, nearly four years into their relationship, any photograph of Kate that appeared in a newspaper or magazine would do so under the caption 'princess-in-waiting'. For the media, it was only a matter of time before Kate Middleton would be William's bride.

In March 2006, the *Evening Standard*, the newspaper I was then working for as royal correspondent, ran a spread of pictures of Kate wearing a fur hat at the Cheltenham races, and pointed out that her fashion sense mirrored the controversial regal fondness for animal pelt. Seasoned royal watchers were less moved by her choice of hat than by the fact that she was pictured in the same exclusive members' enclosure as Prince Charles and his new wife Camilla, now Duchess of Cornwall. William was not with Kate on this occasion as he was continuing his rigorous training at Sandhurst Military Academy. Yet there was Kate, laughing and smiling, and utterly at ease with the royals and their entourage. It only served to underline the extent to which the so-called Firm now embraced Kate. Later, when a reporter from the *Standard* asked a Clarence House official for an on-the-record comment about Kate's fur fashion accessory, the response was as intriguing as it was revealing. They could not comment on the issue, the representative explained, as Kate was a private individual and 'not yet' a member of the Royal Family.

Were it not for that tantalising 'yet', it would have been a predictable rebuttal. As it was, it suggested there was an inevitable outcome of William's relationship, that it would only be a matter of time before they would be commenting on her behalf as a fully signed-up princess and member of the family.

Media obsession with the marriage of an heir to the throne is nothing new, nor is the public's fascination for the partner he or she chooses. Perhaps only the modes of expression differ. Today people can make their views known through opinion polls commissioned by journalists to break down into percentages the nature and strength of the general view. When Henry VIII dumped his Spanish first wife, Katherine of Aragon, to wed and crown his ill-fated second wife, Anne Boleyn, mother of Queen Elizabeth I, things were less scientific. The people gathered on the foul-smelling streets of London to witness the lavish ceremony that took place on 29 May 1533 and to register their displeasure at both Henry's decision to divorce and, worse still, at his choice of new bride.

Of course, King Henry VIII could, and did, wed, divorce and even execute his wives pretty much at will (in fact, two were executed, Anne Boleyn and her cousin Katherine Howard). Henry, an absolute monarch, was not truly concerned about any public backlash. The problems for a young prince today, placed under the scrutiny of less reticent, and at times downright aggressive, media and the public, are far more intense and pressing. Little wonder, then, that the modern royals have not completely abandoned the methods of their more ruthless forebear. On the day of Prince Charles's wedding to Camilla, for example, there was genuine concern that ardent supporters of the late Princess Diana might ruin the day with noisy protest – so much so that a 'friendly' crowd of charitable workers and those known to support the couple were given tickets and allowed to congregate behind barriers inside the walls of Windsor Castle. The cameras were then carefully positioned to ensure these positive pictures were the ones beamed around the world when the couple emerged after the ceremony. Outside, uniformed police, as well as undercover officers, guarded the route. The only person with an anti-Camilla poster was politely asked to take it down.

For a 21st-century prince, finding a balance between public role and private life is all but impossible. In spite of what has gone before, the vast majority of the public still expect their royals to marry for love. This means that a royal's most personal choice is laden with public repercussions and judgement. Set against this is the knowledge that love can make fools of us all. William was aware of this. Whereas marrying the wrong woman can be a cause of heartache and financial strain for the average man in the street, for the future king and his family the impact of getting it wrong can be cataclysmic for the institution they represent. Finding a bride is a fraught business – it is also vital.

An heir to the throne may raise a great deal of money for needy causes and draw attention to important causes dear to his heart, much as Prince Charles has done. Then again, he may strive to implement some level of social change through various schemes and enterprises. He may even represent his crown and country abroad with distinction, supporting his sovereign, shaking hands and giving impressive and thought-provoking speeches before graciously posing for photographs with paupers, presidents and politicians. But no matter how much heat and noise he may generate – and, with his penchant for firing off letters to Members of Parliament and espousing his views on topics such as organic farming, complementary medicine, genetically modified crops and the state of modern architecture, the present incumbent, Prince Charles, certainly does a great deal of that – one simple fact remains: the heir to the throne must find a suitable partner and breed, as distasteful as that sounds. In this respect, he is little more than a farmyard stud, albeit from a top bloodline, in a well-tailored Savile Row suit.

If anybody knows how important the heir's choice of bride has always been both constitutionally and personally, it is William's grandmother and Sovereign, Queen Elizabeth II. She need only look, helplessly, to the generation that preceded her and to the one that followed to see in these bookends of her reign concrete proof that the moments in recent history that have brought the Royal Family to the lip of destruction are those precipitated by the wrong choice of bride. Getting it wrong has brought the monarchy to its knees and laid it bare to ridicule from the people, whose support is necessary if this unelected and undemocratic institution is to survive.

Picking the right bride to become a princess and a possible future queen is not a decision to be taken lightly. A 21st-century princess is a different species from the ones of old. In the past, the system was tried and tested. A prince would marry for political and dynastic reasons, not for love. He would marry a daughter of a foreign king to forge an alliance between nations or pick from a host of suitable, not-too-distant cousins raised to know the score. In time, and in awareness of their respective jobs, they might grow to love each other. Princes found their passion in the arms of their mistresses, usually a discreet aristocrat and invariably somebody else's wife. Newspaper proprietors of old, usually barons and earls themselves, would instruct their editors and reporters to ignore any royal extramarital activity.

In this century, money talks, and sordid sex secrets sell newspapers. Such deals for discretion have long been torn up. Royals and their affairs, as far as the tabloids are concerned, are fair game. For a modern prince like William, the past failures of his ancestors must play heavy on his mind. The consequences have, after all, been almost fatal to the institution he will one day head. The crisis that accompanied Edward VIII's abdication in 1936 and thrust William's great-grandfather George VI onto the throne shook the monarchy to its very foundations.

There is no tradition of abdication in the British Royal Family – and for very good reason. In some European countries, such as Holland, an ageing monarch may routinely retire, as we have recently seen. But it has been drummed into William from an early age that in Britain the only routine separation of monarch from throne comes with death. William, as a child, may have fought against his birthright, and even dreaded it, but his duty was fully explained and his destiny mapped out for him. The abdication of Edward VIII, less than a year after he had ascended the throne, stands alone in British royal history, a cataclysmic event, once unimaginable, now unforgettable. For the many generations that have only ever lived through the reign of his niece, Elizabeth II, it is almost impossible to imagine just how devastating Edward's departure was.

Today, the Duke of Windsor, as Edward became after his abdication, is eulogised rather romantically by some as the king who renounced the throne for love. Films, dramas and documentaries have been made about his and Wallis Simpson's gripping love story, which all seem conveniently to ignore her later infidelities with younger, sexually exotic men, perhaps because they do not dovetail with the love story we all in our hearts want to believe. What we do trust, however, is that Edward loved American divorcée Wallis Simpson beyond reason and because of that love he abandoned his birthright and the heavy burden of responsibility that comes with it. In his riveting memoir, *A King's Story* – the only book ever written by a king, and ever likely to be – Edward reflected that, whatever one's station in life, love must conquer all.

However, there was precious little romance in his sombre 1936 speech informing the nation of his decision to abdicate – perhaps because Prime Minister Stanley Baldwin insisted on having the final say on the wording. There was no romance in his meetings with Baldwin, who relieved him of any hopes of making a queen of Simpson. He told the King, 'The British public will not have her'; and there was no romance in the transference of the burden of monarchy onto the less sturdy shoulders of his younger brother, Bertie, then Duke of York, and soon to be King George VI.

That act – that the much-maligned Wallis herself had counselled against, offering to leave the country for good – tore violently across the empire and the country, striking painfully at the very core of the Royal Family. The institution did not so much wobble as threaten to keel over. It fell to the current Queen's father, the then Duke of York, to lead his small family out of the dust storm. Still mourning the death of his own father, Bertie, as he was known by his family, guided his wife – the stoic former Lady Elizabeth Bowes-Lyon, later Queen Elizabeth, the Queen Mother – along with Princesses Elizabeth and Margaret, blinking into the harsh light of a public life and office for which none had been prepared. As King George VI, he was suddenly the defender of a monarchy in crisis, a monarchy that some genuinely believed to be on the cusp of destruction. With hindsight, it is easy to wonder why there was so much fuss. For the Royal Family, and for the stoic new Queen Consort and her daughters, the answer was, and is, extremely straightforward. The fuss was all about the wrong choice of bride.

In 1996, Elizabeth's youngest child Prince Edward produced and presented a television documentary on the life of the Duke of Windsor, called *Edward on Edward*. It charted his great-uncle's love affair with Wallis Simpson and followed him into exile in France. It was one of the best productions by his controversial company, Ardent, well researched and ably fronted by Edward. But, for all the sympathy Prince Edward personally expressed, there was notably no hint of the Duke of Windsor's behaviour being in any way forgiven or sanctioned by any member of the Royal Family. The Queen did famously visit him before his death, during an official visit to France in May 1972, and, when his body was brought back for burial at Frogmore, his wife was pictured walking in the grounds of Buckingham Palace. But these were acts of common Christian decency on the part of the monarch, his niece. They were not signs that all was forgiven.

Time, for the Queen at least, has done nothing to heal those wounds. Edward VIII made a bad choice, and the Queen's life and those of her children have been defined by it. To a woman as imbued with a sense of duty as the Queen, this fact is compounded by her knowledge that Edward VIII's true crime was that he failed in his duty. He failed to do the one thing that the Prince of Wales simply must do: choose the right woman to be his bride. It was a failure that would, in turn, be repeated by his great-nephew and William's father, Prince Charles. That bears down on Prince William as second in line to the throne with all the weight and inevitability of history.

In the wraithlike figure of Wallis Simpson, King Edward's error was further compounded by the empire's absolute rejection of her. With the still dazzling figure of Diana, Prince Charles's marital folly was compounded by the world's absolute acceptance of her. The danger was not that he would renounce the throne and his people but that they would renounce him. It was a fear to which Charles reacted at times petulantly and rashly. Charles's desperate attempts to regain public favour – or rather the attempts of those working on his behalf – led him and his court into the previously uncharted territory of spin, at times running the risk of damaging not only his mother but the institution of the monarchy itself.

Pragmatists may argue that the marriage of Charles and Camilla on 9 April 2006 – a month after I exclusively broke the story of their engagement in the *Standard* – was the perfect compromise. Unlike his great-uncle, Charles played his cards with a cool head. He was able to have it both ways, the love of his life as well as the chance to reign. Camilla, the restyled, revamped and rehabilitated Duchess of Cornwall, has proved a success. The heir to the throne, so often presented as a middle-aged eccentric, now seems complete with a woman at his side, who he not only loves, but who also believes in him and his many crusades. Charles's succession was a matter of great debate in the months following his divorce from Diana, when damaging revelations of infidelities and the casually inflicted cruelties of their marriage abounded. The debate also resurfaced after Diana's death in 1997.

These days, it may not be a notion greeted with universal joy, but very few genuinely believe that Charles's crown would pass directly to William instead. After all, if Charles was so inclined, it would require an Act of Parliament, not only here, but in each of the realms and dominions. It would also need the Queen to agree it. Crisis over then? No, not quite. Charles may feel entitled to his happiness (of the entire Queen's offspring, he must surely empathise the most with his great-uncle's situation) and as a mother the Queen will want her children to be settled in their personal lives and happy. Unlike his great-uncle, Charles has been allowed to marry his divorcée and keep his position. But it raises the question: at what cost?

The Royal Family, and in particular the court of the Prince of Wales, has been stripped bare for public ridicule, examination and disapproval. The impact has been profound. Spending is scrutinised and tax concessions criticised. There is at times in the country a sentiment perilously close to republicanism. The previous two men to hold the title Prince of Wales have failed catastrophically in their duty to choose a suitable bride. Could the family withstand a third generation making the same mistake? It hardly seems a chance that they are likely to take, nor indeed one that they have had to.

Long before the marriage, Queen Elizabeth had taken a conspicuous interest in her grandson's romance with Kate Middleton. The parallels between William and Kate and the generation preceding them cannot be lost on the monarch. William was 23 and Kate 24 when their love became truly apparent, the same ages as Charles and Camilla were when they first fell in love. The monarch may not be given to whimsy but it must be difficult to resist wondering, what if…? What if Charles had got it right first time around? Then again, there is also the nagging uncertainty: what if William did not?

Prince Charles is understandably determined to shield his elder son from the pressures of such thoughts, from the clamour of the press and the exigencies of royal duties too soon. But already, and perhaps unfairly, William has been touted as a more appealing monarch than his father when his time comes. And, although 88 years and 2 days separate William from his great-great-uncle Edward VIII, he can expect to receive all of the eulogies bestowed upon his notorious ancestor in his prime.

Outside the palace walls, the world in which William exists has been transformed beyond recognition. Yet the imperative that underscored King Edward VIII's life, and the necessity that has governed Charles's, remains William's solemn duty. If he was to avoid the tortuous scandals of the preceding Prince of Wales, he had to find a girl he loves, make sure she is single, respectable and suited to a public role, and produce heirs – magnificently, for the first time, there is no preference of gender to be mentioned here. If his predecessors' failures are anything to go by, it is a career path that is nowhere near as simple as it sounds, and yet William appears to have achieved it beautifully.

Sticking to his narrow job description was not made easier by the fact that William, as heir to the throne, automatically became the country's most eligible bachelor. Eligible bachelors are catnip to a host of decidedly ineligible females. It's easy to go wrong and in these times of telephoto lenses, leaks and appalling betrayals it is easy to get caught if you do. Yet, despite their relative youth and reports of the occasional trial separation, William and Kate's relationship did survive the transition from university life into the real world and now to marriage and a child. In the process, William's 'adorable' Kate, whose role in William's life started innocently enough as just a bit of student fun, has been recast in a far more significant part – that of princess and our queen-in-waiting.

CHAPTER 8

INTO THE
REAL WORLD

'At the moment, it's about having fun in the right places,
enjoying myself as much as I can.'

PRINCE WILLIAM, AFTER TAKING HIS FINAL UNIVERSITY EXAMS

In May 2005, William was putting down his pen after his last gruelling geography exam. Kate had completed hers too, including a well-received dissertation entitled '"Angels from Heaven": Lewis Carroll's Photographic Interpretation of Childhood' (Kate later agreed to make it available to future students on the university website). Unlike William's university contemporaries – perhaps Kate included – who all desperately needed to attain a good grade to help them with their chosen future career, there was only personal pride at stake for the Prince. Whether he got first-class honours, a 2:1 or scraped through with a third was pretty irrelevant as far as his career path to kingship was concerned. Sandhurst, a commission with one of the Guards regiments and then the fast-track into royal duties would follow on from graduation, regardless of whatever the University of St Andrews examinations boards thought of his final performance. But William, a proud and intelligent young man, was desperate for academic success. He was determined not to perform poorly – an eventuality that would inevitably have been met by howls of derision from certain corners of the media and public. William, probably the most academically gifted member of the Royal Family in recent times (a comment that some may think damns him with faint praise), was not about to let anybody down, least of all himself.

He had prepared himself diligently for these exams and as he finished them he let out an audible sigh of relief. Ahead of him were three weeks of festivities and fun, culminating in a lavish graduation ball at the university on 24 June. There would be a traditional ceilidh band, a pop group and disco. And his beautiful girlfriend Kate would be on his arm.

On the night itself, students who had arrived as visions of glamour afterwards stumbled out into the early morning and picked their way across the litter-strewn quadrangle. They linked arms and walked towards the stretch of beach known as Castle Sands. The more foolhardy among them took the head-long plunge into the freezing waters that glimmered as the dawn began to break. Kate, William and flatmate and confidant Fergus Boyd stayed on dry land, wandering down the sands and trying, no doubt, to ignore the fact that day was breaking. With it, a new era in their life was beginning. In many respects, Kate and William were no different now from any other young couple facing the prospect of testing their university romance in the outside world to see if it could stay the course. Neither of them knew what lay in store, only that they were prepared to give it a go. So many university relationships flounder once lectures and common rooms are swapped for working lives. Both were fully aware that their intimacy would diminish; the routine of their lives would never again be quite so in tune as it was through university days. But they agreed that, whatever happened, they would always be the closest of friends and have no regrets.

William knew that his time on easy street was at an end. He had relished the relative anonymity that full-time education had afforded him. For him, graduating had more resonance than for his contemporaries. Whatever he did now, the reality and expectations of impending royal duties could no longer be ignored. At the very least, he would face familial pressure to step up to the mark and shoulder his duties.

A few weeks earlier, he had already acknowledged this point and expressed some anxiety, candidly admitting that he was wary of taking on public duties, 'because I don't want to start too early and then be stuck doing that for the rest of my life'. His university peers might envy William's financial security, as they struggled to find jobs and started paying off loans, eating further into hefty overdrafts, but they at least had the freedom to try on for size different careers or ways of life. Not William. Once he embarked on public life, he would effectively be starting on an apprenticeship that would end with his kingship. And, even though the Prince had learned to combat his self-consciousness with age and experience, he was discouraged by what he had seen of his father's attempts to try to turn that apprenticeship into a meaningful role in its own right. As one of his aides told me at the time, William was put off by what he saw as the relentless belittling of his father's efforts. Would that be his lot, too? If he tried to adopt his father's combative stance when he became Prince of Wales, tried to be a figure with something to say, something to contribute, would he be faced with the same negative treatment?

But, with his university days all but over, William's apparent reticence to assume the business of being a key member of the Royal Family would only ever become more exposed. William had managed to reach the end of his university days – and the grand age of 23 – without actually doing a great deal of anything in the way of public duties for the family. His father, conversely, was a far less natural student, but was, by that time in his life, something of a veteran on the royal circuit. He carried out his first overseas engagement in Australia at the age of 19 and was invested as Prince of Wales at Caernarfon Castle two years later, in 1969.

One royal official at the time explained to me, 'The difficulty for Prince William is that all he wants to do is to keep his head down. He is really torn. He feels very strongly that he has enough of his adult life ahead of him to grow into the role that has been mapped out for him. And if he does not raise expectations about himself too early he might just achieve a degree of normality.'

Prince Charles and his aides have always defended William's stance. His situation is, they say, very different from that of his father, who even as a teenager was heir to the throne. It all seems so much semantics to me. William's place in the succession is writ large in his present as much as his future. On the eve of graduation, opinion polls continued to give out a message that frankly left the young Prince in a state of despair. Time and again, polls showed that almost half the population would rather see William succeed to the throne than Charles, prompting calls for the 'mollycoddled' young royal to finally step out of the shadows. Even Harry had done more photo and interview opportunities than William had at that stage. It was inevitable that, even before his degree results were through, commentators would begin to ask, 'Where does William go from here?'

On 23 June 2005, William graduated in front of his father, stepmother and royal grandparents – as well as several hundred other equally proud parents. Looking nervous and biting his bottom lip, William waited his turn along with 30 fellow geography students. They hovered by the side of the stage in Younger Hall, William dressed in white bow tie and black silk academic gown with cherry-red lining. As the dean of arts,

Professor Christopher Smith, called out the name 'William Wales' from the lectern, the Prince stepped forward to a prolonged burst of applause and flash photography from the audience. In the front row of the lower balcony, Charles and Camilla, who had until then exchanged banter and laughter, fell silent. Sitting beside them, the Duke of Edinburgh studied his programme of events intensely. The Queen, in a brilliant lemon outfit and recently recovered from a cold, adopted that familiar stern look.

William walked to the centre-stage pulpit, grasped its brass handrail bearing the university crest and knelt before Sir Kenneth Dover, chancellor of St Andrews. The ceremony was perfunctory. As with all other graduates, Sir Kenneth tapped William lightly on the head with the ceremonial birretum, a 17th-century scarlet cap rumoured to contain a fragment of the trousers of John Knox, the great Presbyterian reformer. '*Et super te*' (meaning 'And upon you'), Dover intoned as the cloth touched William's head. Then James Douglas, the university bedellus – a kind of glorified head butler – hooked the Prince's red and black academic hood over the kneeling supplicant's shoulders. This act signified that, after four years' study, William was now a master of arts. Within moments, the master was offstage and being handed the scroll of his degree certificate. The culmination of four years of work was over, just like that. William emerged with fellow graduates into the hazy sunshine of the town's main street. Their cosseted undergraduate life was at an end.

William was met by the noise of hundreds of people lining the streets in scenes reminiscent of those that had accompanied his arrival in St Andrews. He graciously glad-handed the crowds on his way to the town police station to thank the Fife Constabulary for looking after him. His student days had been a success, despite the rocky start, and with his upper second he had outranked his father's lower second from Cambridge. As she watched, though, the Queen would have been the first to point out that there are no academic courses on how to be head of state.

After the ceremony, an official thank you was issued by Clarence House on William's behalf. It said, 'I have thoroughly enjoyed my time at St Andrews and I shall be very sad to leave. I just want to say a big thank you to everyone who has made my time here so enjoyable.' He declared afterwards, 'I have been able to lead as normal a student life as I could have hoped for and I am very grateful to everyone, particularly the locals, who have helped make this happen.' More revealing was a chance remark he made to a guest following the ceremony itself. Blinking in the sun as he joined his fellow graduates meeting proud relatives on the clipped grass of St Salvador's quadrangle, he told one guest with some trepidation that it was time for him to go forth 'into the big, wide world'. He would not do so alone.

Seated five rows in front of the Prince, and graduating 80 people ahead of him, was the young woman who, more than anything or anyone, had shaped William's student life. Wearing high heels and a sexy short black skirt beneath her gown, she was called to the stage as Catherine Middleton. She smiled broadly as she returned to her seat, catching William's eye as he flashed back a proud smile.

'Today is a very special day,' William said, 'and I am delighted I can share it with my family, particularly my grandmother, who has made such an effort to come, having been under the weather.' It was a predictably stiff summation of events. Far more natural was the affection with which the Queen patted her grandson's shoulder as he kissed her on both cheeks before she departed. Revealingly, far more natural was the smile on Kate's face as, at William's urging, she introduced her parents to their monarch. It seemed the most normal thing in the world for her to do. But it marked a departure for Kate. She and William had taken a momentous step towards adulthood together that day and Kate was now well and truly part of the fold.

'You will have made lifelong friends,' Dr Brian Lang, vice-chancellor of St Andrews, told the new graduates in an address before they left Younger Hall that day. 'I say this every year to all new graduates: you may have met your husband or wife. Our title as "Top Matchmaking University in Britain" signifies so much that is good about St Andrews, so we can rely on you to go forth and multiply.'

His words were met with laughter of course. But there must have been a few couples in the auditorium that day who prickled slightly at his words and wondered if they referred to them. Were William and Kate among them?

Leaving the security of St Andrews was going to prove a challenge to them both. They had endured a rocky spell in their relationship already, but more trials would lie ahead. William could not postpone forever either duties or decisions. Kate was a bright, determined young woman. She had already invested much in William, but her friends were clear that he would be wrong to assume that she would hang around indefinitely in the absence of any commitment. As for William, he was a young man still struggling to carve out his role in life and horribly conscious that the constitutional clock was ticking. 'I have so many things I want to do,' he said. 'I'm scared, really scared, that I won't have time.'

As late summer gave way to autumn 2005, the uncomfortable process of trying to assimilate real life with royal life was, for Kate, about to begin in earnest. Neither she nor William could have reckoned on it that summer as they luxuriated on holiday in the beautiful country of Kenya, but in just a matter of weeks back home the strain would begin to tell, as Kate's 'double' life would put pressure on her personally, causing tensions between palace and press and taking its toll on her and William's relationship. How could it not? After all, one day Kate would be taking tea with the Queen at Windsor Castle, the next she was catching a ride on a bus, seated next to a complete stranger who was oblivious to the esteemed company she was getting used to keeping. When she was by William's side, she was treated accordingly, afforded every courtesy and even the security normally reserved for a member of the Royal Family itself. She was taken to the best restaurants and the most fashionable clubs and through it all she was embraced by the phalanx of armed Scotland Yard security men. The privilege, and the glamour, would be enough to turn many a young girl's head. But, fortunately, not Kate's. She had been raised wisely and brought up to keep her feet firmly on the ground. However, while her sensible nature may have helped steady her, the turbulence of this strangely conflicting life was still difficult to deal with – especially since her relationship with William was now considered to be moving to a new stage.

In September 2005, I received a tantalising telephone call from a senior Buckingham Palace insider. The source seemed quite upbeat. The news was happy. The informant said that I should be 'on my toes' when it came to Kate. 'The relationship,' the source said, 'had gone to a new level.' When I pressed the informant further, a story unfolded that made me begin to appreciate just how important Kate was and went a long way towards hinting at just how important she may yet become. I was told that Kate had had a 'series of private meetings with the Queen'. The two – joined by William – had had at least two intimate dinners in recent months and the Queen had developed a 'warm and relaxed relationship' with her grandson's girlfriend. One of the dinners was said to have taken place at Windsor Castle. This is the Queen's favourite royal residence and the one that she truly regards as home. This was significant in itself.

'Keep a close eye on the situation,' I was told. 'The fact that Kate has met with Her Majesty several times and has dined with her privately should not be underestimated. Her Majesty takes a loving interest in her grandson and heir and she is delighted he is so happy with Kate. Kate has a wonderfully relaxed manner and to be so relaxed in the company of the Queen is a good thing. It speaks volumes about how the Queen feels about her.'

It was a very important steer and proof, as if proof were needed, that in the world of royal reporting the story does not stand still for long. Outside castle walls, Kate continued to act like an ordinary girl: independent, intelligent, possessing a certain degree of class perhaps, but not so very different from swathes of smart young women. She was often spotted browsing in shops on the fashionable King's Road, sometimes alone, sometimes with her mother or friends, before heading back to the Chelsea flat where she was now living. There was no armed guard by her side. She was equipped with only her wits and growing savvy. This, by the autumn of 2005, was the dichotomy of Kate Middleton's new life. There is no more vulnerable or conflicting position than this, to be hovering, half in, half out of the Royal Family. But, for the most part, Kate coped remarkably well with her newfound and always shifting state.

Kate and William tried to develop their own routine. After all, whatever William's status, they were like any couple trying to figure out what their relationship meant in the real world beyond the university gates. At its core was a need for secrecy and a continued game of cat-and-mouse with the pursuing paparazzi. William began to stay overnight with Kate at her white stucco-fronted apartment opposite a bus stop in Chelsea. They would do what any young couple might. Sometimes they would head out to nearby clubs, such as Boujis or Purple, drink vodka and cranberry and enjoy the release of a throbbing dance floor and a mindless night of fun with friends. At other times, they would relax at a local restaurant. The Pig's Ear, a discreet and classy gastropub known for its good food and Chelsea-bohemian clientele, was one of Kate's favourites, and William's too. He was often seen there supping his Breton cider. On other occasions, they would stay in; William would cook as he often had at their St Andrews house, or they would order in pizza, watch a film and try to emulate the simplicity of their university 'marriage'.

It was all a far cry from the privilege and attention that the Prince would receive when staying at the home of his father or grandmother; but after four years of freedom this was how he liked it. His 'double life' was one of choice; Kate's was imposed upon her. For there was one significant difference from their carefree university days: the press, or rather the press's attitude to the couple. As far as freelance photographers were concerned, the gloves were off. William – and by extension Kate – was no longer shielded by agreements fixed by courtiers. Editors were now ready to test the water and see just how far they could go, and just how much money they could make in the process.

At university, the press had fulfilled their gentlemen's agreement and kept their distance. They had allowed William to go about his daily business free in the knowledge that he and his companions were not being followed. Now the paparazzi were out in force and Kate, for the first time, would learn just what it really entailed to be the beautiful girlfriend of a future king. Her Chelsea flat and its environs may have been vetted by William's Scotland Yard security officers, but nothing stops a paparazzo with the scent of his prey – and his pay – in his nostrils, as Kate would find out to her dismay shortly after the wedding.

Up to five such astute photographers had tracked Kate down to her home, having trailed doggedly after her through town. They sometimes worked as a team, thus reducing the risk of missing a picture – but it meant having to share the spoils if successful.

They would pitch up outside in the early hours of the morning, sitting quietly in their cars, sometimes with blacked-out windows, engines off, patiently waiting and watching. As soon as Kate or William emerged, they would act – firing off a few frames from the distance. If Kate was on her own, they would invariably follow. Her photograph had now earned something of a premium – not as much as the Royal Family and their advisers might estimate, but enough to make securing and selling it a worthwhile venture. Glossy magazines and newspapers had woken up to the fact that Kate was now newsworthy. Their readers wanted to know more about her: what she was wearing, where she shopped for her clothes, where she had her hair and makeup done. It all became part of an almost daily news diet.

Kate's arguably stunning image began to appear alongside snaps of footballers' wives and girlfriends or the latest girl band member or pop sensation. At first, the pair let it ride. To some extent, William was of the opinion that the media attention went with the territory – for him, after all, it always had, and it was the brief respite during student days, rather than this renewed onslaught, that marked a break from the norm. Besides, when they were together, it was easier to handle. There was always a waiting car and a royal bodyguard on hand to deal with any eventuality. Pictures of William and Kate climbing into a car after a night out together had rapidly become a staple of the picture editors' morning schedules. It was more difficult for Kate, though, when her protective boyfriend and his security entourage were not there to assist her. She had become unnerved as some of the photographers began to follow her more openly. It was as though she were being stalked – not aggressively but a tricky situation nevertheless. The photographers were professionals and knew the rules. To some extent, Kate had to work them out as she went along.

At William's behest, Clarence House officials tried to form a strategy to cover Kate. They wanted to prove harassment, so privacy specialists from royal lawyers Harbottle and Lewis were called in to advise. Everyone at the palace, including Prince Charles, knew how fraught any sort of legal recourse could be. In October, Harbottle and Lewis sent newspaper editors a pre-publication warning, suggesting in the strongest possible terms that Kate should be left alone and that some of the photographers who persistently pursued her had breached guidelines from the Press Complaints Commission. William was determined to push things further. He was being briefed on privacy issues by Paddy Harverson, his father's communications secretary, and was interested in finding out how a landmark ruling won by Princess Caroline of Monaco in a Strasbourg court the previous year might impact upon him and his girlfriend. The ruling, after years of alleged harassment by the paparazzi, effectively banned the German press from publishing photographs of Princess Caroline and her children. Might William be able to argue the same for his girlfriend? He discussed the problem with Kate and her family and within weeks had instructed royal lawyers to examine the possibility of taking some form of legal action through the courts to place Kate firmly off limits. In December 2005, the broadsheet *Sunday Telegraph* was tipped off about the move, and its chief reporter, Andrew Alderson, penned a report that Clarence House would be proud of.

'William may turn to the human rights court to protect Kate,' it read. The information could only have come from William's own officials, and the *Sunday Telegraph* is a favoured publication for official leaks. The article continued, 'Prince William is personally masterminding attempts to ensure that his girlfriend, Kate Middleton, can pursue a "normal" life and career away from the prying lenses of the paparazzi. The *Sunday Telegraph* has learned that the prince has mastered complex privacy laws and may ask lawyers to go to the European Court of Human Rights if the situation worsens. According to his friends, Prince William feels that Miss Middleton's future happiness and the survival of the relationship depend on protecting her from overly intrusive photographers.'

It read as a barely concealed threat to Fleet Street's tabloid editors to consider themselves put on notice – if they continued to publish images of Kate, the palace would use the courts to act. When I checked this story out at the time, one courtier told me, 'Actually, the level of intrusion has calmed down quite a bit but it's something William is very concerned about. He can cope with it but he's always been anxious about the impact on others who have suffered intrusion simply because of being linked to him.'

William's concerns may have been understandable but they also proved a source of slight tension between him and his father. Prince Charles sympathised with Kate's lot but he felt recourse to the European Court of Human Rights was ill advised and could open a whole new can of worms for the Royal Family, who, after all, depend on positive publicity for their very existence as a privileged, expensive and unelected institution. Besides, Prince Charles has never been a great fan of laws that he views as all too often abused by the undeserving at a cost to the greater good, and to the detriment of his country's sovereign laws.

Much to the relief of all, it seemed that, as Christmas approached, the problem was abating. Reporters and their editors did seem suitably chastened. But just before Christmas, as the palace began to relax, I revealed a story that put privacy issues back in the spotlight and sent alarm bells ringing all the way to SO14, Scotland Yard's elite Royalty and Diplomatic Protection Department. I revealed that William had demanded to know how photographs pinpointing the location of his girlfriend's London home had come to be printed in a down-market German magazine. The pictures showed William leaving the apartment following a night spent there with Kate, and crudely indicated the exact location of the flat with a big red arrow and the caption 'Das liebesnest' – the love nest. Senior protection sources condemned the story, printed in the Hamburg-based Das Neue, as 'grossly irresponsible' and the episode prompted an immediate review of the Prince's security. William was furious at the magazine's 'stupidity' in publishing such personal information at a time when security fears in the capital were at their peak in the aftermath of the city's 2005 bloody 7/7 terrorist bombings.

Kate and William had been back in the real world barely five months and already it seemed to be closing in on them and threatening their relationship. William knew that his father was uncomfortable with his proactive approach to the press and it was a source of some friction between them. But it was not the only element of William's life that seemed out of kilter. This period of adjustment was proving tense and uncertain as far as his continued relationship with Kate was concerned. In September, I had been told to keep an eye on the situation and had been informed that the relationship was moving rapidly on.

It was only a matter of time, it seemed, before the 'M' word was mentioned. When it was, it came in the form of a snippet in the Mail on Sunday's feisty gossip columnist Katie Nicholls's page. 'Prince William's turbulent relationship with Kate Middleton is more gripping than any soap opera,' she wrote. 'Whether they will stay together is the question on everyone's lips,' she continued, before taking the giant leap and claiming that senior courtiers at Buckingham Palace had started discussing the prospect of a marriage and that 'contingency plans' for a wedding had been put in place. She allowed herself the safety net of pointing out that the palace plans for all eventualities (preparations for the Queen Mother's funeral began in 1969), before going on to suggest that an announcement was being readied for spring 2006, with a wedding in the autumn. Of course, it was wildly speculative, but it was not entirely without foundation. And it showed just how far Kate Middleton had come in the few short months since graduating from university.

However keen she and William may have been to maintain her privacy, by the end of the year, even the broadsheet newspapers – known for their restraint in comparison with their more energetic cousins, the tabloids – were publishing profile articles about Kate. The *Independent on Sunday* referred to her as 'Her Royal Shyness'. William, they claimed, frequently conveyed the impression that, if the monarchy could be persuaded to call it a day before it was his turn to lift the crown, he would happily step out of the aristocratic limelight. He was, they said, a commoner by instinct if not by birth. This seemed to me a theory too far. However much William was a product of both his mother's and father's opposing influences, he was a royal through and through. His desire for privacy and for his version of normality was, if anything, akin to wanting to have his cake and eat it too. His attraction to Kate and his continued relationship with her was, perhaps, evidence of a certain fascination with 'normality' but he could hardly be the sort of 'republican prince' envisaged in the article. Still, it was clear that William felt irresistibly drawn to the daughter of decidedly middle-class, self-made entrepreneurs in a way that he was not when in the company of, say, some obscure Ruritanian princess with a triple-barrelled name and several shaky connections to the extended family tree.

Under King William, commentators mused, and possibly Queen Catherine, we might yet see a move away from the present, expensive, fake-ancient patronage and pageantry (much of which dates back no further than the 19th century and Queen Victoria's adoration of pomp and history, however faux). In its place, we could expect a move towards a more modern Scandinavian-type monarch, but perhaps at the cost of being far less secure.

Undeterred, the *Independent on Sunday*'s article ran, 'The People's Princess may be replaced, in Kate, by a real princess of the people: a non-blue-blood. For republicans who prefer to be citizens rather than subjects and who hoped, after Diana's death, that the demise of the monarchy was imminent it's not the happy-ever-after they envisaged. But it might yet be for William.'

But, even as the newspapers got ready to crown Kate and lauded her for her normality, it was this, not her proximity to royalty, on which she seemed determined to focus. Speaking of her plans to design her own range of children's wear with her parents, one friend revealed, 'She had this fashion idea and she's decided to see it through. She's always loved clothes and has a good eye for design. Working with her parents means she won't be spied on if she and William do stay together. Kate believes she can make good money as well.'

She had William's backing, it seemed. 'He's determined she should be able to lead a "normal" life,' another source told me. Yet this harping on about normality was beginning to irk some sectors of the press. Kate's normality might appeal for now, but it would begin to pall pretty quickly if she, or her boyfriend's emissaries, turned it into a weapon with which to jab back even the most well-intentioned of press enquiries. In a matter of months, the palace had fired a variety of warning shots across the bows of Fleet Street's finest and it seemed that they were playing a dangerous game in the process. In his desire to protect Kate and to indulge her fantasy that it was possible to date the future king and still lead a life unaltered by that reality, was William really doing Kate any favours? The sheltered university days were over. Their relationship was moving on to another level. Kate might still cling to her identity as a private individual but her relationship, their relationship, was not a matter for them and them alone.

CHAPTER 9

IN THE ARMY NOW

*'The last thing I want to do is be mollycoddled or be wrapped up in
cotton wool, because, if I was to join the army, I would want to go where my
men went, and I'd want to do what they did. I would not want to be kept
back for being precious, or whatever — that's the last thing I would want.'*

PRINCE WILLIAM TALKING ABOUT HIS MILITARY CAREER

Prince William put his arm around Kate, pulled her towards
him and kissed her full on the lips, apparently oblivious of
anything or anyone around him. Perhaps it was the mountain air
or his determination to enjoy his last moments of real freedom
before starting his military training; or perhaps he was simply too
exuberant and too in love to let this impulse pass without action.
Unbeknown to them, his touching moment of romance was
captured on film and was destined to be recorded as their first
public kiss – the first time that the young lovers had let their
guard down and shown their intimacy.

After four years together, their commitment to keeping their
distance from each other in public was such that at times they ran
the risk of seeming rather staid and middle-aged, a couple so
comfortable with each other that one might be forgiven for
thinking that all passion was a thing of the past. But this moment
in January 2006 put paid to that notion. If they were worried

about privacy, for once it took a back seat to the overriding mood of the moment.

Separation was looming, with William only days away from starting his military training at Sandhurst Military Academy. His brother, Prince Harry, was already a cadet there and well into the year-long course on which William would soon embark. No doubt Harry had filled in William on some of the rigours that awaited him. But in the meantime William could turn his attentions to Kate and to a carefree skiing holiday together in a modest chalet in Klosters. The location may have been a familiar enough choice, but William and Kate's pre-Sandhurst break was actually a far cry from his family holidays there with his father, who, over the past 17 years, had always telegraphed his arrival by pitching up at the five-star Walserhof Hotel with a sizeable entourage in tow. This time, the tone was low-key, simple and normal.

Much to the young couple's amused delight, they had initially given the media the slip, as scores of photographers and reporters had made the expensive trek from Britain to the Swiss ski resort of Verbier. They had followed a hunch that the young lovers might return to one of their favourite haunts over the New Year. But William and Kate had shunned the resort's bars and restaurants, intent on spending as much time together in cosy intimacy as possible. For the press, it was a costly error, and no doubt William and Kate rather enjoyed the thought of the assembled media all those miles across the Alps, replete with skis and salopettes, wanting for nothing but the all-important story.

When the press pack finally did track them down, they made up for it by getting the perfect story, in the form of that first kiss. William's romantic gesture had come on the penultimate day of their holiday. After an invigorating morning spent tackling some of the resort's most challenging black runs, they had decided to go off-piste on Casanna Alp to enjoy the powder before stopping for a bite of lunch. And then, that kiss. One onlooker said, 'As Kate caught her breath, William placed an arm around her shoulders and pulled her close for a long, slow kiss on the lips. It was very romantic and lasted several moments.' They had come a long way together: from the heights of young passion, to the lows of trial separations, uncertainties and wobbles. Now, as this open, confident kiss signified, William knew he had found a girl he could love and who loved him in return, not for his status, wealth or title, but just for himself. William knew that he would soon begin the toughest physical test of his life at Sandhurst and that he would effectively be banned from seeing Kate for five weeks. (Cadets are not allowed any leave until the first five weeks of their training is completed.)

With their thoughts turning towards the immediate future, William and Kate allowed themselves to consider more distant possibilities. 'Although their lives are about to change, they are determined not to let that spoil what they have got. They know they have got something really special and nobody and nothing will come between them as long as they are honest with one another,' a close source told me at the time.

On 8 January 2006, the day before Kate's 24th birthday, William arrived with his father at Sandhurst Military Academy for the start of his 44-week officer training course. He was the most senior member of the Royal Family to train at the academy, and he was taking his first step towards accepting the future inheritance that would make him head of the armed forces. But, in the first instance, the 23-year-old Prince, one of 269 other officer cadets to enrol at the famous Surrey institution that day, was faced with the less than grand ordeal of having his head shorn of hair: exposing, in the process, that other Windsor crown to be handed down by his father – his bald patch.

William was assigned to a company and platoon and banned from leaving the camp for the next five weeks. He underwent a gruelling schedule, which saw him living in the field, improving his fitness and polishing his boots until they gleamed. By the end of his first term, the second in line to the throne would be proficient in using a hand grenade, an SA80 5.56mm rifle and a Browning 9mm pistol. He would have absorbed lectures on first aid, tactics and war studies given by some of the country's most knowledgeable officers and more fearless taskmasters. Lieutenant Colonel Roy Parkinson, an instructor at Sandhurst, laid it on the line. He told the media who had gathered at the academy to witness the Prince's arrival that Prince William would get 'very little sleep' in the first few weeks of training. Officer Cadet Wales, as he would be known, would receive no special treatment and his drill sergeants would not go easy on him. 'We receive people from all backgrounds,' Parkinson explained, 'but background goes right out the window once training begins. It's a team effort here. If someone steps out of line, they're stamped on, whether they're a prince or not.'

In the next day's papers, one wag predictably joked that the Prince's time at Sandhurst was going to be a 'battle of Wills'. Ahead of him lay one of the toughest experiences of his young life, physically at least.

Just six weeks into training, he faced one of the most grim and notorious exercises, the 'Long Reach' – a 24-hour march in sleet and snow on the Welsh hills. Carrying a pack as heavy as himself, deprived of sleep and on minimal rations, William was testing to the limit his resolve and physical and mental reserves. Pictures appeared of him, his body bowed against the icy wind as he and his platoon struggled through awful conditions. However, there was never any question of following his uncle Edward's lacklustre performance while training and failing to be a Royal Marine. The army's motto is 'Be the Best', and William had to prove himself equal to that challenge. He had once flirted with quitting university, but he knew now that, however tough the task, quitting was not an option. After almost a day and night slogging through the bitterly cold Black Mountains of Wales, pale, exhausted and surviving on bites of chocolate and precious little else, there was a real determination about the young Prince. He had inner strength and he wanted to prove to himself, and to his fellow cadets, that he had what it takes. At one point, close to collapse during one steep climb, he sank to his haunches to gather his breath. Typically, he urged on his fellow cadets before gathering himself up and getting back on track. This was, after all, a team-building pursuit during which the young cadets marched more than 65km (40 miles), navigating between nine checkpoints and sleeping, when they could, under the stars. Such are the demands of the exercise that up to a third of the 269 cadets who started failed. William was not among them.

While William threw himself into military training, Kate had her own battle on her hands. In some respects, hers was the more perilous of the two. For, while William's life was mapped out and rigid in its military discipline, Kate faced the rather daunting prospect of working out just what to do with herself while he was at Sandhurst. Her position in his life was still, officially, rather up in the air. She still had to contend with the life of contradictions presented by her strange, uncomfortable status of middle-class-royal-in-waiting. 'She is not, and never has been, somebody who would rest on her laurels,' one source close to the couple admitted at the time. 'But it's fair to say that this was a difficult period for both of them. William had his route pretty much mapped out.' Kate did not. She loved him of course, of that she was certain. But she could not sit around waiting for her prince to come home and sweep her off her feet. She had already toyed with and rejected the idea of working in an art gallery; this after all was a girl with a degree in art history from one of the most respected universities in the country. She was no fool, happy to while away her hours dreaming about her prince. She resurrected her idea of setting up a business venture of her own, working in the meantime with her parents at Party Pieces. But, more than ever, she found that her movements were scrutinised, however robust previous attempts to deter paparazzi and reporters may have been.

As she was by now well aware, the smallest detail could be spun into a story, however throwaway it might seem. The salon where she had her hair and nails done was now news. It provided a light-hearted moment when Kate, out with her mother in London's Sloane Square, found herself accidentally and somewhat prematurely ascending a throne of sorts. At Richard Ward's up-market hair-and-beauty emporium, a favourite salon of Prince Edward's wife, Sophie, Countess of Wessex, and Prince Marie Chantal of Greece, the spa treatments involve sitting on a raised 'throne' while having a manicure. The gossip columnists thought it hilarious when this detail emerged about the young woman who, as far as they were concerned, was destined to be the future queen. Even Kate must have seen the humour in the moment. 'Kate drops in with her mother Carole,' said an inside source at the salon. 'She's very down-to-earth. You wouldn't say she was a preener by any means, but she always looks great.' It was true. Kate always seemed to hit the mark. She was just glamorous enough. Her association with royalty lent her a certain sparkle, but in her own right she possessed that tantalising blend of understated style and a glint of self-confidence that turns a pretty girl into a sexy young woman. She never looked as if she was trying too hard. But she was never caught on camera looking anything other than great.

William's decision to join the army had marked a compromise on his part and an acknowledgement of his royal duty. He had resisted pressure to join the Royal Navy, a move that would require months at sea, away from his 'adorable Kate'. Joining the army had been a victory of sorts for William. But he still had many personal bridges to cross as he faced gruelling training, miles away from Kate. Each mud-soaked step, each teeth-chattering night in the wilds, each barked order obeyed, served to remind him that this was not the life he would have chosen but one forced upon him by birth. William let it be known from a very early stage that if he were to enter the army his ultimate aim was to join the Army Air Corps as a helicopter pilot. He was not interested in taking the more traditional route of serving in a Guards regiment, as his younger brother Harry had done when he joined the Blues and Royals.

In fact, it was Harry, rather than William, who proved himself a natural soldier and leader of men. This came as a surprise to critics who always considered Harry something of a joke. He had long since been regarded as the feckless younger brother, with no real job, no real responsibility and absolutely no qualms about capitalising on the fact. But, at Sandhurst, Harry knuckled down and bloomed. He impressed his superiors and proved popular with his peers, though he was far from a saint. 'He can be a lazy little shit,' one senior officer admitted. Yet, for all that, Harry's time at Sandhurst passed in the sort of uneventful fashion that must have had Clarence House aides offering prayers of thanks on a nightly basis.

As the brothers endured their personal trials at Sandhurst, Kate's profile was about to rocket with one picture that underlined just how much she was a part of the royal firmament, with or without the presence of her royal boyfriend. The moment came on 17 March 2006 at the Cheltenham Gold Cup races.

Camilla was due to present the winner's trophy and so the engagement was down in her and Charles's diaries as an official event. Kate had arrived for the famous Friday race day with a girlfriend and her girlfriend's parents, entering through the punters' entrance and mingling with the rest of the day's spectators. She was particularly smartly dressed and looked absolutely stunning. Veteran royal photographer Mark Stewart spotted her in the crowds and mentioned her presence to Amanda Neville (now Amanda Foster), a friendly long-serving member of Prince Charles's press team. According to Stewart, Amanda looked a little surprised by the news that Kate was at the races as well as her royal boss.

By the second race, Kate, much to the photographers' surprise, had appeared on the balcony of the royal box, where Lord Vestey, a friend of the Prince, was hosting a lunch for Charles and Camilla. Camilla's daughter Laura and Laura's then fiancé, Harry Lopes, were there, as were Tom Parker Bowles and his wife Sara, Zac Goldsmith, Ben Elliot and Thomas van Straubenzee, one of William's best friends, who was locked in conversation with Kate. It was the first time that Kate had been invited to adopt such an elevated position on her own. She had arrived. It was Camilla's most high-profile social engagement yet, but she did not seem bothered by the presence of the younger woman who threatened to steal her limelight. Quite the opposite: she appeared warm and welcoming. If anybody could understand the nerves that Kate might have been experiencing, it was Camilla. She was a past master – or rather mistress – when it came to hovering publicly on the edges of royalty.

The pictures from that day, with Kate in full view, were the first to present a 'new' Royal Family of sorts. It was fresh and surprisingly attractive, more representative in its blended nature of the social realities of its subjects. Here was a ragtag group, each member with a tale to tell: some of marital strife and infidelity, some of young love, some of privilege squandered but recovered. Here was a new cast, or at least assorted members of the old cast, playing new roles: the mistress as wife, the petulant prince as doting stepfather, husband and, perhaps, father-in-law-to-be.

'It was astonishing to see how relaxed and comfortable Kate was around the heir to the throne,' said Mark Stewart. 'It just goes to prove how serious her relationship with William is. It also shows how fond Camilla is of her, too. After all, it was Camilla's first year of presenting the Gold Cup but she didn't appear to be remotely put out at being overshadowed by Kate's presence.'

Unsurprisingly, Kate's impromptu appearance in the royal box sparked a betting frenzy, with at least one bookmaker forced to slash the odds on Kate and William getting engaged before the following year's festival from 40–1 to 25–1.

Although it is easy to forget it with Prince Harry for a brother, there is a rebel that lurks in William. On 14 and 15 April 2006, it was William and not, for once, his younger brother whose partying thrust him onto the front pages of the morning tabloids.

It should have been all about Harry. Friday, 14 April was, after all, the day that he passed out at Sandhurst, the day that Officer Cadet Wales became Second Lieutenant Wales of the Blues and Royals and paraded in front of the Sovereign – or 'Granny', as Harry called her. There had been the predictable, good-natured jokes at the young royal's expense: 'A red-faced Harry passes out; no, it's not what you think' – that sort of thing. In fact, after completing his 44-week training, Harry deserved his moment of self-pride and recognition and he deserved it to be unsullied by bad behaviour or scandal. It was a shame he did not receive it. The Queen gave a speech to the cadets where she described the parade as a 'great occasion'. 'This day marks the beginning of what I hope will be highly successful careers,' she said. 'My prayers and my trust go with you all.' She then presented the prestigious Sword of Honour to the best cadet and also handed out the Overseas Medal and the Queen's Medal, before addressing the newly commissioned officers. It was the first time in 15 years that she had attended a parade, and there were no prizes for guessing why she had chosen to present at this one.

The passing-out parade was Harry's graduation moment; the revelry that followed was his graduation ball. It is, of course, a well-rehearsed tradition at Sandhurst, and the day began well enough with the ceremonial Sovereign's Parade. Harry had, in accordance with custom, invited a party of ten family and friends to join him. His girlfriend, Chelsy Davy, was not among the elite group who watched Harry march, as she was spending the afternoon at the hairdresser in anticipation of the lavish black-tie event that evening. But Prince Charles was there along with Camilla, Harry's former nanny Tiggy Pettifer (née Legge-Bourke), family friends Hugh and Emilie van Cutsem and Prince Philip. William was there, of course, along with the rest of the officer cadets, standing to attention and beaming with pride as his brother passed out. Kate had been invited to the afternoon's events but, much to the surprise of many there, she did not turn up.

According to one person who was there, 'Everybody was expecting her but she did not show. In fact, she was still expected at about five p.m. that evening but, to be honest, I think there was a little bit of relief among the top brass that she did not come because the thinking was that, if Kate did not go, William would not and it would be less of a nightmare in terms of security later on. It made sense that William and Kate would not want to upstage Harry and Chelsy either, as it was Harry's day.' If the desire not to overshadow her royal boyfriend's younger sibling had been behind Kate's decision not to go to the ball that evening, then her sacrifice was in vain.

Once the passing-out ceremony was over, Harry and his fellow new officers changed into the mess suits that, until then, they had not been entitled to wear. Dressed in the tight-fitting trousers, stiff waistcoat and bright-red dress jacket, Harry looked every inch the officer as he chatted happily with the men of his platoon at the drinks that preceded the evening's party. His grandparents had expressed their pride and left early, as did the rest of his personal party of guests, except Chelsy.

After drinks in their individual platoon houses, the cadets and their guests headed across to the college's gymnasium, where the real party was waiting to happen. It may sound rather low-rent, the equivalent of a school disco held in a gym, but the building had been transformed into a breathtakingly lavish venue. A series of covered walkways connected the network of themed rooms that had been plotted throughout the vast space to cater for every taste and mood. In one area, a live band played in front of a chequered dance floor, surrounded by high tables, uplit in red. In another, there was jazz. Elsewhere, the partygoers could play roulette or blackjack in the casino, drink vodka from an ice bar or eat chocolate from a chocolate fountain. Outside, the discipline of military life had been turned over in favour of an amusement park, complete with roller-coaster thrill rides and a hamburger van. It was an extravagant setting, but Harry had eyes only for Chelsy. She was dressed in a sheath of turquoise satin that clung to her curves, scooped low at the back to show off her flawless tanned skin, and flowed, mermaid-like, out and down to the floor. Her makeup was minimal and her earrings simple. She had flown into the country the previous afternoon, landing at Heathrow, and was met by the sort of security usually reserved for members of royalty, heads of state or – for that matter –

wanted criminals. It had been weeks since she and Harry had been in each other's company, so there was little wonder that they seemed reluctant to take their eyes, or hands, off each other.

'Harry's bodyguards stood around him as he and Chelsy danced and kissed. They were snogging, hugging and holding hands, massively and openly affectionate,' one partygoer recalled. 'I suppose he's used to that by now but it did seem odd. He was joking with other cadets and is obviously very popular. He was happy to talk to anybody who approached him, although he did seem keener to talk to the girls.' He posed happily for pictures when asked by pretty guests and laughed good-naturedly when one girl, the worse for wear for drink and urged on by her friends, cheekily took a pinch at his bum. 'Instead of being annoyed,' one girl said, 'Harry just pinched her bum back and she ran off giggling.'

At midnight, the party moved outside, where a vast display of fireworks lit up the night sky and the new officers ripped the velvet strips that had been covering the officers' pips on their suits. It was a traditional rite of passage and a moment of whooping celebration amid an increasingly chaotic party, as some cadets and their guests were by now showing signs of flagging.

Among the strugglers, to the dismay of his senior officers, was Prince William. Harry was drinking and smoking and partying with the best of them. But he was, those who witnessed it maintained, a perfect gentleman throughout. He was not brash, or loud, or inappropriate. He was focused on Chelsy. He was proud of his achievement and that of his brothers-in-arms. The same could not be said of William and some of his civilian friends who had pitched up to join the fun. One college source recalled, 'One of William's civvy pals impersonated a brigadier all evening and tried ordering people about. He and the royal gang thought it very funny. Another found it highly hilarious to brag about a stag-night encounter with a prostitute and losing his wallet. Nobody else found them funny.'

Their behaviour was found so distinctly unfunny that, as 2 a.m. approached, William was advised by a senior officer that it would be best for him to call it a night. It was a humiliating rap on the knuckles for William and worse was to come. Hours later, Sandhurst's commandant, General Andrew Ritchie, rang Clarence House and apparently demanded an explanation for the raucous behaviour of the previous night. Pictures appeared in a morning tabloid of William, apparently the worse for drink, having a go on one of the thrill rides. Reports about 'upper-class twits' and the older Prince's behaviour soon began seeping out. Harry had, by all accounts, been 'as good as gold' and had played by the rules. William had not.

Twenty-four hours later, William and Harry, joined by Kate and Chelsy, were continuing the party back in London, and were pictured having a boozy night out at their favoured club, Boujis, in South Kensington. William was seen leaving with Chelsy, not Kate. Harry, it seemed, had sneaked out of a back door. It was the Princes' way of playing with the waiting paparazzi, throwing them off their guard. Harry had something to celebrate: Sandhurst was over and he and Chelsy would soon head off on holiday together. But for William things were different. For once, he was the brother who seemed selfish, thoughtless and down-right badly behaved. He had gone too far the night before and here he was carrying on as if he could do whatever he pleased without fear of criticism. It may sound harsh and some would argue that William was still just a high-spirited young man approaching his 24th birthday having fun with his brother and their girlfriends. Possibly, but he was not beyond reproach, either. With his lack of self-control and his inability to rein in his friends, William had spoiled Harry's moment of glory. He had turned the story away from his brother in the most negative fashion. Significantly, Kate had not been by his side when it had happened. Would William have been in the same position had she gone to the ball? It seemed unlikely.

Suddenly and subtly, it became clear that the balance of their relationship had changed. Once, Kate's glamour and image was dependent on William's presence. But the night of Harry's passing-out suggested that this had begun to work both ways. The public liked Kate and they had a limited tolerance for playboy princes, whatever their parentage. Kate was now irrevocably linked with William as far as press and public were concerned. Could it be that we all liked William a little bit more with her by his side?

William was always very keen to stress his youth when it came to talk of marriage and his royal duties. He may cite the fact that the average age for marriage in Britain is 32 and claim that, at 24, he had many years of bachelorhood to look forward to. But there was nothing average about William or his position. This is something that William – like his late mother – does not want to hear. Diana famously parted company with William's first nanny, Barbara Barnes, when she pointed out that in trying to raise William as a 'normal' little boy Diana was fighting the forces of nature. Diana had a clear idea of how she wanted her sons to be raised. Barnes, a traditionalist, protested, 'The Princes need to be treated differently because they *are* different.' She may have been speaking out of turn but she was speaking the truth: William was not, and never would be, 'normal'.

CHAPTER 10

THE WAY AHEAD

'She's been brilliant, she's a real role model.'

PRINCE WILLIAM COMMENTING ON THE QUEEN

They arrived at Kew Palace to the strains of Bach, Wagner and Donizetti, played by harpist and flautist. The music played as the light began to fade in the exquisite Royal Botanic Gardens that surround the palace, and the family progressed through the Queen's Boudoir, known as the Sulking Room, and on into the King's Drawing Room. The table was set to perfection – bathed in the soft light of a myriad candles. Spring blooms brought fragrance and colour to the room; silverware placed with military precision shone and glassware gleamed. This was the scene of a very special dinner, in honour of a truly remarkably woman, and everything had to be perfect. It was the evening of 21 April 2006 and the guest of honour was Queen Elizabeth II, there to celebrate her landmark 80th birthday in the bosom of her close family.

Appropriately for a woman proud of her Scottish ancestry, the menu included a starter of timbale of organic Hebridean smoked salmon. There was juniper roast loin of venison from the

Sandringham estates served with a port-wine sauce, steamed young cabbage and spring vegetables, and fruits from Prince Charles's Highgrove estates were used in the dessert. William sat next to his grandmother. His father sat on the other side of the woman who had reigned supreme as monarch and matriarch for 53 years. She must have surveyed the family gathered around that burnished table with real delight, and not a little relief that, after a bumpy start to the year, here at last was an occasion that had drawn together her family in undiluted joy, pride and celebration.

The event's co-hosts, Charles and Camilla, had been first to arrive, swiftly followed by William and Harry, the Duke of York and his daughters, Beatrice and Eugenie, looking elegant and more grown-up than ever. After them came the Earl and Countess of Wessex and then the Princess Royal with her husband, Rear-Admiral Tim Laurence, and her children, Peter and Zara Phillips. The children of the late Princess Margaret, Viscount Linley and Lady Sarah Chatto, the Queen's nephew and niece, were also among the guests.

Throughout the dinner, a selection of Handel's *Water Music* was played by 12 musicians from the London Chamber Orchestra, conducted by a thrilled Christopher Warren Green. As the meal drew to a close, those present raised their glasses in a toast to a 'wonderful' monarch and a 'darling mama and grandmother'. The day had been one of great pageantry and joy. Earlier, the focus of world media attention had fallen on Windsor. Again, I was commentating on an historic royal event, standing on a box, perched high on the roof of the Best of Britain shop opposite the castle, and a temporary set for CNN. As the Queen emerged, the band of the Irish Guards, resplendent in scarlet tunics and bearskins, oompahed out 'Happy Birthday' on the stroke of noon, before the Queen began a walkabout through the town centre.

Around 20,000 people had congregated behind police barriers.

Some were so eager to catch a glimpse of the Queen on her birthday that they had pitched up six hours earlier and patiently waited as the crowds grew and the hour drew near. From my vantage point, I could see how the street before the castle teemed with red, white and blue patriots. Some gripped the steel barriers in excitement; others waved miniature flags or held banners aloft. Flowers were thrown and gifts proffered as the Queen, dressed in cerise and with a sprightliness that belied her years, walked past. She walked by the bronze statue of Queen Victoria outside the King Henry VIII gate dominating the front of the castle – set high above the tarmac road, walkways and the High Street, seeming to survey the scene with imperious approval. It was hard to believe that our own smiling monarch was now just one year shy of the age reached by her iconic great-great-grandmother.

I felt a change coming as I watched her celebrate her momentous birthday on that overcast April morning, and I have watched the cogs turn quietly as the royal machine prepares to change gear. One well-placed source told me, 'The decisions have already been made and the process in which the Queen will step back and out of public life has already been set in motion. The Queen is 80 and Philip, while he's remarkably fit for his age, is an old man. The key to the monarchy as the Queen sees it is making changes without anybody seeing the joins.'

That's exactly what's been happening and she is effectively moving into semi-retirement. The Queen realises her place in history and knows that the time has come to adapt or risk the monarchy falling into disrepair. A handover of power is happening right in front of us and only the very few within the Royal Family and their closest confidants and advisers are even aware it is happening. The changes are subtle but seismic.

It's powerful stuff and nothing has been left to chance. It never is. It is no coincidence that the Queen has been spending more and more time with her grandson, of whom she is very fond. The Queen recognises a simple, for Charles, painful, fact that the role for which her eldest son was born has all but passed him by, however much public opinion may have softened. History, fate and his own spoilt nature have conspired to place Charles in an unenviable position. For years, his own parents seriously doubted his suitability for the throne. He was, according to one royal insider, regarded as something of a loose cannon: too quick to anger, given to tantrums and driven by an almost revolutionary zeal to 'make his mark' on the country with his various initiatives, causes and beliefs that many believed teetered dangerously on the brink of quackery.

Charles's apparent need to be viewed as a shaper of ideas and political influence was a serious source of concern to his advisers, too. Former deputy private secretary Mark Bolland has admitted that during his time in the Prince's service he 'tried to dampen down the Prince's behaviour in making public his thoughts and views on a whole range of issues'.

He wrote, 'The Prince's expressions of his views have often been regarded with concern by politicians because we would be contacted by them – and on their behalf. Private secretaries to government ministers would often let us know their views and, typically, how concerned they were.'

Charles may have done some good. Certainly, he has raised the debate on important issues such as genetically modified crops, religious tolerance and saving the environment, but he will have to keep all his undoubted passion to himself when he ascends the throne. He is well aware of this fact. Yet, despite the partially successful efforts to rehabilitate Charles and Camilla, the fact remains that the spotlight is now turning increasingly towards William and the court that he will establish. Whatever happens, the focus seems destined to fall only briefly on Charles and

Camilla. No doubt it won't be easy for a man as opinionated as Charles to bite back his views, but he must if he is to keep the institution of the monarchy safe for the next generation – safe for William and Kate.

According to one former courtier, 'There was a time after Diana's death, and even more recently than that, when many staff at Buckingham Palace were quite convinced that they were serving the penultimate monarch, that Charles wouldn't have a crown left to hand down to William.'

I do not think this doomsday scenario is given any serious credence now. However, mindful of her lengthening reign, the Queen was prompted to urge a resolution to the 'Camilla problem' through marriage. Mindful of his duty, Charles complied. This was a smoothing of the way forward to the next generation, not simply the glorious resolution of Charles and Camilla's enduring grand romance. It was made clear to Charles that he had to fit in with the bigger picture and accept the shifting shape of the monarchy as envisaged by the Queen. It was a calculated risk and it appears to have paid off. The reception given to Charles and Camilla on their Indian tour was warm, if not excited; the press coverage of Camilla is increasingly gentle but never effusive. There is no escaping the lingering feeling that, while Charles may have many supporters, his greatest asset is also his greatest weakness. Camilla as consort and Duchess of Cornwall is a constant reminder of the failings of the past. She undoubtedly gives strength to Charles but, no matter how optimistic palace spokespersons try to be, Charles and Camilla have both brought far too much baggage to the relationship for it to be presented as anything approaching love's young dream.

Still, the general feeling is that with Camilla at his side Charles is a less abrasive, spoilt figure, and behind the scenes the ground-work has been laid for the shift in power from the Queen to

Charles and so to William. Key members of staff from Buckingham Palace have been moved to Clarence House. It seems to me that Charles's court is being bolstered and strengthened as the Queen prepares to hand over much of her power. 'Right now a complete transformation is taking place at the heart of the monarchy,' explained one royal observer at the time. The Queen is about to step back, although not abdicate, and Charles is considered a safe pair of hands. However, the real focus – the real hopes – for the future of the monarchy, are on William – and Kate.

William increasingly started to undertake the duties of his public life that, for a while, he seemed to be avoiding. He was deemed to have conducted himself brilliantly on his first official tour in New Zealand in 2005. He has been to Sandhurst, which showed that he finally accepted the fact that, as future head of the armed forces, he must have a uniform himself. Significantly, he also took on the presidency of the Football Association. That has always been a position relegated to a more minor royal in recent years. William took over from his uncle, Prince Andrew, but just look at the timing: his incumbency came in the year of the World Cup and it is a role that both George V and George VI took. The role is very much part of William's presentation as a modern monarch-in-the-making. The message his presidency gave was clear: he doesn't just play polo, like his father, but he's into football as well (although Kate's not so keen and, when asked why she did not play polo, she told writer Kathy Lette, 'I'm allergic to horses'). William, for all his privilege, is a man for – if not entirely of – the people. He has trained with Premiership team Charlton and has revealed he is an Aston Villa supporter. It gives him and the Firm an edge and a contemporary feel. 'He's not outmoded, like his father may appear,' one commentator put it. 'He's very much in touch – just look at his girlfriend.'

Kate could hardly be a more middle-class consort if she tried.

Her family is neither landed nor aristocratic. And she is from the sort of 'stock' that a previous generation of royal heir would have been allowed to consider only as mistress material. That is not to say that she lacks the qualities laid down for a royal bride. In some respects, she ticks the boxes: she has no lurid past and has conducted herself with poise and discretion through a relationship that, in all likelihood, was passionate and romantic long before their secret leaked into the public domain. Charles pressed upon his son the notion that duty must be paramount when choosing a bride, but the rebel in William – the product of his two, frankly wayward, parents – made him question whether a truly modern monarchy should endure the sort of self-sacrifice made by previous generations. He argued that he should be allowed to make his own choice in his own time and that his family, and his country, should have confidence in his ability to do so. William's stubborn determination not to be pushed around seems fair enough to contemporary sensibilities. But so, too, is his father's gentle reminder of the responsibility that comes with his title.

We were not prepared to tolerate indefinitely the playboy prince rolling out of nightclubs at 3 a.m. or, like his brother, thrusting his head between strippers' breasts. Bar bills of £2,500 at exclusive members-only clubs like Boujis in west London began to lose their novelty value. As for the Queen, too much high living is all too reminiscent of her dashing, playboy uncle and his desertion of duty all those years ago. No one has ever read a story about the Queen collapsing outside a bar. Her conduct, past and present, has always been befitting of a monarch. William had, and to a certain extent still has, to look out for the pitfalls that come with confusing royalty with vacuous celebrity. If he treats his situation like the latter, the public might begin to question what they are paying for in maintaining the young royals.

The Royal Family needed a dose of youthful romance, not

relentless debauchery. In the clear-skinned Kate and the strapping figure of William, they found it.

'There is a real sense,' one aide told me before that announcement of their engagement, 'that there's no reason why Kate shouldn't have the sort of impact on the monarchy and its popularity that Diana had. Only she is older, more self-assured and, let's face it, far more intelligent, at least academically, than Diana ever was.'

In William, she has a husband quite clearly concerned with protecting her in a way that, perhaps, Charles just was not equipped to do with Diana.

Charles will be king and Camilla will be his queen consort alongside him, make no mistake. William believes very strongly that his father will be a good king, while he himself remains rather reluctant about rushing into an official role.

William has admitted, 'I'm very much the person who doesn't want to rush into anything without really thinking it through. I don't shy away from doing particular events but I do like to go to the ones that I really feel passionately about.'

Without doubt, William's contribution to royal life was, and is, much smaller than either his father's or his grandmother's was at the equivalent age. At some point during the day, he attends to his correspondence. He does respond promptly to personal letters from family and friends, and if he has spent a weekend as a guest at someone's house he will always write a thank-you note with a fountain pen. He will also spend an hour or two studying papers that the Queen and Charles have sent him. These are not state papers, but documents and articles that they have carefully selected to help him prepare for his eventual role as king. It is not a chore he enjoys, but one that he simply has to knuckle down to, one of the less glamorous trappings of royalty.

In his 2003 book *God Save the Queen: Monarchy and the Truth about the Windsors*, the writer and journalist Johann Hari made an astonishing claim. He said that Prince William, his father, brother and 20 per cent of the British people were all supporters of republicanism. He wrote, 'One man has the power to destroy the British monarchy – and he's not a politician. The man who will finally herald the Republic of Britain is a soon-to-be 21-year-old named William Windsor [it should be William Wales of course] – or, as the history books might record him, William the Last. It is time we all admitted three basic facts: William does not want to be king; he hates the idea of being king; he will not be king – ever.'

He went on, 'So what happens to the monarchy if William quits? Constitutionally, the throne could easily pass to William's younger brother Harry. But all the evidence suggests Harry is even more wilful, individualistic and ill-inclined to sublimate his energies into a pleasureless life of "duty". The crown could pass to Andrew Windsor. But, really, won't most people conclude that it's time to call it a day?'

It is hard to discern the factual basis for these claims. He wanted the Royal Family out and he came up with the premise that William agreed with him in order to argue that the monarchy was doomed. Unsurprisingly, given such contentious views, the book was well publicised, however ill founded it was. It also rattled a few cages at the palace, including William's. His response spoke volumes about his comprehension of the role that was unalterably his.

William used an interview set up to mark his 21st birthday to assert his desire to serve his country in a deliberate rebuttal of Hari's remarks. He cut to the chase: 'All these questions about "Do you want to be king?" It's not a question of wanting to be, it's something I was born into and it's my duty. Wanting is not the right word. But those stories about me not wanting to be king are all wrong. It's a very important role and it's one that I don't take lightly. It's all about helping people and dedication and loyalty which I hope I have – I know I have.

'Sometimes I do get anxious about it but I don't really worry a lot. I want to get through university and then maybe start thinking seriously about that in the future. I don't really ever talk about it publicly. It's not something you talk about with whoever. I think about it a lot but they are my own personal thoughts. I'll take each step as it comes and deal with it as best I can. The monarchy is something that needs to be there. I just feel it's very, very important. It's a form of stability and I hope to be able to continue that.'

He is seen, probably because of his youth, to be a moderniser. But, however 'radical' his choice of partner, William is far from the revolutionary that Hari has envisaged. William has said, 'Modernisation is quite a strong word to use with the monarchy because it's something that's been around for many hundreds of years. But I think it's important that people feel the monarchy can keep up with them and is relevant to their lives. We are all human and inevitably mistakes are made.

'But in the end there is a great sense of loyalty and dedication among the family and it rubs off on me. Ever since I was very small, it's something that's been very much impressed on me, in a good way. People say it's not ambitious, but it is actually quite ambitious wanting to help people. Trying to keep that going is quite tricky and it's something that, without the whole family, is harder for just one person to do. It would be dangerous to look a long way ahead and predict changes in the monarchy.'

William may be relatively inexperienced but he has been around long enough to recognise that the monarchy has to be seen as relevant to its people. In my view, he was right to be reticent about looking ahead too far. Perhaps the death of his mother will always make it difficult for him to look to the future with any real faith and conviction. But, if he is to be a successful monarch, there are certain things which he will have to face up to – sooner rather than later. The succession is one of them.

William has grown from being his late mother's loyal little consort, to awkward teenager idolised by screaming young girls, to assured young prince and husband. He has joked around with his father, doing more for Charles's popularity in those happy, natural family moments than a lifetime of PR campaigns ever could. He has been the naughty schoolboy, the model pupil and the student struggling for normality. Eventually, though, he will be king. 'I am worried about it,' he has said, 'but I don't really think about it too much because there's no point in worrying about things which are not really present yet. It's not that I never want to do it, it's just that I'm reluctant at such a young age, I think anyway, to throw myself in the deep end.'

The crown is an ever-present reality in William's life, however much he may try to convince himself and others of the contrary. William's place in the succession defines him and the responsibility that he faces is awesome. More and more, he frets about the steady slipping away of normality that must come with the preordained path set out for him. He worries that he will be unable to remain grounded and hopes to emulate his grandmother in her strength, his father in his passion and his late mother in her empathy and warmth. He holds back and he holds his breath and hopes that he will know when, as he puts it, the moment has arrived to throw himself in at the deep end, not realising that he is already there. In reality, Prince William has no choice; he cannot be allowed to sink, so he must swim. The only decision still left for the young Prince, until not long ago, was whom he would choose to swim alongside him. That decision has now been made.

CHAPTER 11

MAKING THE GRADE

'He's lucky to be going out with me.'

KATE MIDDLETON ON DATING PRINCE WILLIAM

It was perhaps the most important date so far in the life of the girl now very publicly acknowledged as William's princess-in-waiting, a fact that Kate Middleton must surely have recognised. The official business of the crisp clear day – 15 December 2006 – dictated that it was William's proud hour, as he passed out at the Royal Military Academy, Sandhurst. However, the future king was not the only one seen to make the grade, for this was the first time that Kate, then almost 25, would attend a public engagement alongside the Queen and the rest of the senior royals. The apparent significance of this 'joining the Firm' did not pass unnoticed, and even the most hard-nosed of hacks allowed themselves a moment of romantic indulgence: the *Daily Mail*, for instance, in a rare moment of whimsy, observed that Kate's scarlet coat echoed the sash worn by William that day. The synchronicity of her wardrobe and the simple fact that she was there on such a significant day in her royal lover's life was, it asserted, 'the strongest sign yet that she and Prince William could marry'.

Until that day, William's hugely protective attitude towards his girlfriend had ensured that, given the intensity of the relationship, they were seen out in public together comparatively rarely – save for the occasional night out or trip to the polo. But that December day William extended his most public invitation to Kate; little wonder, then, that many people read so much into the move. She arrived with her parents, Michael and Carole, and the Prince's private secretary, Jamie Lowther-Pinkerton, moments before the Windsor party. Although the Middletons did not sit next to the royal party – which included the Duke of Edinburgh, Charles and Camilla – there was a certain pomp to her arrival. All the other guests were already seated as Kate was ushered into her place in the front row accompanied by William's best friend, Thomas van Straubenzee, and two of his godfathers, King Constantine of Greece and Lord Romsey. Kate and, tellingly, her family were in lofty company indeed. In truth, the arrival of the glamorous, assured young woman dressed in vibrant red completely overshadowed the royals, even the Queen.

So too did her assessment of her boyfriend's appearance in his smart passing-out uniform, when she chatted with a friend after the ceremony. It seemed there was no limit to what the media – and not just the press – would do to get a story. Britain's ITV network hired lip-reading experts who discerned that Kate had apparently declared, 'I love the uniform, it's so sexy.' Whether this is what she really said, it showed that, like Diana before her, Kate was more than capable of stealing the show – even when all the Royal Family's star performers were out in force. It was something that not only members of the family but also the palace courtiers noted with some trepidation.

That day, the 24-year-old William was among 233 cadets

commissioned at the Royal Military Academy marked by the Sovereign's Parade. Like his younger brother, Harry, he was destined for a commission in the Household Cavalry's Blues and Royals regiment, where he would train to become a troop leader in charge of armoured reconnaissance vehicles. Unlike Harry, who was due to deploy to Iraq in 2007, William, as second in line to the throne, is barred from going to any frontline war zones. However sincere William's devotion to his military training, it is always destined to amount to a flirtation never consummated in warfare. Instead, he was expected to serve little more than a year in the army before moving on to the Royal Air Force and Royal Navy as part of his wider training as future head of the armed forces.

For all that, as he stood in the shrill winter sun that day, William looked every inch the soldier prince. Standing 6ft 3in tall, he was placed at the end of his platoon as an 'escort' to the banner, as well as acting as marker to ensure his colleagues marched in a straight line. Like his fellow cadets, he wore a smart blue uniform, cap and white gloves, but carried a rifle instead of a sword and wore a scarlet sash. He also wore the blue-and-white Jubilee medal given to him by his grandmother to mark her 50th anniversary on the throne. Reviewing the young soldiers lined up before her, the Queen paused briefly as she walked past her grandson and whispered a 'Hello' that left William beaming.

Significantly, Clarence House sources indicated that, after the parade ended, Kate and her parents joined the royal party for a family lunch for the first time. It was something Buckingham Palace later strenuously denied. Amid a row over snobbery by the royals towards the Middletons, the palace would seek to claim that the Queen had never actually met Kate's mother – a claim that dumbfounded many royal reporters, including this one. After all, at the time, the Royal Family's spin machine was happy for the story of that convivial lunch to be written.

To mark his passing-out, Clarence House released photographs and footage of the Prince taken on his last major exercise at Sandhurst. They also arranged for interviews with fellow cadets to be released to the press in which he was described as a 'normal guy'. Junior Under Officer Angela Laycock, 24, who was in William's Blenheim platoon, told how he fitted in with other cadets. She said, 'I've not really noticed anything different, to be honest. The first loaded march, we had a bit of a detour to avoid some photographers. He's just a normal guy and gets stuck in like everybody else.' Describing how William joined in training with the other cadets, she added, 'On a riot-training exercise he was grabbing potatoes and lobbing them at the force protection people just like the rest of us.'

Of course, he is not a 'normal' guy at all, and at that moment his girlfriend was far from just a 'normal' girl. For the focus of the national newspapers was not on the royals, but on Kate. It seemed they had found their new princess. That night, she and William partied at the traditional passing-out ball, as Harry and Chelsy had done in such style earlier in the year at his own graduation from Sandhurst. As they sipped champagne and celebrated, there was nothing to suggest that this romance was any less perfect than it appeared. The *Daily Mail* best summed up the mood of the moment with its headline, ON WILLIAM'S BIG DAY KATE MAKES THE GRADE, TOO. The *Sunday Times* went further and a few weeks later published a piece on Kate entitled THE GIRL WHO WOULD BE QUEEN.

Perhaps it was inevitable, but, as the outcome of the affair between William and Kate seemed such a certainty, his passing-out parade was also the day that focus began to shift from Kate and the Royal Family she seemed about to join to Kate and the family she was bringing with her. However uneasily the notion of class and breeding sits with modern sensibilities, it is fated never to pass without comment, especially where issues of Crown and State are concerned. And so the backlash of soft, deft blows began.

Carole Middleton, it was observed, was chewing gum as she watched her possible future son-in-law passing out. The veteran royal commentator James Whitaker, for one, suggested it was 'common'. Others pointed to the fact that Carole was trying not to smoke and, therefore, as she was probably chewing nicotine gum, she should be praised rather than criticised for the lapse in social niceties. Others still viewed the whole discussion as ludicrous and peripheral. William and Kate were, after all, very much in love – weren't they?

Just a few weeks after her starring role at Sandhurst, the newspaper quoted senior sources as saying William felt he had to make a decision one way or the other. 'In frank discussions between the Prince, his private secretary Jamie Lowther-Pinkerton and other key aides,' a source said, 'William has been presented with two "ideal" scenarios: he could announce an engagement in the New Year, or cool his romance with Kate during his military service with the Household Cavalry at Bovington Camp, Dorset.' It was to prove prophetic and alarming stuff for Kate, and apparently prompted a heart-to-heart between her and her mother. When William failed to show at the Middletons' family gathering in December, the chill thought must surely have seeped into Kate's heart that perhaps he was not as serious about her as she had once thought, or indeed as he had once so genuinely appeared. Perhaps he was having cold feet. Perhaps Kate's heart was about to be broken.

Carole Middleton is an astute, down-to-earth woman who realised she would have to have a long, hard talk with her beloved eldest daughter. Carole has the reputation of being nobody's fool. She is worldly wise, having travelled widely during her career as a flight attendant. Therefore, when she saw what was unfolding, she made it clear to Kate that, if William did not want to commit, it was not wise for her to drift along in the relationship indefinitely. Carole has always had a special relationship with her daughter. Later, much would be made of Carole's 'social ambitions', with the suggestion that it was her fierce desire to climb the social ladder that guided her actions when it came to Kate. This is unfair. No mother likes to see her daughter taken for granted and not receiving the respect and consideration she deserves. Kate, after all, is an intelligent girl who had put her life on hold for the sake of William and her willingness to make their relationship work.

Kate's Monday-to-Thursday job as an accessories buyer for Jigsaw, the Kew-based high-street store run by family acquaintances John and Belle Robinson, was hardly a challenging role, and one that Kate had taken primarily for the freedom it afforded her to visit her boyfriend near his Dorset barracks. As 2006 turned to 2007, it must have been a difficult period of renegotiation between Kate and William, as both nursed their own trepidations over just how significant their romance was and exactly where it was going. However, they had been down this rocky road before and always pulled back from the brink of actually breaking up. They still loved each other and, despite his reservations concerning commitment, William did not want to lose Kate. She was simply too precious to him. They had a shared history. They understood each other. He needed her.

At the beginning of the year, at least, these private reservations did not deter the media, and everybody hoped for a successful conclusion. The speculation intensified and rumours of a possible imminent engagement led to increased paparazzi attention outside Kate's apartment. It reached fever pitch on the day of her 25th birthday on 9 January 2007, with more than 50 paparazzi and TV cameramen positioned at the door of her Chelsea flat as she walked to her car to leave for work that morning. It was a birthday surprise that alarmed Kate. She tried hard to accept it with her trademark smile. The 'cult of Kate' had never been so visible or so palpable and for the first time she was elevated from 'girl next door' to commercial trendsetter. The £40 Topshop dress she wore that morning sold out within days, proving she had a following all of her own. The scenes outside her flat prompted William, fearful that his girlfriend was being forced to endure the same media pressure experienced by his late mother, to express his concern at the 'harassment' of his girlfriend. He issued a statement saying he wanted 'more than anything' for her to be left alone. Her family had already employed law firm Harbottle and Lewis to urge the media, both in Britain and abroad, to use restraint. This time, however, there were not just a few freelancers on Kate's doorstep, but representatives of newspapers and those from respected agencies such as Associated Press and the Press Association. There were also at least five TV crews, including a team from ITN, which produces news bulletins for ITV and Channel 4. The BBC did not send a camera crew but used footage supplied by the agency APTN. Sky News also used footage in its bulletins. The palace sat up and took notice. Her lawyers were in close contact with the Press Complaints Commission and stopped short of making an official representation on her behalf. Sources said they hoped to use 'persuasion' rather than legal action to protect her. The similarities with the problems faced by William's mother were clear.

The ugly scenes on Kate's birthday prompted the late princess's aides to speak out in a chorus of disapproval and a call for action. My good friend, Inspector Ken Wharfe, the retired former bodyguard to Princess Diana, was in no doubt that the number of photographers pursuing Kate, coupled with the lack of any control, put her in danger of becoming the victim of a Diana-style tragedy. He said at the time, 'History appears to be repeating itself, despite claims that lessons have been learned after the loss of Diana. As far as I can see, the warnings have not been heeded.' He said it was imperative for Prince Charles to employ former royal protection officers to guard Kate until she became engaged to William and full-time official Scotland Yard security became available. After their brief split, he wrote to Carole offering to protect Kate until the furore died down. Patrick Jephson, Diana's former private secretary, echoed Wharfe's views: 'I think that any reasonable person would be horrified about the situation and what Miss Middleton has to endure. I think the attempts to use legal, regulatory and informal methods to deal with the situation will help. Nothing is more effective than proper control on the ground. That is the lesson of the Diana experience, including her death. That level of control on the ground is the only method which will work effectively for Kate.'

Perhaps fearing a backlash, News International immediately announced that all its publications, including the *Sun*, *The Times* and the *News of the World*, would not use any paparazzi photographs of Kate in future. Executives at the corporation hoped this move would curry favour with senior Clarence House aides, too, and perhaps lead to their getting the tip-off about a future royal engagement. Unusually, Charles's office at Clarence House took the decision to comment on the move to back off Kate. An official spokesperson said, 'We are pleased that News International has agreed to stop using the paparazzi pictures. What Prince William wants more than anything is for the paparazzi to stop harassing her.' There was even speculation that Kate's situation was being manipulated in a test case involving harassment laws, in an attempt to protect her privacy and curtail the activities of photographers.

William and Kate couldn't stop smiling as they announced their engagement to the world.

(© Arthur Edwards)

Above: The changing of the guard: Charles was on exceptional form at the Queen's Diamond Jubilee concert, creating this heart-warming moment.

Below: William and Kate enjoy a slightly different carriage ride from what they are used to.

Leaving stars star-struck at a BAFTA event in LA.
(© Arthur Edwards)

Above: The proud grandparents. Although Prince Charles can often be very reserved in public, he has been effusive in his enthusiasm for becoming a grandfather.

(© Arthur Edwards)

Below: The perfect moment, topping off a perfect day.

(© Press Association)

Above: Princess Diana, as ever, is sorely missed on occasions such as these.

(© Arthur Edwards)

Below: William has always been very close to his father and brother. He will be hoping to recreate iconic images such as these with his own family now.

(© Arthur Edwards)

Above left: A pregnant Kate wore all green, including a shamrock, for St Patrick's Day at her first solo military engagement. *(© Arthur Edwards)*

Above right: Proud new parents William and Kate prepare to have their first child, HRH Prince George of Cambridge, christened at St James's Palace in the presence of the Queen. *(© Getty Images)*

Above right: Kate looks on as her husband rings a bell to start the Ring O'Fire Anglesey Coastal Ultra Marathon in her first official public engagement after the birth of her son. *(© Getty Images)*

Above: It has been a long time since the last heir was born. Here Charles and Diana are pictured playing with Prince William when he was just ten months old.

(© Arthur Edwards)

Above: More than 30 years later, Prince William arrives in Wellington, New Zealand, with his own wife and son, at the start of their tour of Australasia, 7 April 2014.

(© Getty Images)

William, Kate and George bid farewell to Australia and New Zealand after a three-week tour, the first official trip overseas with Prince George.

In the inevitable dissection of these events, many royal commentators rallied protectively round Kate. The issue of privacy and press intrusion became the focus of the House of Commons' Culture, Media and Sport Select Committee for its investigation of media invasion of privacy on 6 March 2007, during which leading media figures were called to give evidence. One of those was veteran royal photographer Arthur Edwards – the contributor of photographs to this book in return for a donation to his favourite charity, who was recently honoured with a lifetime achievement award by his peers. During the proceedings, Edwards, whose astute reading of the nuances of the royal story in the previous 30 years is second to none, was met by somewhat condescending titters from committee members when he said William had told him he intended to marry Kate. As ever, he was right.

'She is a private citizen and she is in love with Prince William and I am sure that one day they will get married. I have talked to him about this. He has made it clear that he wants to get married and I believe what he says, and they should be left alone,' he said. He added that he had heard from Kate's friends about her distress at media intrusion and said photographers had followed her shopping, and even climbed onto buses to photograph her. But by this time there was pandemonium. Moreover, as he tried to clarify his comments – saying the Prince had said it would not happen until he was at least 28 years old – the political reporters had already left the room to file his comments to the news wires.

There was something missing in all this well-meaning attention and earnest endeavour to get it right, this time, in terms of coverage and acceptable levels of interest. I was not alone in thinking that, as she left her flat that morning, Kate seemed curiously isolated, miles from her barracks-bound boyfriend. Yes, William had swept in to make his statement and attempt to redress the balance, pull the press up short and remind them that this girl was very special to him. But there were some who felt this 'chivalrous' gesture was rather too little, too late. Might Kate have felt so too?

There are also those who believed that Kate was enigmatic at best, boring at worst. 'What are her interests?' asked a newspaper editor. 'All she seems to do is go to the gym and go to either Boujis or Mahiki [the current favourite nightclubs for wealthy twenty-somethings in London]. She does not have a job. She does not go to the theatre. We don't really have any idea of who she really is, and what we do see is rather shallow.'

Then came another signal that perhaps Kate was positioning herself for a change in status. In May, it emerged that Kate had asked people to call her 'Catherine'. The press were quick to point out the obvious: 'Catherine' is a far more regal name than 'Kate'. A defensive Paddy Harverson, Prince Charles's communications secretary, strenuously denied all these reports. Nonetheless, *Sunday Express* columnist Adam Helliker, who wrote the 'Catherine' story, insisted he had heard about – but had not seen – a 'gentle' email sent by Kate to her friends, saying she was reverting to the name she had had until she was in her mid-teens. Helliker said, 'It was just a very jokey thing.' He defiantly stood by his story. Another, potentially more damaging, report emerged soon afterwards and claimed that Kate's lack of industry was causing the Queen some irritation. The report stated that the Queen wanted Kate to get a full-time job. In fact, she was quietly working, as her lawyer Gerrard Tyrrell confirmed, already: getting up each morning in Bucklebury, driving to the Party Pieces office in Reading and putting together the catalogues for her parents' company. She also took a technology course to learn how to make digital catalogues. Under the circumstances, it was probably about the only job Kate, as a princess-in-waiting, felt safe doing.

'She's been offered every job under the sun,' I was told. Everyone from Russian oligarchs to top fashion designers wanted her. But Kate was well aware that taking such positions could open her up to accusations of using her association with William for financial gain, an accusation that could come back to haunt her. Until William formalised their relationship, she was left in an awkward spot. She was not officially entitled to any royal benefits paid for by the taxpayers, such as security, yet she, perhaps more than some of the minor royals, was exposed. She had no spokesperson or official guidance on what to wear or how to conduct herself in royal circles. Yet, because of her boyfriend, she was already a celebrity, having to cope with the difficulties that fame brings. Her main lifeline was the media lawyer Gerrard Tyrrell, whose clients included British model Kate Moss and Roman Abramovich, owner of Chelsea Football Club. Any time Kate felt harassed, as she claims she did on her 25th birthday, it was to Tyrrell that she turned. His response was often swift, sending letters to newspaper editors warning them that Kate was a 'private' citizen and as such had a right to privacy.

In March, around the time William started army training in Dorset, the couple attended the Cheltenham Gold Cup races in traditional tweed suits. The press covered their attendance ironically, noting how much like Charles and Camilla – nicknamed 'Fred and Gladys' – the pair looked in their old-fashioned clothes. William was said not to be amused. A few days later, Kate, looking far more youthful and modern in a warm coat and Russian-style fur hat, went to the races on her own. Lord Vestey, a friend of Prince Charles, was hosting a lunch for Charles, Camilla, Camilla's children, Tom and Laura, as well as Zac Goldsmith and Camilla's nephew Ben Elliot, among others. When the royal party heard Kate was there, she was invited to join them in the royal box.

Unlike Diana, Kate has almost never seemed to be rattled by the cameras. Photographer Niraj Tanna revealed, 'Even in the early hours of the morning, when William and her pals look a little worse for wear through drink or just tiredness as they leave their favourite nightclubs, Kate always looked immaculate.' She would never let herself go. She would drink cautiously, and carefully touch up in the women's toilet before facing the cameras that would inevitably be waiting for her.

In July, her boss at Jigsaw, Belle Robinson, gave an interview about Kate, portraying her as down-to-earth, even though Kate had asked for a job with 'an element of flexibility to continue the relationship with a very high-profile man and a life she can't dictate'. Yet the older woman liked her part-time employee. 'She sat in the kitchen at lunchtime and chatted with everyone from the van drivers to the accounts girls,' Robinson told the London *Evening Standard*. 'She wasn't precious. Many people have distorted it to say we're friends with her parents, but I've only met them four times. I have to say I was so impressed by her. There were days when there were TV crews at the end of the drive. We would say, "Listen, do you want to go out the back way?" And she'd say, "To be honest, they're going to hound us until they've got the picture. So why don't I just go, get the picture done, and then they'll leave us alone."'

Throughout 2006, Kate and William had tried to keep their heads down with regard to the media. They were tracked down and photographed mostly on holiday, leaving nightclubs or on the polo field. Harry, too, was caught, having been out partying perhaps a little too often. These images increasingly began to leave a somewhat negative impression – the British media referred to the young Princes as 'boys' or, even worse, as 'playboys'. It did not sit well. The future hopes of the British Royal Family were being openly mocked in lots of circles as just a pair of prize silly Sloane Rangers spending oodles of cash celebrating on cocktails. For young men purporting to be serious soldiers, they appeared to spend an awful lot of time in nightclubs. Interestingly, of the tight-knit royal clique who hit the clubs with increasing frequency, perhaps the most aware of the bad impression they were creating was the media-astute Kate. On holiday in 2006, Prince William and Guy Pelly, an old friend in the group, often simplistically referred to as the 'court jester', were racing around on mopeds at the villa of Kate's uncle, Gary Goldsmith, in Ibiza. Kate came out of the house and, matron-like, told them to stop. Anyone, after all, could be watching. Like chided schoolchildren, they did what they were told. William may not have liked it, but he could not fault her judgement.

Kate's confidence in her role as the royal girlfriend steadily grew. She was more self-assured – buoyed by the confidence her mother instilled in her. She met the Queen, who liked her, as did Charles and Camilla. Harry, according to one friend, took longer to warm to her. Kate, with her demure outfits, fitted jackets over a dress, drop pearl earrings and self-control, was the complete opposite of Harry's blonde Zimbabwean girlfriend, the wealthy Chelsy Davy, who dressed in a far more provocative style. Chelsy never shied from photographers, with a glass in one hand, a cigarette in the other. At times, she may have looked like an unmade bed, but she has raw, earthy sex appeal – something Kate lacks. The passionate attraction between Harry and Chelsy fizzled, but in public, at least, the same could not be said of William and Kate.

CHAPTER 12

THE PRINCESS BRIDE

'A multitude of rulers is not a good thing.
Let there be one ruler, one king.'

HOMER, THE ILIAD

16 NOVEMBER 2010, ST JAMES'S PALACE, LONDON

Tightly holding the arm of the only man she had ever truly loved, Catherine Elizabeth Middleton tried her best to maintain her poise. With a beaming smile and, gently leaning on her royal prince – Royal Air Force Flight Lieutenant William Wales – they looked a couple deeply in love, completely at ease with each other. He had given countless interviews in the past, but they were usually with his younger brother Prince Harry, a natural performer in front of the camera, stealing the show with one-liners and derogatory quips about his older more considered brother.

Giving 'the boys' that experience had been part of palace strategy, to help both Princes, second and third in line to the British throne, to learn the ropes of royal life, as well as how to cope with the ever more demanding modern media. In the past, royals didn't do interviews – Queen Elizabeth II still hasn't after

60 years on the throne – but this new generation has no choice but to do them unless it wants to seem completely out of touch.

This time, William took the lead, gently guiding his bride-to-be through the minefield of her first outing before the unforgiving British press. After all, this was a new experience for Kate, but it was one that she would have to get used to. She knew her every move and nuance was being scrutinised, her every word reported around the globe to millions of television viewers, who, until now, had seen her image only in glossy magazines and newspapers; but they were now at last hearing her voice for the first time. She was clearly nervous; who wouldn't be? But she was not about to show it. After all, Miss Middleton was honed from sterner stuff.

That morning, William's father, the Prince of Wales, had released a press statement that had made headlines on the 24-hour news channels around the globe. It began, 'His Royal Highness Prince William of Wales and Miss Catherine Middleton are engaged to be married.' It continued, 'The Prince of Wales is delighted to announce the engagement of Prince William to Miss Catherine Middleton.' One of Prince Charles's former aides said he was a very *laissez-faire* father' to his two sons. 'He likes Kate a lot, but she won't be getting any "training" or guidance as to how to behave.'

At last, the marathon courtship of the second in line to the throne, more than eight years in all, was over. Life for this handsome young couple, both 28, would never be the same again.

Prince Harry, who had been in flying training at Middle Wallop that day – the young man with whom he had suffered so many of the slings and arrows of outrageous fortune in life, not least their mother Princess Diana's death in 1997 – was the first to comment on his big brother's happy news: 'I'm delighted that my brother has popped the question! It means I get a sister, which I've always wanted.'

Back in London, Kate was taking her first tentative steps in public life. 'It's obviously nerve-racking,' she admitted in a cut-class, English, public-school accent when asked whether she was excited or nervous about marrying into the Royal Family. She said the Queen had been 'welcoming', as too was her new father-in-law Prince Charles. Now, with Princess Diana's 18-carat, oval sapphire ring on her finger, she had realised her destiny. Containing 14 small diamonds surrounding the blue stone, in a cluster setting from the royal jewellers Garrard, the engagement ring had cost Prince Charles £28,000 thirty years earlier, when he had placed it on the finger of the shy Lady Diana Spencer, a young woman not long out of her teens. In today's money, it would have cost £100,000, so perhaps in this age of austerity giving his fiancée a recycled ring wasn't a bad PR move. But that had not been William's motivation.

'It was my mother's engagement ring, so I thought it was quite nice because obviously she's not going to be around to share any of the fun and excitement of it all – this was my way of keeping her close to it all,' he said. It was a touching gesture that some commented on: some negatively pointed out that it had been an ill-fated ring that marked an ill-fated marriage and doomed match. However, it took Kate's breath away when William produced it from his rucksack out of the blue while they holidayed together in Kenya. 'It's beautiful. I just hope I look after it. It's very, very special.' In a single, deeply significant gesture, William had brought his iconic mother right back into the public consciousness and onto the newspaper front pages that she had graced during the latter part of the 20th century, when she ranked as one of the most famous people in the world.

Kate had already suffered the heartache and public ignominy of a very public split with her Prince in 2007. They had split up a couple of times before that, too, but every time the power of their love, like a magnet, had pulled them back to each other during their roller-coaster eight-year courtship. This English lady was a new breed of outsider who dared to marry into the Royal Family. She may be compared to the 'People's Princess' throughout her royal career as she tries to carve out her own role and reputation, but in truth she is a true 'Princess of the People'. She is a middle-class girl born and raised in the country from loving, solid, hard-working parents with high aspirations, who had worked tirelessly to earn the money to do the very best for their three children. Catherine, the eldest, had simply met and fallen in love with a prince – a very simple story really. Now she is our new 21st-century princess and in line to be our future queen consort. What's more, she will be mother and grandmother to future sovereigns, too.

Kate and William's first public appearance as a newly engaged couple was all but outshone by a shocking blaze of camera flashes from the battery of handpicked photographers invited from the world's media outlets to meet them in a state room at St James's Palace for their first official joint engagement. They had tried their best to answer the quick-fire questions, but they were almost drained by the frenzied clicking cameras shutters. A little earlier, sitting in a quiet side room at Clarence House, his father's London home, it had been a calmer atmosphere, although the questioning, while soft, was still testing. William and Kate gave the first glimpses of the intimacy of their relationship. Seated side by side in their first interview together, the happy couple spent more than 15 minutes chatting informally to ITV News's political editor Tom Bradby, a newsman the Prince liked and had chosen as the conduit of his good news, much to the chagrin of the BBC. Relaxed, and often sharing a joke together, William and his bride-to-be talked about their happy news and revealed that they wanted to start a family. That, of course, was a foregone conclusion for a prince entrusted with securing the line of succession of one of the oldest and most celebrated monarchies in the world, with a thousand-year history. Now, at his side, looking stunning in a beautiful peacock-blue dress by her favourite designer label Issa, was the woman with whom he would start that family.

The proposal had been truly romantic. It was exactly out of the textbook for princes on white chargers sweeping their chosen damsels off their feet. His mother, whose step-grandmother Dame Barbara Cartland made a fortune peddling such stories in slushy romantic novels, would have been proud. William revealed in his engagement interview, 'It was about three weeks ago on holiday in Kenya. We had been talking about marriage for a while, so it wasn't a massively big surprise. I took her up somewhere nice in Kenya and I proposed.'

Kate added, 'It was very romantic. There's a true romantic in there. I really didn't expect it. It was a total shock... and very exciting.'

Bradby asked, 'And he produced a ring there and then?'

She replied with a beaming smile, 'Yes.'

William explained, 'I'd been carrying it around with me in my rucksack for about three weeks before that and I literally would not let it go. Everywhere I went I was keeping hold of it because I knew this thing, if it disappeared, I would be in a lot of trouble; and, because I'd planned it, it went fine. You hear a lot of horror stories about proposing and things going horribly wrong. It went really, really well and I was really pleased she said yes.'

But why had he waited so long to propose? 'I wanted to give her a chance to see in and to back out if she needed to before it all got too much. I'm trying to learn from lessons done in the past and I just wanted to give her the best chance to settle in and to see what happens on the other side,' he said.

In fact, his proposal plan had been truly adventurous and wildly romantic. He had selected a remote spot beside a shimmering African lake in Kenya to ask the most important question of his life. Just five miles from the equator and 11,500 feet above sea level, Kenya's peaceful Lake Alice is so far from civilisation that only a handful of sightseers witness its astounding beauty each year. The lake has stunning turquoise waters and is surrounded by lush green hills, against the backdrop of a snowy Mount Kenya. It is not difficult to see why the Prince had selected this destination to propose to his future wife.

Helicopters usually land on a rough shingle beach at Lake Alice's southern tip. Once the rotor blades have stopped spinning, passengers are treated to the kind of silence that can almost be heard. With no other humans for several miles in any direction, the only sounds that are made are those of nature – a rare passing bird or the splash of a fish or frog. Meanwhile, the lake's waters bob with unusual floating rocks – lightweight black stones serving as a reminder of its volcanic origins. With a blazing blue sky and a brisk mountain breeze, William and Kate used borrowed rods for fly fishing from the pebbly beach before the Prince plucked up the courage to ask for her hand in marriage.

Most who go to Lake Alice fall in love with the place on sight. The peace is breathtaking. It is a unique place where one feels as if nobody else has ever been there. It takes so much effort to reach the place it feels virtually untouched by man. It is a hundred per cent seclusion and a hundred per cent romantic. William had spent weeks planning his trip to Kenya, where the couple stayed in a romantic log cabin. Without air transport, Lake Alice is at least a four-hour journey from the nearest tarmac road – 20 miles on slimy dirt roads accessible only by four-wheel-drive cars, before a gruelling two-hour uphill trek.

But the Prince decided instead to arrive in style and flew in a chartered helicopter, carrying his mother's sapphire engagement ring in his rucksack.

It was, as Kate said, truly romantic.

Lying in the top of a long-extinct volcano, Lake Alice is surrounded on all four sides by a ring of ridges, which protect it from the icy high-altitude winds. Poking out from behind one of the nearby peaks is Mount Kenya – the second-highest mountain in Africa – whose snowy summits are famously difficult to reach. Lake Alice was formally discovered in 1935 by British explorer Kenneth Gander-Dower. William enlisted the help of family friend Ian Craig, who owns the nearby Lea game reserve, where the couple spent most of their holiday, and who arranged for their helicopter ride. Details of William's romantic proposal came as the staff at a secluded Kenyan lodge where the couple stayed revealed how they spent their final romantic day before the Prince popped the question.

Stunned staff at the isolated Rotunda lodge said they had no idea they were hosting the heir to the throne when William arrived with his future bride – just hours before he asked Kate to marry him. The peaceful hotel consists of just two simple wooden cottages nestled high in the Mount Kenya range, around three miles from Lake Alice, and is permanently staffed by three local workers, who live on site to greet the guests and tend to their every need.

But the royal couple were undemanding. William and Kate asked for virtually nothing as they enjoyed a back-to-basics stay, during which they tucked into a simple supper home-cooked by the future king. Jackson Kimutai, 28, one of the members of staff, said the pair's only request was to be taken fishing for trout from the back of a rickety rowing boat. And he added that the team believed William and Kate were just another ordinary young couple when they arrived at around 3 p.m. on 20 October in a rented Toyota Landcruiser. The Prince was dressed in a casual shirt and chinos, while Kate wore a summer dress. Kimutai recalled, 'They came by road and jumped out of the car. The man introduced himself and said, "Hi, I'm Willy." She was very smiley and happy and said her name was Kate. We took their luggage to the cottage for them – it is transported over a gorge on a special rope runway. Then we showed them the place. We had no idea who they were and they gave us no reason to believe they were anyone special.'

He added, 'We only get supplies here once a month, so all of our guests must bring food and drink with them. William and Kate had a box of things which they put in the kitchen.'

The staff said the royal couple first spent a few minutes relaxing in Rutundu Lodge's rustic wooden surroundings. The couple's cosy chalet was fitted in a comfortable but basic fashion. Bare polished wooden floors in the living room and bedroom are covered with warming fluffy rugs, while the bathroom includes a large bath and a toilet, which seeps into a septic tank. Guests book in on a strictly self-catering basis and have use of a basic kitchen attached to the cottage. Most meals are cooked on two simple gas ring burners, while essentials are chilled in a traditional 'fridge' – several wooden shelves in an external cupboard.

The cottage overlooks the stunning Lake Rutundu, another mountain pond stocked with trout and surrounded by rolling hills. Rutundu worker Cosmos Kiecan, 30, said a cheerful William and Kate later went to the water for a fishing trip. And they abandoned any idea of grandeur as they cast their rods from the back of a decades-old wooden rowing boat.

He said, 'When they arrived they said straight away that they wanted to fish, so after they had settled in we took them down to the lake. It is a big lake and well stocked with trout. Some of them are up to four pounds and most of the guests want to try and catch some for their supper. We allow two to be taken and eaten every day and the rest are thrown back.

'Some people fish from the jetty or the banks, but William was keen to go out in the boat, so Jackson and I rowed them out to the middle of the lake. It is a small boat but it works very well.

'They sat at the back facing the water so they could flick their rods for fly fishing. We were at the front and rowing for them. They were having a great time. It is only fly fishing which is allowed and he spent some time showing her how to do it. Sometimes she was flicking her rod wrong and he helped her to do it better. You could tell they were very close and happy to be together. She kept looking at him and smiling and he was happy too,' he added.

The couple spent around an hour on the water before eventually heading back to shore empty-handed. Kimutai went on, 'Sadly, they didn't manage to catch anything. We went back after an hour and they hadn't had a single bite, but some days it is like that. We told them it is hard to catch a fish in Lake Rutundu and they laughed. After that they went back to their cottage to relax.'

The peaceful lodge's staff are well versed in their evening procedures to keep guests warm despite the biting mountain breeze and lack of electricity. At sunset each day, they leap into action – lighting a fire underneath an external water tank for hot water and burning lamps to flood the cottage with romantic light.

'We always get hot water for the guests and light two fires inside – one in the main room and one in the bedroom,' Kimutai added. 'The only light is by paraffin hurricane lamps but people seem to like them. Although we are not cooks, we always offer to help the guests with their meals.'

As darkness fell, William and Kate ran themselves a hot bath and snuggled up beside the front room's roaring fire. The Prince cooked them up a simple meal that they tucked into using the cottage's off-white plates and tarnished, well-used cutlery. Meanwhile, the staff said the couple didn't even have any wine – choosing instead to sup mugs of tea made from hot water left for them by the workers in a battered vacuum flask.

'He was very happy to cook,' Kimutai said. 'They had brought their own supplies, although we did not see what. We usually ask people to leave their dirty plates and things in the sink so we can wash up for them, but they hardly left any mess. Sometimes there are also lots of empty bottles of wine or beer but we didn't see any sign of any alcohol from these guys. We think they just drank the tea we left them and enjoyed themselves by the fire.'

Later, the couple retired to the bedroom, where a rustic wooden four-poster stands alongside a set of bunk beds for families with children. At night, the cottage is enveloped by total silence, broken occasionally only by the flapping of nocturnal birds or the occasional wandering buffalo or antelope. Lying at the heart of the Mount Kenya National Park, Rutundu is protected by three permanent rangers, who watch for intruders or poachers and use a radio link to summon armed colleagues when required. The site's blissful tranquillity is ensured, as the nearest mobile signal is only receivable from a rocky outcrop about a 30-minute walk away through the bush. But by night the presence of deadly animals means guests are warned not to attempt the journey and advised instead to stay tucked up inside their cottage.

The next morning, William and Kate emerged blinking into the African sunlight before enjoying a simple breakfast on the terrace prepared by the Prince. The staff said they took the couple for a second, shorter, fishing trip before they left – in time for the 10 a.m. checkout.

Kiecan said, 'They had obviously had a really lovely time and had burned a lot of wood for the fire. We took them down to the lake again and then they left. Willy was joking that they had heard a tapping on their window when they woke up. He pulled back the curtains to see who it was and it was a weaver bird banging at the glass. They are bright yellow and often come up to meet the guests. Willy said after that it went around to all the other windows and tapped on the glass there, too. The whole time the couple were here they were really chatty with us, and very friendly. He was joking about the weather because he said he had been here before and got cold. Although it's usually sunny, it's very high here so it does get cold – especially at night. This time he said he had brought two jumpers and she also had some clothes for the evening with her.'

The staff only found out later who the special guests were and were amazed. The trip to Rutundu was one of several excursions planned by the Prince during their holiday at the nearby Lewa wildlife park, where William had spent a month working during his gap year before he met Kate at university. Ian Craig, the owner of the reserve, is believed to have put the royal couple up for part of the time in his personal house on the 55,000-acre site, which is home to dozens of animal species, including lions, giraffes, zebra and antelope. William and Kate also spent several nights at the spectacular Sirikoi game lodge, where they shared a romantic tented room in the wilderness. Happy locals have told of their joy that the Prince chose Kenya to confirm his commitment to the future princess. David Kamau, 23, works at a craft stall in the Lewa reserve and said he was delighted when William came in to buy hand-crafted local decorations for the couple's Christmas tree.

He said, 'Everyone is so pleased that they came to Kenya to get engaged. To have a prince and princess staying was wonderful. I met William when he came to my shop. He chatted to us for ages and then bought a pack of ten wire angels and a pack of ten beaded Christmas trees. It is great that we know they got engaged in our place – and even better to know our work will be decorating their Christmas tree.'

Both wrote in a visitors' book after their romantic trip to the log-cabin hideaway. Kate wrote, 'I had a wonderful 24 hours. Sadly no fish to be found but we had great fun trying. I love the warm fires and candle lights – so romantic! Hope to be back again soon.' William's note, dated 20–21 October 2010, said, 'Such fun to be back! Brought more clothes this time! Looked after so well. Thank you guys! Look forward to the next time, soon I hope.' He signed it William; she signed hers Catherine Middleton. Now, of course, she has a different name and title as she has joined the House of Windsor.

What followed was an extraordinary attempt by the couple to keep their engagement a closely guarded secret. Even the Queen was kept in the dark for over two weeks. 'We're like sort of ducks,' said William, 'very calm on the surface with little feet going under the water. It's been really exciting because we've been talking about it for a long time, so for us it's a real relief and it's really nice to be able to tell everybody. Especially for the last two or three weeks – it's been quite difficult not telling anyone, keeping it to ourselves. I was torn between asking Kate's dad first and then the realisation that he might actually say no dawned upon me. So I thought, if I ask Kate first, then he can't really say no.'

William even kept his big news a secret from the Queen as he and Kate excitedly made their plans for a future together. He was determined to do it his way, and protocol went out of the window. It also gives us an insight into how the new-look House of Windsor will be led from the front by William when he becomes king. One senior member of the Royal Household told me, 'He did not tell his family until the last minute because he knows once it was official there was a danger he would lose control of it all. William is determined his wedding to Catherine is going to be their day as well as one of public celebration.

'He knows it is a public event but it is also going to be their special private moment, too, and they don't want that to be forgotten by the courtiers charged with the organisation.'

The happy couple were all smiles for the cameras when they arrived for their pal Harry Meade's wedding. They were already secretly engaged as they boldly strolled through the front of the church before a battery of waiting photographers. But Kate, of course, did not have on Princess Diana's sapphire engagement ring.

A week later, on 30 October, William invited Kate's parents to Birkhall on the Queen's Balmoral estate in the Scottish Highlands. It was there, in the Queen Mother's favourite old royal retreat, that William — knowing his bride-to-be had accepted his proposal — asked her father Michael for his daughter's hand in marriage. They were preparing to announce the news on Wednesday, 3 November, once he had told the rest of his family. Just four days later, on 7 November 2010, I penned an article in the *News of the World* breaking the story. The headline read, WE WILLS WED NEXT SUMMER, with a strapline deck below that read, 'Royal engagement to be announced Xmas'. The opening line of the story could not have been clearer. It read: 'Prince William and his patient girlfriend Kate Middleton will announce their engagement before Christmas, the *News of the World* can reveal.' Nine days later, I was to be proved right. In the past, the dates and venues are announced simultaneously. But in typical William style he wanted it his way.

Palace officials — who still had not been told of the arrangements — refused to confirm the story. The otherwise happy story was not without tragedy, however, with the death of Kate's paternal grandfather, Peter, on 2 November, aged 90, in his home in the village of Vernham Dean, Hampshire. Kate and the rest of her family were devastated by his loss and all focus was switched from her big day to the preparations for the funeral on 12 November. A close source said, 'It's not clear at this point if [Kate's father] Mike had actually told [her mother] Carole, because William and Kate had asked them not to say anything.' Kate herself admitted that there was an interesting period when even she was not sure if her mother knew. 'We had quite an awkward situation because I knew that William had asked my father but I didn't know if my mother knew.' So she came back from Scotland, where they had been photographed on the royal Balmoral estate on a shoot. Carole did not make it clear to her daughter whether she knew or not.

Then, on his last solo engagement before the big news broke, William flew to Afghanistan along with the Defence Secretary, Dr Liam Fox. In a surprise visit to Camp Bastion in Helmand Province, he joined about 2,500 servicemen in the remembrance ceremony, laying a wreath to remember his own friends and others who had lost their lives. He returned on Monday, 15 November, and that night he telephoned the Queen to tell her the good news. She was delighted. His father, too, was happy, although the Prince of Wales's comment that his son and future daughter-in-law had 'practised long enough' was a classic illustration of his emotional limitations. That, coupled with the timing of his comment that he did expect his wife the Duchess of Cornwall to be queen when he is king raised eyebrows, and suggested possible future tensions between his and his son's rival courts.

On 23 November 2010, I attended a St James's Palace press briefing where they announced that the marriage would take place on Friday, 29 April 2011 at Westminster Abbey. They were keen to stress that the Royal Family would pay for the wedding, with the Middletons chipping in too. It was, they said, a precedent set by the marriages of the Prince and Princess of Wales in 1981 and Princess Elizabeth and Prince Philip in 1947. Jamie Lowther-Pinkerton, the sharp, former SAS officer turned courtier, revealed it would be a 'classic' royal wedding with all the pomp and pageantry the world expected of the British. He said the couple, who were 'over the moon', were very much in charge of the arrangement. They wanted it to be their wedding and, even though it would take place at Westminster Abbey, the Royal Family's church, at the high altar, it had the feel of an English parish church. They wanted everyone to enjoy the day and welcomed Prime Minister David Cameron's suggestion that it should be a public holiday, allowing everyone to celebrate. 'This is their day,' Jamie said. 'They are calling the shots.'

A CLASS APART

'Being a princess isn't all it's cracked up to be.'

DIANA, PRINCESS OF WALES (1961–97)

He is a prince with vast wealth, ancient ancestry and coveted royal title, once dubbed the world's most eligible bachelor. She is a beautiful middle-class Englishwoman of unexceptional family background who is now catapulted into an extraordinary world of global celebrity and royal duty. Together, they will indubitably become one of the most enduring double acts of their generation, instantly recognised wherever they go. The marriage of Prince William Arthur Philip Louis of Wales and Catherine Elizabeth Middleton is therefore an enormously important moment in the history of our *modern* monarchy.

This union bucks historic trends, with the direct heir to the throne choosing a bride outside his social circle and class, a commoner no less. It is a marriage born of love, not one like those of English princes of old: forged for dynastic or diplomatic reasons. Kate is not even an aristocrat like William's late mother Diana, Princess of Wales, who was the last commoner to wed a direct heir to the throne. When she arrived at St Paul's Cathedral to wed, she was Lady Diana Spencer.

William's choice of a commoner bride signals his clear intention to be his own man when he ascends the throne. He will reign *his* way and has made it clear he will not be 'an ornament', but is determined to get more involved with public life than his predecessors. Effectively, he wants to get his hands dirty. So will Kate. Those close to them insist this couple, more than any other royal couple, will become the embodiment of modern monarchy, and in doing so will silence the growing band of republicans who demand a democratic replacement of the sovereign, and the end of the monarchical system with an elected, accountable head of state.

It is true that both William and Kate are people of their generation, albeit privileged ones. Only time will tell whether William's statement of intent that he made as a 27-year-old will be easy to live up to, especially as the demands of the formal side of his role engulfs him. Many believe that, as a couple, William and Kate have the ability, intelligence and desire to drag the institution into the 21st century. The comparative youth, good looks and experience will, courtiers hope, make it more relevant to the people that it, after all, exists to represent, as a symbol of unity and national pride. It is the people who pay for the royals' privileged lifestyle and so they can expect value for that money. There will always be detractors, but, with William at the helm and Kate at his side, this ancient, hereditary institution can perhaps still justify a place in our new British society, a society where social mobility is not just a buzzword but a reality.

Like his mother, Princess Diana, William has the heart and natural grace to become a beacon of national hope for a new, more demanding generation – if you like, a 'people's prince'. With that in mind, his choice of bride is perhaps both significant and crucial. If he had wed a European princess or aristocrat, inevitably people would see them and the children they produce as elitist. But, like him, Kate is a woman of her generation, possessing the perfect pedigree and lack of stuffiness to convince people that this modern monarchy is for real, an institution that has a future as well as a past.

That is why this marriage is a defining moment for the British Royal Family. Together, they will be world stars, the most famous couple on the planet in historical terms, ranking alongside the likes of Charles and Diana, John F. and Jackie Kennedy and, latterly, the Obamas. Their arrival as an official couple immediately gives the Royal Family a younger, fresher and more relevant feel. As king, when that day comes, William will reign with Kate at his side as queen consort. Through William and Kate's union, perhaps for the first time since Charles and Diana kissed on the balcony of Buckingham Palace on their wedding day in 1981, the British monarchy is back under the global media spotlight for the right reasons.

Only once in our history has a future British sovereign married a commoner, and then it was in very different circumstances. In what was then a religious society divided, the relationship between Catholics and Protestants was at best an uneasy one. In 1659, at Breda in Holland, James, the Duke of York, secretly wed, while the Royal Family remained in exile following the English Civil War and Cromwell's Interregnum. James's brother, later King Charles II, insisted his wayward, weak-willed brother marry Anne in an English ceremony, saying that her strong character would be a positive influence. This commoner would hold a significant place in history, becoming the mother to two queens.

Much more recently, in the 20th century, the woman who later became known as the Queen Mother was technically a commoner too when, as Scottish aristocrat Lady Elizabeth Bowes-Lyon, she married the then Prince Albert, Duke of York, later King George VI, in 1921. At the time, her husband's older brother, the Prince of Wales, later Duke of Windsor, was heir to George V.

Placed in historic context, William and Kate's love match is therefore significant. It is a royal marriage where, thankfully, love and royal duty truly entwine. It is a modern marriage that started from a chance meeting and shows just how far monarchy has evolved. This clunky institution seems at last to be prepared for real change.

Gone are the days of forced royal marriages. Gone, too, are the days when it was very acceptable for princes to live with their mistress for love. The last King called William, William IV – who came to the throne in 1830 – lived with the actor Dorothea Jordan for 20 years, and she bore him ten children, who took the surname FitzClarence.

The world has changed, even the royal world. William and Kate's marriage is a truly modern match – ironically, a trend started by his grandmother the Queen, who, as a teenager, fell for the dashing Philip Mountbatten (his real surname was the Germanic Schleswig-Holstein-Sonderburg-Glücksburg) at first sight. Almost from that moment, Princess Elizabeth was determined to marry him. It helped, of course, that he was a great-great-grandson of Queen Victoria and a nephew of the Machiavellian Lord Mountbatten.

William and Kate, however, come from very different backgrounds. Kate is a woman who descends from both working-class and middle-class roots, unique for a royal bride and something William's great-great-grandfather George V would not have believed possible. Would he have condoned his great-great-grandson's marriage to a commoner? I doubt it.

Equally, if Kate and William had come from an earlier generation – and she had had a title of course – their long courtship would never have taken place. It would have been sealed in marriage years ago. In their time together, they have been relatively free to experience a loving relationship before committing to marriage.

Placed in the context of the British Royal Family's colourful and illustrious history, Kate's ascendance is quite simply extraordinary. She is destined to be one of the most famous women in the world, a British royal and, one day, expected to reign alongside King William V (should he decide to use that name). Kate certainly appears to possess the media savvy and natural grace needed to navigate the rough and tumble of the often brutal royal world, where her every public move, and some private ones, are caught on camera.

As soon as it became clear that Kate's relationship, despite very public blips and splits, had the necessary staying power, genealogists began to look even deeper, tracing her family history in earnest further and further back, hoping to find contrasts to William's royal bloodline. What they discovered made interesting reading. For in the year that Prince William's illustrious ancestor, his great-great-great-great-grandmother Queen Victoria, was born at Kensington Palace in 1819, a young man named James Harrison took his first nervous steps down a coalmine in County Durham in the north of England. For the next 120 years, Harrison and his descendants served the nation diligently, facing daily jeopardy underground. His origins could not have been lowlier. He came from solid working-class stock, where life was often cheap and short – the very opposite of the glittering court life of Britain's monarchy at the time. Yet Harrison's bloodline was strong. Now, more than two centuries on from his birth, this miner's descendant is the new bride of the future king.

Kate can also trace her lineage to the literary world. She is a distant cousin of the late children's author Beatrix Potter, but is also a long-lost relative of *Swallows and Amazons* creator Arthur Ransome. Ransome's sister Joyce was married to Hugo Lupton, the cousin of Kate's great-grandmother Olive.

Though polished, sophisticated and in every way fit to accept William's proposal of marriage, Kate brings to the Royal Family a vital lineage that will qualify her to be truly titled the Princess of the People. Her family's story is an uplifting one, a story of one family and its road from obscurity and poverty all the way to the steps of the British throne.

William was christened by the Archbishop of Canterbury, Dr Robert Runcie, raised in a palace and educated at top prep schools and Eton College; Kate's childhood and upbringing was obviously very different. She had a traditional middle-class family background, comfortably well-off and privately educated. However, when one digs a little deeper, one finds – as with most families – one or two skeletons in the ancestral cupboard. Their errors, of course, are no reflection on her. You can, after all, choose your friends but not your family. One of Kate's forebears had a prison record. Another, even closer to home, was Kate's fun-loving multimillionaire uncle Gary Goldsmith, then 49, her mother's brother, who heaped shame on the family in 2009 when he was exposed in a sex-and-drugs sting by the redtop *News of the World* in which he bragged of his niece's royal associations.

It is fair to say there is nothing in her ancestry and family history that would have helped predict that Kate's life would take such a remarkable course. Prince William's great-great-great-grandfather was the notorious womaniser monarch King Edward VII; Kate's was a jailbird. As Prince of Wales, William's Victorian-born ancestor had infuriated his mother Queen Victoria with his lavish, extravagant and often hedonistic lifestyle. He scandalised the monarchy, becoming the first British royal to appear, in 1891, as a court witness in a case brought by William Gordon-Cumming, a friend found cheating at baccarat, Edward's favourite, but illegal, game of chance. A decade earlier, Kate's great-great-great-grandfather, according to the 1881 census, another Edward – Edward Thomas Glassborow – then 55, went one better than a court appearance, for he was doing hard labour in London's Holloway Prison.

Prison records have not survived from that era, so it is impossible to know why the father of seven, who worked as a messenger for an insurance company, had ended up behind bars. In those days, Holloway was the destination for prisoners of both sexes sentenced at the Old Bailey or Guildhall Justice Rooms. Glassborow, who lived in Hackney, east London was one of 436 inmates when the census was taken. It is unclear when Kate's ancestor was released, but by the time his third son Frederick – Kate's great-great-grandfather – married on 1 June 1886 he was free. For by then Edward was describing himself as a 'gentleman of independent means', which was quite an extraordinary turnaround for a former felon. Glassborow died aged 72 in 1898, with Frederick at his bedside. The cause of his death was recorded as apoplexy, the result of chronic rheumatism.

Frederick's eldest son, also named Frederick, conscripted to the army at the outbreak of World War I, went, like thousands of his contemporaries, to Belgium, to fight the Hun on the frontline. When peace came, he returned to his job as manager of the London and Westminster Bank, where he met and married a young woman named Constance Robinson. The couple travelled across Europe because of Frederick's work. Kate's grandmother, Valerie, and her twin sister, Mary, were born in Marseille. In 1942, at the height of World War II, the family returned to Britain, where Frederick was transferred to Leeds to become manager of the Westminster Bank. Valerie eventually married

Peter Middleton, the son of a wealthy Yorkshire solicitor, who served as an RAF pilot during World War II and worked as a commercial pilot after he demobbed. Peter had just ended his career as a commercial pilot and had taken up a job as a pilot instructor with the Air Service Training.

Kate's father, Michael Francis Middleton, was born on 23 June 1949 in Chapel Allerton Nursing Home in north Leeds. The family home, where Peter lived with his wife, the former Valerie Glassborow, was the aptly named King Lane in an affluent suburb of Leeds in West Yorkshire. He was raised within walking distance of three golf clubs – Headingley, Moortown and Sand Moor, close to the Eccup reservoir – with his older brother Richard, born two years earlier. Michael Middleton, Kate's father, eventually married a glamorous air hostess, Carole Goldsmith, Kate's mother.

Carole Middleton's side of the family makes interesting reading too. Unlike her husband, Carole has unmistakeably working-class roots. The daughter of a lorry driver, Ronald Goldsmith, and housewife Dorothy, formerly Harrison, she was born in Perivale maternity hospital ten miles west of central London, six years after her future husband, on 31 January 1955. A decade on from VE Day, with a young Queen Elizabeth II on the throne for only three years, the country was emerging from the depressing recovery post-war. There was more prosperity, and working-class people, whose aspirations had been strangled by the class divide before the war, believed they could make something of themselves. The British Empire no longer ruled the waves or the world. Many youngsters were taking their lead from America, where rock and roll was the new sensation. 'Change' was certainly the buzzword of the time.

When Carole Middleton was barely a toddler in July 1957, Prime Minister Harold Macmillan reflected the mood of the country with his famous optimistic speech in which he said, 'Our people have never had it so good.' True, as with all politicians, Macmillan was painting a rosy picture of Britain's economy, while urging wage restraint and warning that inflation was the country's most important problem of the post-war era. Carole's family home was a modest property, 73a Dudley Road in Southall. Ron, as family and friends knew him, had ideas for bettering himself and had plans to become a builder even then. Kate was raised by her family to be a lady, but certainly, given their background, Kate's grandparents would not have dreamed it possible that one day their granddaughter would become the future Princess of Wales and, ultimately, queen consort.

CHAPTER 14

THE FIRST TOUR

*'I can only say that the experience of this past seven days
has exceeded all our expectations.'*

PRINCE WILLIAM ON LEAVING CANADA

If she was nervous, she did not show it. She may have been the
new (royal) kid on the block, but Kate – now Her Royal
Highness the Duchess of Cambridge – took to the job of roving
royal ambassador as if it was second nature. She looked every
inch the picture-perfect princess and did not put a foot wrong
while accompanying her husband on their first joint tour to
Canada. Together, they were the Royal Family's new golden
couple. If the far-flung Commonwealth realms are to sign up to
a continued affiliation with monarchy in the long term, the
people have to believe in them. With that in mind, the young
husband and wife had something of a mission to fulfil – to take
Canada by storm.

Canada is a well-trodden royal path. In 1939, the Queen
Mother, then Queen Consort, toured the vast and beautiful
country from coast to coast with the King. She immediately fell
in love with the place. The tour, then, was designed to bolster

transatlantic support in the event of war, and to reaffirm Canada's status as a self-governing kingdom, albeit with a British monarch at its head.

During a walkabout, a certain Boer War veteran asked the Queen Consort, 'Are you Scots or are you English?' to which she replied, as quick as a flash, 'I am a Canadian.' Kate would have to learn quickly if she was to follow in the esteemed footsteps of the last so-called 'Commoner Queen' (despite her aristocratic roots, the Queen Mother was technically a commoner because she was not of royal blood), whose quick wit and consummate PR skills were legendary.

I covered William and Kate's tour as an accredited correspondent. From what I saw up close, they were a safe pair of hands too, as they worked the huge and excitable crowds who gathered to see them with aplomb. In an opinion poll taken just before they touched down, almost half of Canada's citizens thought the monarchy was 'a relic of a colonial past that has no place in Canada'. If that was truly the case, then that half must have stayed at home. Thousands turned out just to try to catch a glimpse of their future king and queen when they arrived on 30 June 2011. Further crowds lined the route up to the residence of the Governor General, Rideau Hall, fervently waving their Canadian flag hours before the couple had even arrived. Some had travelled for many hours across the enormous country in order to be there to welcome the royal couple.

The excitement was palpable. From what I witnessed, Canadians appear to be happy to continue their love affair with royalty, despite what that poll claimed, and indeed perhaps more so than any other realm. Victoria Doherty and Olivia Dale, both 13, and Jasmine Starks, 14, drove with their families for six hours from Waterloo, Ontario. Jasmine said, 'We love Kate. She's so down to earth and very beautiful. We got up at four in the morning to watch the royal wedding. I can't wait to see what she's wearing as it's what everyone will be talking about.'

Pat Cook, 64, from Hamilton, Ontario, said, 'I think William and Kate have really renewed interest in the monarchy in Canada. They seem very in love and Kate has so much self-confidence and will fit right in with the royals. We've been here since nine this morning to get a good spot.'

Just before they arrived, the 300 VIP guests, made up of military families and people who worked for charities close to the couple's hearts, took their seats, and the guard of honour did some last-minute rehearsing.

The official car drew up along the red carpet and waiting to greet them was Canada's Prime Minister Stephen Harper and his wife Laureen. Around 10,000 people cheered wildly as William and Kate stepped out. A tanned and healthy Kate looked particularly delighted at the warm reception and waved shyly. The four of them then approached the Tomb of the Unknown Soldier and stood in quiet contemplation as a solo trumpeter sounded the last post. William carefully placed a large wreath on the monument, while his wife leaned forwards to put down a small posy of flowers. She warmly greeted the woman who had handed it to her, Mabel Girouard, who had been chosen by the Canadian Legion as their Memorial Silver Cross Mother after her son Bobby, 46, was killed by a suicide bomber in Afghanistan.

The royal couple left the memorial and began to undertake the first of many joint walkabouts. At first, Kate looked apprehensive – with a fixed smile on her face, she stepped forward to work the crowd under the watchful eye of the private secretary Jamie Lowther-Pinkerton and her protection team. Before long, though, she had sent the crowd into a frenzy of excitement, although there were just as many screams for William. Kate visibly began to relax after a few minutes as she grew into her role and was handed armfuls of flowers and gifts. Each time, she said, 'Thank you so much. We are so delighted to be here.' As if she was seeking reassurance, she occasionally looked over to catch William's eye on the other side of the crowd, perhaps to make sure she was moving quickly enough, but there was no doubt that she was performing admirably. William himself smiled as one woman told him, 'Canada is so happy you are here,' to which he replied, 'Thank you. That is so kind.'

As she waited for the Prince to finish, Kate chatted with the Prime Minister and his wife, telling them, 'That was so amazing, there were so many people there... How many do you think? We have been on the go since 7.30 a.m. this morning, so it's been a long day.' As the couple got into their official car, her first test over, Kate leaned into her husband's shoulder and grinned broadly.

The next stop, by State Landau, was to Parliament Hill. The cheers subsided for a few seconds and a woman, five yards from the carriage, shouted out, 'Happy Birthday, Diana,' adding, 'We love you, Will and Kate.' The day, of course, would have been Princess Diana's 50th birthday. Just as her late mother-in-law had done so many times on her travels with the clothes she selected, Kate embraced Canada's birthday celebrations by wearing a stylish outfit in the country's national colours.

Kate was wearing an elegant cream Reiss dress – the same one that was worn for her official engagement pictures by celebrated photographer Mario Testino – and a red hat by Lock and Company's Sylvia Fletcher that appeared to feature a maple leaf, worn in honour of Canada Day in Ottawa. She matched the hundreds of people who were also dressed in the national colours that had turned out for her first engagement with her husband, a citizenship ceremony. The Duchess finished off her look with a Maple Leaf diamond brooch, which the Queen loaned her for the tour and that had first been worn by the Queen on her visit to Canada in 1951. As with all royal tours, the pace was relentless. At one point, Kate wilted in the heat and her make-up began to melt. She gestured towards her cheeks and told Prime Minister Stephen Harper's wife Laureen, 'I'm just so hot. It's incredible.'

The Canadian Museum of Civilisation in Gatineau was the next stop. There they were serenaded by a tune that had been penned by a Canadian piper, designed to remind them of their days as a courting couple. As they came down an escalator into the attraction's Great Hall, Pipe Major Bethany Bisaillion's great highland bagpipe wheezed into life as she began her piece, entitled St Andrews Courtship. Ms Bisaillion, 44, from the Sons of Scotland Pipe Band – who had played for the Queen in the past – said after the performance, 'It's a lively march in honour of their time at university – it is uplifting and fun. I play at many citizenship ceremonies and I thought it would be a great way to mark their visit by creating something unique.'

William and Kate then joined Governor General David Johnston and his wife, Sharon, on stage as 25 new citizens, surrounded by their families and friends, swore allegiance to the Queen and, poignantly, her 'heirs and successors'. As they were called forward, William gave the new Canadians a large national flag, while Kate presented them with a small handheld one. After the ceremony, the couple posed with the group and the Prince made them laugh when, told by an official he was standing on the wrong step, he turned to those behind him and said, with great humility, 'Sorry.'

Royal aides were keen to pace Kate on her first ever tour, and so they ensured that the couple would enjoy some private time as well. For a few hours, they, William and his new bride, were alone. He rowed her across a stunning lake to an island where they spent hours together in a romantic log cabin, complete with a packed picnic. They had even managed to ditch their Scotland Yard bodyguards, who gave them radios and kept a discreet distance so that the young couple could wander off into dense woodland completely alone. 'They took food and drink with them and just disappeared together,' a senior source said. The secret hideaway was on Harrington Lake Estate near Lake Meech, where Canadian Prime Minister Stephen Harper has a private retreat – his version of Chequers – 35 miles from Canada's capital Ottawa. The cabin – built in the 1920s as a hideaway for a lumber baron, which has its own bedroom, bathroom and kitchenette – is nestled in an area known as Gatineau Park, amidst the Gatineau Hills, and is complete with the most breathtaking views. It is a royal favourite, and has been used by people ranging from the Queen to a multitude of Canadian Prime Ministers as a quiet place to go fishing and, simply, to chill out. The couple, who had only just wed in April, watched by 2 billion globally on television, looked rejuvenated after this much-needed mini-break.

Later, Kate, at an open-air pop concert on Parliament Hill, Ottawa, wore a purple Issa jersey dress and thrilled the ecstatic 100,000 crowd as she arrived with William, dressed casually in an open-necked shirt. Kate, seen by now as a natural royal performer, looked relaxed and happy as the royal couple took their seats in the VIP section. As they sat down, Canadian singer Alan Doyle, of local favourite band the Great Big Sea, shouted to the crowd, 'Put your hands up. We're in the presence of royalty for God's sake.'

As the TV panned onto them, showing the couple on the big screen for the crowd, the show host, CBC radio star Jian Ghomeshi, joked, 'We have to keep introducing you because we like having you here.'

Throughout the concert, William and Kate were tactile – chatting lovingly to each to each other as the Canadian bands entertained them.

They completed their trip to Ottawa, with Kate by now dubbed 'Catherine the Great' by the Canadian media, by visiting veterans at the Canadian War Museum. After planting a tree at Rideau Hall, they paid their respects at the headstone of the Unknown Soldier. Inside, they mingled with 150 veterans of World War II, the Korean War and Afghanistan, together with their families. They listened to harrowing stories of heroism and injury, and were informed of how rehabilitation programmes help Canadian veterans.

Everywhere she went, Kate drew comparisons with Princess Diana – most notably when she visited sick children and babies at the Sainte-Justine University Hospital in Montreal, the largest mother-child centre in Canada. Kate appeared, understandably, slightly unnerved by the experience. William, with a tender stroke on her back, stood by her side as the two of them met gravely ill children in the hospital cancer unit, and he was able to reassure her. They first spent an emotional hour privately visiting babies in the hospital's premature-baby unit, and then the couple spent at least twenty minutes with six children, taking care to spend time showing each child individual attention. There was a particular touching moment when William gently reached out to his wife as the pair spoke to a shy Jak Kilow, a two-year-old, in the playroom of the hospital.

The couple, just like William's late mother, sat at the children's level on small chairs, leaning in to ask questions. One patient, Laurence Yelle, 14, who was diagnosed with a brain tumour and was wearing a headscarf after having lost her hair through gruelling chemotherapy, said, 'Kate was so lovely, she spent a lot longer talking to me than I thought she would. She asked me questions about the artwork I was doing and also about my illness. It was easier than I thought to talk to her, she was the most normal person.'

The fast pace of their first tour continued relentlessly. It was almost like a military operation. The royal entourage, too, had a very masculine and military feel to it. The aides all had military backgrounds; Jamie Lowther-Pinkerton, a former SAS Major who had served with distinction in Colombia, ran the show. But even the press supremo, Miguel Head, had cut his teeth at the Ministry of Defence. What this meant was that there appeared to be a distinct lack of female support staff for Kate. While her husband, a guardsman attached to the RAF as a search and rescue pilot, had a services background, it felt to me as though Kate was being expected to keep up with their schedule, rather than have them adjust the tour pace to allow for her relative inexperience. She is fit and intelligent, but she needed stamina to run with this royal pack. Fortunately, she had it.

On 3 July, after spending the night aboard the Canadian frigate HMCS *Montreal*, in which they sailed up the St Lawrence from Montreal to Quebec City, William and Kate began their day by joining the ship's company of around 200 sailors for a Sunday-morning prayer service. It was predictably named a 'love boat' in the press, but it was hardly that – Kate later admitted that she barely got a wink of sleep on the naval vessel. At City Hall in Quebec's picturesque old town, where the couple received the freedom of the city, they also witnessed their first anti-royal demonstrators on the trip. Only a handful turned out, though, and they were kept back behind a cordon. Besides, supporters of the Royal Family vastly outnumbered them.

Kate teetered carefully down the ship's steps in her four-inch stilettos to meet a line-up of Quebec dignitaries, including the Grand Chief of the Huron-Wendat Nation, Konrad Sioui, who was wearing traditional dress. He said, 'Kate was very interested in my hat and she wanted to know what feathers it's made of. I told her turkey feathers. I gave William a document that is the treaty that was signed between our two nations by our ancestors in 1760. It is a treaty to say we will live in peace and friendship as brothers.'

It was here that Kate spoke publicly for the first time since her engagement interview with ITV correspondent Tom Bradby, and, interestingly, she spoke of her hopes of starting a family after meeting the father of a 'beautiful' little girl. Perhaps as a sign of things to come in the near future, she appeared a little broody after being presented with a bouquet by Raffaela, the two-year-old child of British ex-pat David Cheater, 28, during a walkabout. The proud dad wished her luck on starting a family and Kate thanked him saying, 'Yes, I hope to.'

The couple went on to visit the town's Province House, the venue for the Charlottetown Conference in 1864, where the idea for the nation of Canada was born. Taken on a brief tour of the building, which is where the Prince Edward Island's legislature met for the first time in 1847, and, in fact, still do today, they were shown the Confederation Chamber, where the Charlottetown Conference was held. On the other side of the building, in the Legislative Assembly, where the politicians sit, Speaker Kathleen Casey explained the history behind the building. When told there were only two opposition members, William joked that they were not 'doing very well'.

Outside, William made his first major speech on the trip. 'It is quite a moment for Catherine and me to be standing here in the Atlantic Canada, in front of Province House, where the Canadian Federation was forged,' he said. 'Here, in the crucible of Canadian nationhood, we look forward to meeting many of you. We have both so looked forward to this day, and discovering more about your beautiful island.'

Following this, they then set off by helicopter to the beautiful Summerside Harbour where there was a spectacular search and rescue demonstration, made extra special by having William at the controls. The backdrop was straight out of one of Kate's favourite childhood books, *Anne of Green Gables*, which is set there in 1870. While her husband showed off his flying skills, Kate remained on land, chatting with Captain Josh Willemsen. On one occasion, William brought the helicopter around in front of the watching Duchess – perhaps trying to impress his young bride – banked slightly so that she had a good view into the cockpit and flew off.

In what would become a feature of their future royal tour style, the couple later rolled their sleeves up and gave the waiting photographers just what they had been waiting for. Each climbed into separate boats to join crews in a Dragon Boat race on Dalvay Lake. This was the new, young and vital Royal Family for all to see. Both gave it their all – William was given a position as a rower, while his wife was in charge of steering in her boat. The Prince seemed delighted that, despite the wet and miserable conditions, his team had emerged victorious. Heather Moyse, the Olympic bobsled gold medallist, shared a joke with the Prince as she presented him with a bottle of champagne for winning the race. She said afterwards that he had said that the island should be named Prince William Island following his stunning performance, if he could arrange it with his uncle. She added, 'Both he and Kate are very competitive. As a female athlete, I would be really annoyed if someone let me win.'

This was, as has been mentioned, a fast-paced, whistle-stop tour. They crisscrossed the vast nation, taking in Yellowknife, the sparsely populated capital of the Northern Territories, where they were welcomed with traditional Native Canadian drumming, in a performance by the Dene tribe at the Somba K'e Civic Plaza.

Members of the Inuktitut and Chipewyan tribes were among the greeting party too. A quick change out of the formal wear and into casual clothes, Kate in an olive fitted shirt, skintight jeans and cream and white deck shoes, they took a float plane to Blachford Lake, a remote Ranger outpost in the vast wilderness of the north, situated right on the edge of the tundra. This was a fine example of the extraordinary life that Kate had signed up for.

On 8 July – nine days into the tour – William and Kate joined the colourful Calgary Stampede, complete with white Stetsons and the best country garb, including jeans and checked shirts. It was a spectacular triumph. William agreed. 'I can only say that the experience of this past seven days has exceeded all our expectations. We have been hugely struck by the diversity of this beautiful country, from Ottawa to Quebec, from Prince Edward Island to the Northwest Territories and now the excitement of Calgary. And what about these fantastic white hats!' Canada, he said, had far surpassed all that they were promised. 'Our promise to Canada is that we shall return.'

Having finally left Canada, after what can only be regarded as a fantastically successful trip, the world's most famous couple's next stop would be another first for them. They were heading to the City of Angels, the capital of celebrity, Los Angeles.

Drawing a crowd better suited to rock stars, complete with near-hysterical screaming, William and Kate arrived, and they were undoubtedly the toast of Hollywood. This was the city of A-list multimillionaire superstars, but their celebrity seemed to eclipse them all. They were about to take America by storm.

They were joined by 200 guests for drinks and canapés in the garden of the British Consul General Dame Barbara Hay's residence in Los Angeles. Among them was England footballer David Beckham, actor and comedian Stephen Fry and Lord

Freddie Windsor, son of Prince and Princess Michael of Kent, who lives in the city with his actress wife Sophie Winkleman.

Beckham, who was playing at the time for the local LA Galaxy team, told William, 'Victoria really wanted to come but she is just so tired at the moment. She sent you both lots of love. How was Canada? It looked amazing.'

The Prince replied, 'Don't be silly, send her all our love and tell her good luck with it all. It's been an amazing few days – we've been so lucky with all the incredible places we've been able to see, and we've met so many fascinating people. It's been amazing, amazing.'

Beckham then spoke about the media frenzy surrounding the birth of his first daughter. 'I woke up on Wednesday to a ton of messages on my voicemail from our friends congratulating me on the birth of our daughter. I turned to Victoria and said, "Did I miss something?" Apparently it's being reported every day that she's already been born. One way or another, fingers crossed, she'll be with us in the next few days.'

William listened with interest – David thought the media intrigue surrounding his children was hard to deal with. The media storm that gathered ahead of William and Kate's first child was to be on a whole different level.

Sir Nigel Sheinwald, Britain's ambassador to the US, said, 'They have had a fantastically successful trip to Canada and they will have a great welcome in California. They will meet a huge range of people, from the governor to people working in the projects of Skid Row. They will get a good snapshot of life in this part of California.'

He was right; there was near-hysterical screaming everywhere they went, from Los Angeles's Beverly Hilton Hotel, where they arrived for a new media summit, to a glitzy charity polo match to raise money for their charities.

The highlight of the weekend trip came when they rubbed shoulders with the Hollywood acting elite at a BAFTA event. They arrived to deafening screams from crowds held behind crash barriers as they walked along the red carpet.

Kate looked stunning in a lavender-coloured dress, by Alexander McQueen, and William was smart in his dinner jacket and black bow tie. William took to the stage to give a speech to the guests, and shared a joke with them to begin with, drawing on the huge success of *The King's Speech*. Speaking in a slightly husky voice, he made the audience laugh when he said, 'Before I start I should just like to thank Colin Firth for my perfect opening line – "I have a voice".' He went on, 'As President of BAFTA, I am immensely proud of the success Brits have had in the fiercely competitive world of film, television and video games. Their creative and hi-tech achievements have contributed greatly to our national wealth, not to mention our personal pleasure. Tonight I celebrate them: but I particularly celebrate the fact that, hard on their heels, comes another wave of enormously talented Brits, whom you have the chance to meet this evening. They deserve equal success and, with your help, will surely achieve it. Let's continue the winning formula. Catherine and I have been hugely looking forward to tonight's event with its exciting cast, British and American. Thank you all so much for coming. I believe great things will result. And now, as they say: "Lights, Camera, Action".'

When William stepped down from the ballroom stage, one of the first groups the royal couple talked to was Jennifer Lopez, Tom Hanks and his wife Rita Wilson, and Barbara Streisand – not an everyday occurrence for either group. Everything was just so. The menu blended British tradition with a touch of California cuisine – a courgette and mint titan with a lemon and pine nut gremolata, shaved manchego and a courgette blossom flower garnish to start; followed by a filet of beef with creamed leeks, pickled garlic, asparagus, turnip, baby onions, potato fondant and a red wine sauce. For dessert, guests enjoyed a version of the British dessert Eton Mess featuring English rose meringue, strawberries, cream, sugar-dusted edible rose petals and pulled sugar. The dishes were washed down with fine wines – Villa Maria Private Bin Sauvignon Blanc and Villa Maria Private Bin Merlot Cabernet Sauvignon. Hotel Chocolat even provided chocolate BAFTA masks on the tables.

They were a big hit. Hollywood A-lister Nicole Kidman gave her verdict on William and Kate as she arrived at the sparkling BAFTA bash. Asked what she thought of the royal newlyweds, she replied, 'I just think they're lovely. I was just on the phone to my mum and she said, "It's so good you're going" because we're Australian. It just makes you smile.' They certainly did. It had been their first joint American visit, and they had done extremely well. The couple finally boarded their British Airways flight back to London where they posed for a few moments before walking inside the first-class cabin. Their relief was palpable, their mission certainly accomplished. They well and truly deserved a break.

CHAPTER 15

A 'GROTESQUE' INTRUSION

'Any such publication would serve no purpose other than to cause further,
entirely unjustifiable upset to the Duke and Duchess of Cambridge.'

SPOKESMAN FOR THE TRHS THE DUKE AND DUCHESS OF CAMBRIDGE

Elegant in an ice-blue lace dress by designer Alice Temperley, her hair pulled back in a bun and held in place with pearl-headed pins, Kate sipped tea and chatted to several guests, including shoe designer Jimmy Choo, a favourite with Princess Diana. Somehow, Kate managed to keep her composure, smiling and laughing her way through a Diamond Jubilee tea party at the British High Commission in Kuala Lumpur. Inside, however, Kate was distraught, humiliated by the actions of the paparazzi. She had every right to be grim-faced after the French magazine *Closer* published intrusive topless pictures of her on holiday with Prince William. It was devastating, but she was not about to about to allow her tears of frustration to flow in public.

William, on the other hand, looked less composed. He was not about to let it rest. Earlier, he and Kate had been locked in private talks with aides who were travelling with them on the Far East Jubilee tour of Singapore, Malaysia and the Solomon Islands. They had been utterly shocked when private secretary Jamie Lowther-Pinkerton broke the news. Communications were immediately sent to the offices of both the Prince of Wales and the Queen, in London. William wanted decisive action. He called the photographs a 'grotesque breach of privacy' and said he and his wife felt 'violated' during a 'highly intimate moment during a scene of married life'. He was simply not prepared to let the paparazzi hound his wife as they had his late mother.

Their Diamond Jubilee tour had started well enough. The couple arrived in Singapore on 11 September and were greeted by large, animated crowds everywhere they went. In Kuala Lumpur, Kate notched another first – she delivered her first overseas speech with aplomb at Hospice Malaysia. During it, she stressed the importance of palliative care in transforming the lives of sick children. Kate – Patron of East Anglia's Children's Hospices in the UK – also used her speech to announce a UK-Malaysian partnership between the two hospices, an announcement that won enthusiastic applause from her audience. 'Providing children and their families with a place of support, care and enhancement at a time of great need is simply life-changing,' she said. 'With effective palliative care, lives can be transformed. Treatment, support, care and advice can provide a lifeline to families at a time of great need.' Then, in an instant, the whole mood of the tour changed.

At first the couple, guided by their aides, were not sure what action to take against the photographer (alleged to have been Valerie Suau, from the newspaper *La Provence*) and the magazine that first published the shots. But they were convinced of one thing; the pictures taken as the couple relaxed at Viscount Linley's retreat, Chateau d'Autet, in Provence a few days earlier were a complete violation of their privacy; privacy that they could reasonably expect. After consulting their legal team, the couple took the bold step of announcing on 14 September that they had launched legal proceedings against the publisher of the French magazine. While Kate was able to look relaxed, in public at least, William was noticeably unsettled. He had, it seemed, the weight of the world on his shoulders. As they watched a traditional Malay tea-pouring ceremony before heading to the next leg of their South-East Asia tour, they certainly looked distracted.

A few commentators questioned the wisdom of going to France and parading topless in a country where the paparazzi have perfected the 'fine art' of taking intrusive photographs. But, on the whole, the reaction was sympathetic. Away from the tea party, the young royals showed the strain of the day's revelations and appeared downcast as they left for the airport. This was the first big media test since they had married in a whirlwind of positive reaction. Their response had to be a fine balancing act – they wanted action but they did not want it to overshadow the overseas Jubilee mission they had been sent on.

I myself had flown ahead to Borneo. Logistics meant that the tiny press pack on that leg of the trip had to advance. I was up early after spending the night in bunk beds in a wooden dormitory in the Danum Valley, usually reserved for university research students. The tour was to go ahead as planned, we were told. By now, the topless picture controversy was the story; the news relevance of what the couple planned to do in the jungle was becoming increasingly less relevant.

The jungle itself was a mystical place. As I crossed the Rain Forest canopy bridge at dusk, I watched in awe as a flying squirrel, scientifically known as Pteromyini, leapt from tree to tree. My colleague, photographer Ken Goff, had earlier photographed an adult orangutan as it had walked past him, just a few metres away. It was like stepping back in time to another age entirely. However, the jungle did have its disadvantages for a reporter – there was no communications for starters — so I was unable to keep abreast of developments as the topless photographs row unfolded. It was, however, about to take a dramatic twist.

As the royal couple received a briefing on conservation in the Danum Valley, the small press pool had a briefing of our own from the couple's advisers. We were left in no doubt whatsoever about the anger that the two of them felt. William's spokesman said he felt really strongly about privacy and harassment, and told us that he was prepared to pursue a criminal prosecution against those who had snooped on his wife if necessary. 'It's part of a very long-standing and heartfelt position by the Duke and Prince Harry, given their past, to do everything they can to protect themselves. They've always said they don't have an issue with the mainstream media just doing their job, but they have always had an issue with paparazzi whose work intrudes on their privacy.'

The Borneo jungle seemed a symbolically fitting backdrop to their troubles. No one could have guessed though, from watching them in public, that the previous 24 hours had left the royal couple 'livid' and 'violated'. As the scandal surrounding the photographs raged elsewhere — with more pictures being published in the Irish edition of the *Daily Star* — William and Kate spent the day smiling and joking as they photographed orangutans and admired exotic flowers.

At one point, the young couple were fitted with special harnesses and helmets before being hoisted 138 feet up into a giant Parashorea Tomentella tree using a 'counterweight pulley system', which had been set by technicians to their combined weight, believed to be about 23 stone. Having been winched high into the jungle canopy, William spotted the official photographer Ken Goff, who had been granted permission to perch in an adjacent tree. As they waited in their harnesses, the Prince looked at his wife and quipped, 'Girls don't have the same wardrobe malfunctions as men do. I hope I don't have any wardrobe malfunctions.' To their great credit, even while they must surely have been seething with anger, the pair could make light of the events in front of the cameras.

Meanwhile, the royal lawyers went into battle to seek an injunction in a French court. At the same time, they also tried to halt the publication of what was being billed as a '26-page photo special' in an Italian magazine. The female French photographer who took pictures of the Duchess sunbathing at the chateau – but not, she says, the topless ones – tried to distance herself from the affair. Valerie Suau's only work, which she insisted was 'decent', was published in *La Provence* newspaper the previous Saturday with no complaint from the Royal Family. It was clearly a false trail from Valerie. Months later, she would face a French magistrate and would have to face the consequences of her actions.

Back home, the affair had become so far-reaching that even the Church had waded into the controversy. The Archbishop of York, Dr John Sentamu, said, 'It would be a very sad day when we are taken into the gutter of believing that every woman wants to flaunt her body for all to see. The only time we cannot escape revealing our nakedness is when we are born. Beyond that our culture has said that the only other time should be in the privacy of our homes.'

Borneo had been, to an extent, a sanctuary from the excesses and intrusions of the outside world. It was also a testament to how impressive their control was in front of others, that they were able to continue touring so professionally. They even wanted to stay the night, but their schedule prevented it. Because of the threat of bad weather causing them to miss their flight to the Solomon Islands, William and Kate had to travel on, leaving the comparative peace of the jungle.

The next stop was the South Seas. When Kate arrived on the

Solomon Islands, she was immediately crowned with a headdress of fresh flowers. In an instant, the tension, which had been building, lifted. They couple seemed in a much brighter mood. They first headed for an overnight stay on a remote luxury resort for some much needed, and deserved, down-time, before leaving the next day for their trip to the tiny island of Tuvalu. There the couple, in grass skirts and flower crown, tried hula dancing Polynesian-style. The nine coral atolls that make up the tiny nation of Tuvalu, where the British Queen is still monarch, boast a population of just 10,000 – but that day it seemed as though most of them had come out to see their future king and queen.

The royal couple arrived by plane, where Arthur Edwards was the only photographer allowed to join them. He took, by his own admission, some of the best photographs of his long and illustrious career, a few of which can be found in the picture section of this book. William was carried through the streets on a 'carriage' with a thatched roof made of leaves, hoisted on the shoulders of 25 strapping young islanders. The Prince greeted their hosts by saying 'talofa', a traditional Samoan greeting, and described Tuvalu as the highlight of their nine-day Diamond Jubilee tour, which came to an end that day. He told them the whole world remembered the warmth of their welcome for the Queen when she visited in 1982. It was one of the 'iconic images of her reign'. Then, in an unusually informal 'state dinner' hosted by the island chiefs, the couple threw themselves into the celebrations. With a shimmering shake of the hips, they seemed to put all of the drama of the last few days behind them, and they danced their worries away. They had passed the first big test of their marriage, and now, thankfully, they were going home.

CHAPTER 16

BABY ON BOARD

'Their Royal Highnesses the Duke and Duchess of Cambridge are very
pleased to announce that the Duchess of Cambridge is expecting a baby.
The Queen, the Duke of Edinburgh, the Prince of Wales, the Duchess of Cornwall
and Prince Harry and members of both families are delighted with the news.'

St James's Palace, 3 December 2012

Marriages and births are at the heart of monarchy, crucial in a very obvious way to the survival of the ancient institution. As one royal historian rather bluntly put it, the first 'duty and ambition' of someone in Kate's position was to produce an heir. It is not quite as brutal as in the days of Henry VIII – when failure to give birth to a son often resulted in an unfavourable outcome for the queen – but the pressure was still there. From the moment they wed, the next pressing question to which newspapers dedicated pages of newsprint was: 'When will Kate fall pregnant?' If recent royal history was anything to go by (the Queen and Princess Diana both fell pregnant within a year of their wedding), the palace would very soon be announcing a royal pregnancy. But the editors were to be disappointed. Their first anniversary came and went, and the newspapers seemed to back off. The royal pregnancy, or lack of it, became the great unsaid.

It was completely out of the blue, then, that I received a call from an impeccable source on 23 November 2012. The caller was a long-term royal contact and what they told me both excited me and filled me with dread. He was convinced that the Duchess was pregnant. He had spoken to a number of people close to the couple and they were convinced too – but I needed more. I pressed him further: 'Has anyone heard it from William and Kate's lips?' He had always given me accurate information in the past, and he was a good source because he never embellished what he had heard in royal circles. In this case, he had not, and this time I said I really needed more. I knew that, if true, William and Kate would guard this secret extremely closely. To break the royal pregnancy story in the same way that I had revealed that the Prince of Wales and Camilla were to marry, I needed to be 110 per cent sure. Any less than that would have been unprofessional, unwise, and almost certainly career suicide. In this case, I wasn't able to be that certain.

By St Andrew's Day, 30 November 2012, without definitive proof, I was sure an announcement was imminent. There was something different about the Duchess; her face seemed fuller and her hair softer, flopping over her face. I could tell that this was going to be a difficult story to nail down.

The Duchess was returning to her pre-prep school, St Andrew's in Berkshire, where she had been something of a star pupil, winning awards for both sport and music. If my source was right and she was pregnant, her visit would have to be a sedate affair.

I was not the only one primed for the big story. Veteran *Sun* photographer Arthur Edwards, whose sources are also impeccable, was convinced too. But, like me, he could not nail it down. At the school, Kate met teachers and students privately over lunch before visiting the pre-prep school for under-5s. There was something noticeably different in the way in which the palace staff were handling this trip; the photographers' close access was restricted for one. Arthur smelled a rat, but, when he – just as I had done – pressed palace officials hard, there was a flat denial. If she was pregnant, they did not know about it.

At first, it was all very relaxed. She asked them if they kept pets at school and told how, when she was at St Andrew's, the school had had two guinea pigs. 'There was one called Pip and one called Squeak, so my sister was called Pip and I was Squeak,' she said. Laughter followed. Then, in a short speech, she described her time at St Andrew's as some of the best years of her childhood. 'It is such a treat to be back here at St Andrew's. I absolutely loved my time here; they were some of my happiest years, which makes it so incredibly special to be here today. In fact, I enjoyed it so much that, when I had to leave, I told my mother that I was going to come back to be a teacher. While that didn't quite happen, I was thrilled to have been asked back today on St Andrew's Day.'

Then Kate threw a definite curveball to Arthur and me. Dressed in green tartan in honour of the celebration of the patron saint of Scotland, she toured the school privately before observing some of the school's 'Progressive Games', which were games played indoors by the school's teachers and students on St Andrew's Day, a tradition stretching back to when the school first opened. Staff set up a number of short, five-minute games, and small groups of mixed-age children progressed around the games earning scores as they went with a winning team declared at the end of the day. Kate, the school's former hockey captain, then formally opened a new Astroturf playing field by unveiling a plaque. She was so delighted to be back on the hockey pitch that she just had to have a go, despite the fact she was wearing high-heeled boots. It certainly wasn't the requisite footwear, but it didn't bother her. How could she possibly be pregnant and still be so active with the children, we asked ourselves. I couldn't have been more wrong.

Then the waiting was over. A few days later, on 3 December 2012, the couple capped what had been a wonderful Diamond Jubilee year by suddenly announcing that they were expecting their first child. The news apparently caught even the Queen and Prince Charles by surprise. William and Kate had wanted to keep it secret so badly that they even kept their closest family in the dark. Unforeseen circumstances meant they had no choice but to reveal their most cherished secret. It emerged later that William had to break the news to his grandmother, father and brother in hurried telephone calls just minutes before making the announcement to the world after his wife was taken to hospital suffering from acute morning sickness. It is not uncommon for pregnant women to experience morning sickness, particularly during the first few months of pregnancy. She was suffering from hyperemesis gravidarum or HG, a very severe form of the problem, which needs specialist hospital treatment. The main danger is dehydration – it can be difficult to keep enough fluid down orally and can causes weight loss during pregnancy.

William did not want to take any chances. He took his wife to London's King Edward VII's Hospital and spent several hours with her. Outside, a massed phalanx of photographers and camera crews gathered and waited outside in the freezing conditions behind a steel barrier on the opposite side of the road. She was less than 12 weeks pregnant and was expected to stay for several days at least, being cared for by gynaecologist Marcus Setchell, who had delivered the Countess of Wessex's two children. St James's Palace was being careful about how much detail to divulge, refusing to be drawn on when the royal couple had become aware of the pregnancy, only saying 'recently'.

As Kate was being treated in hospital, the wider world was

thrilled by the news. Prime Minister David Cameron wrote on Twitter that he was 'delighted by the news...They will make wonderful parents.' Labour leader Ed Miliband, not to be outdone, tweeted: 'Fantastic news for Kate, William and the country. A royal baby is something the whole nation will celebrate.' William's uncle Earl Spencer, the brother of Princess Diana, said the pregnancy was 'wonderful news and I am thrilled for them both'. The Archbishop of Canterbury, who married the couple, said, 'The whole nation will want to join in celebrating this wonderful news. We wish the Duchess the best of health and happiness in the months ahead.' Even the White House chipped in. President Barack Obama's press secretary, Jay Carney, said, 'On behalf of everyone here...beginning with the President and First Lady, we extend our congratulations to the Duke and Duchess of Cambridge on the welcome news we received from London that they are expecting their first child.'

I was broadcasting for Australia's top morning show, *Sunrise*, at the time. It meant I was outside the hospital for a long time, doing live crosses to Channel 7's headquarters 'brekkie central' in Sydney in the early hours when most of the others had packed up for the day. The news, however, was limited. All we really knew was that Kate was inside and that she was being cared for. The daily comings and goings of her husband and family were the only action of any note. All was rather quiet. Then followed a dramatic and, ultimately, tragic series of events that nobody could have seen coming.

Two presenters from Australian radio 2Day FM called the hospital pretending to be the Queen and the Prince of Wales, and were put straight through to the Duchess's ward in the early hours. Neither the receptionist who put the call through nor the nurse treating the Duchess suspected anything was amiss, despite the distinctly amateur impersonations of the Queen and the

Prince's voices. One of the presenters even barked, pretending to be a corgi, while the 'Queen' wrongly referred to the Duchess as 'my granddaughter'. The nurse looking after the Duchess gave confidential details of her treatment and of her condition, and even talked about what time it would be convenient for the 'Queen' to visit.

This seemingly rather humorous story at least gave the media something to talk about. A spokesman for the hospital said, 'This call was transferred through to a ward and a short conversation was held with one of the nursing staff. King Edward VII's Hospital deeply regrets this incident.' The hospital's chief executive, John Lofthouse, said, 'This was a foolish prank call that we all deplore. We take patient confidentiality extremely seriously and we are now reviewing our telephone protocols.' It was mean and in bad taste, and the radio station immediately apologised, but not before it replayed it time after time in order to get maximum publicity.

Mel Greig, one of the two presenters of the *Summer 30* show, who pretended to be the Queen, spent around two minutes talking to the nurse. She began by saying: 'Kate, my darling, are you there?' The nurse replied, 'Good morning, ma'am, this is a nurse speaking. How may I help you?' The 'Queen' said, 'Hello, I'm just after my granddaughter Kate, I wanted to see how her little tummy bug is going.' After the nurse gave her some details, she said, 'OK, I'll just feed my little corgis then,' followed by barking from co-presenter Michael Christian. She asked when a good time would be to visit, and the nurse replied, 'I would suggest that any time after nine o'clock would be suitable, because the doctor will be in in the morning, and will just be getting her freshened up in the morning. I would think any time after nine.' Michael Christian, who pretended to be the Prince of Wales, asked the nurse, 'Is Wills still there, or has he gone home.

I haven't spoken to him yet.' The 'Queen' interjected, 'When are you going to walk those bloody corgis?' The Charles impersonator replied, 'Mumsy, I'll go and take the dogs outside.'

This type of prank had been carried out before. Even the Queen had been fooled once, by Canadian DJ Pierre Brassard posing as Canadian Prime Minister Jean Chrétien, asking her to record a speech in support of Canadian unity ahead of the 1995 Quebec referendum. But, in truth, the security was at fault. Royalty protection should have locked down the switchboard so that no calls could be put through. There was no need anyway, because a protection officer was with the Duchess at all times, and all calls should have gone through him first.

Michael Christian himself admitted he was 'completely shocked' to be put through to the ward, adding, 'I thought we'd get hung up on!'

When William arrived at the hospital for his daily visit the next day, he was told about the hoax but he did not seem unduly bothered. He, most likely, had more important things to worry about. The palace said it would not be making any comment on the episode, but it did not make a formal complaint to the radio station.

Prince Charles seemed to capture the mood perfectly. When asked about the pregnancy as he was boarding HMS *Belfast* in London to cross over to the *SA Agulhas*, where he met Sir Ranulph Fiennes to wish him well on his latest Antarctic exhibition, he teased reporters, joking, 'How do you know I'm not a radio station?' before going on to say, 'I'm thrilled, marvellous. A very nice thought of grandfatherhood at my old age, if I may say so. So that's splendid. And I'm very glad my daughter-in-law is getting better, thank goodness.' It seemed the story would just evaporate.

Then the mood changed. Suddenly, this was no joke. It emerged that the nurse at the London hospital who took the hoax call had been found dead. Jacintha Saldanha, 46, left a handwritten note addressed to her managers at the Edward VII's Hospital, which read: 'Please accept my apologies. I am truly sorry. Thank you for all your support. I hold the Radio Australians Mel Greig and Michael Christian responsible for this act. Please make them pay my mortgage. I am sorry. Jacintha.' She then, tragically, took her own life.

It sent shockwaves around the world. It was the lead item on news shows everywhere. The Duke and Duchess of Cambridge said in a statement they were 'deeply saddened' by the death of the nurse. The St James's Palace statement said the Duke and Duchess 'were looked after so wonderfully well at all times by everybody at King Edward VII Hospital, and their thoughts and prayers are with Jacintha Saldanha's family, friends and colleagues at this very sad time'. A palace spokesman later added, 'At no point did the palace complain to the hospital about the incident.' The statement added, 'On the contrary, we offered our full and heartfelt support to the nurses involved and hospital staff at all times.' The hospital paid tribute to 'a first class nurse who cared diligently for hundreds of patients'. The DJs were immediately suspended.

King Edward VII's Hospital chief executive John Lofthouse said mother-of-two Mrs Saldanha, who had worked at the hospital for more than four years, 'was an excellent nurse and well-respected and popular with all of her colleagues. Everyone is shocked by the loss of a much loved and valued colleague.'

The Twitter accounts of both presenters were deleted and all references to the prank call recording removed from the 2Day FM website. Their company SCA said on its Facebook page it was 'deeply saddened by the tragic news' and had extended 'deepest sympathies to her family and all that have been affected'.

This somewhat macabre media circus had to end. The best way

was for Kate to leave the hospital. After a visit from her mother, Carole, the next morning, she did just that. Saying she felt 'much better' and wearing a scarf and holding a bunch of yellow flowers, she paused to smile for photographers alongside her husband. From now on, nothing would be the same for the pregnant Kate and her husband William.

With the changes in the laws of primogeniture taking effect, the media looked for any clues of the unborn child's sex. Although Kate had become accomplished at keeping secrets, on a day trip to Grimsby she appeared to let slip the sex of the baby. Fresh from her break in the Swiss Alps, she had flown by helicopter into a fog-bound Grimsby where her first engagement was to visit the National Fishing Heritage Centre. But, during a 10-minute walkabout in front of a 2,000-strong crowd, local woman Diane Burton handed her a teddy bear. Next to her was Sandra Cook, 67, a grandmother-of-two, who said, 'She was just so natural it was like talking to a friend. She moved on to the lady next to me and that is when she almost let slip the secret.

'The lady gave her a teddy bear and I distinctly heard her say "Thank you, I will take that for my d…" Then she stopped herself. She stopped abruptly. I couldn't help myself and butted in, saying to her, "You nearly slipped up then." She said, "What do you mean?" And I said, "You were going to say daughter, weren't you?" She kept smiling throughout, but said, "No, we don't know what it is." I said, "Oh, I think you do," to which she replied, "We're not telling!" I only hope that she doesn't now give birth to a boy or I'm going to look pretty stupid. But she definitely said 'd…'.

As speculation swirled about the sex of the unborn baby, Kate's royal apprenticeship was also gathering pace. With Prince William away, working as an RAF search and rescue pilot, Kate was asked to support the Queen and the Duke of Edinburgh on engagements. Her Majesty had been taken ill, hospitalised after a bout of gastroenteritis, but this was never going to derail her for long. For the Queen, the need to do her duty is elementary, almost part of her DNA. It was fitting, then, that she returned to work at Baker Street tube station – famed for links to Sherlock Holmes – to mark the 150th anniversary of the London Underground.

Kate looked blooming as she walked a step or two behind to add that touch of glamour to the occasion. Right on time at 11.30 a.m., the royal party viewed a restored 1892 underground coach, and met staff and apprentices involved in the restoration project. All three royals then walked through a brand-new S7 train, before the Queen unveiled a plaque, naming the train 'Queen Elizabeth II'. At the end of the visit, London Underground's chief operating officer Howard Collins presented Kate with her 'Baby on Board!' badge, and Kate said, 'Oh yes, I've seen this before – how do they work? … I will have to wear it at home.'

CHAPTER 17

PRINCE THE ELDER

'You have got to remember his age, both of their ages, you know …
what they do at their age – they do a lot more than most other pensioners of
their equivalent age. If occasionally there is the odd engagement cancelled, it
shouldn't come as such a surprise, given the workload.'

PETER PHILLIPS, THE QUEEN AND THE DUKE OF EDINBURGH'S
ELDEST GRANDCHILD, 6 JUNE 2013

When it comes to health, the Royal Family has a 'keep calm and carry on' attitude. It must run in the family – they don't believe in making a fuss. So, when Buckingham Palace announced, on 6 June 2013, that the Duke of Edinburgh had been taken to the exclusive Harley Street London Clinic, it was done with the minimum of trouble. After all, Prince Philip is fairly old school; his catchphrase is 'just get on with it'. That is exactly what he expected the Queen and the rest of his close family to do while he underwent an exploratory operation following abdominal investigations. It was, though, in my view, a watershed moment.

The Duke had earlier attended a garden party for 8,000 at Buckingham Palace and spent the afternoon cracking jokes with guests. Decked out in his top hat and tails, he looked dapper as always, defying his great age. He could pass for a man 10, perhaps even 15, years younger. Towards the end, he slipped away privately, leaving the event at around 5.30 p.m. He changed out of his morning suit and was driven to the private London clinic.

After news of his hospitalisation was made public, Buckingham Palace issued a rather matter-of-fact statement, saying simply that 'the results will now be analysed. At this early stage he is progressing satisfactorily. Further updates will continue to be issued when appropriate.' When I pressed a senior member of the Royal Household further about the Duke's health, the aide remained tight-lipped. How serious was it? What is the precise nature of the Duke's condition? The aide was brief, but he did not mince his words: 'He's old.' In a world where what isn't said is sometimes more telling, these words spoke volumes to me. It was clear, I should prepare for all eventualities, although perhaps not immediately. There was cause for concern, for a man of the Duke's age to be operated on under general anaesthetic was worrying enough, and this latest bout of ill-health for the Royal Family patriarch had far-reaching implications.

At his age, the Duke counts every day as a blessing. He is a firm believer in the Latin phrase *carpe diem*; he seizes every day with gusto. But on his 90th birthday he said, 'I reckon I've done my bit.' He said he would be 'winding down' and reducing his workload. Up until now, there has been scant evidence of that. He not only carries out hundreds of public duties – and even made a solo trip to Canada this year – but he also performs scores of private functions. Not only that, but Philip is also the Queen's rock. They have been married for 65 years and met in 1939 when she was just 13. At her coronation, he vowed to be her 'liege man in life and limb' and she has described him as her 'strength and stay'. They have an indefatigable partnership. There is no question she loves him dearly and relies upon him. Now, it seemed, more than ever, our 87-year-old Sovereign would need the support of her immediate family.

The Queen did exactly what he asked of her. As ever, she stoically put duty first, as her beloved husband prepared for major surgery a few miles away. She was understandably 'concerned' about him, but went ahead with her planned engagements anyway, without him at her side. For once, rather than having their reporters out chasing stories, it was the BBC itself that was the focus of attention. Hundreds gathered outside the BBC's new £1 billion headquarters at Broadcasting House, which was flying the Royal Standard, cheering loudly as the Queen's car arrived right on cue at 11.10 a.m. Inside, the *Sun* newspaper's Arthur Edwards was the pool photographer to record the moment for posterity. It was, of course, an engagement the Duke had been due to attend. 'Her Majesty was the picture of serenity. So calm. She was magical.' He went on to say, 'She was obviously concerned for the Duke, but she was not about to show it.' She had a professional job to do. She even pulled a surprise of her own when two BBC presenters, Julian Worricker and Sophie Long, who were going out live on the BBC news channel, realised she was right behind them. After finding they had a special audience, the pair acknowledged her presence with a nod of the head before continuing the broadcast. It was a wonderful, unscripted, light-hearted moment.

Her Majesty, in a powder-blue coat and hat, then made a short address broadcast live by the BBC in the UK and around the globe via the World Service. She referred to a previous visit to Broadcasting House with Prince Philip shortly before her coronation 60 years ago. That was to be her only mention of her husband. BBC Trust chairman Lord Patten and BBC director general Lord Hall, who made a short address in which he wished the Duke a speedy recovery, escorted her throughout the visit.

She began the tour by visiting Radio 1 and meeting hosts including Nick Grimshaw, Trevor Nelson and Sara Cox, before being led to the station's well-known Live Lounge to watch a performance by The Script. At the end, she chatted briefly to lead singer Danny O'Donoghue, a judge on BBC1 show *The Voice*. When the Queen learned he was playing the Glastonbury festival, she joked, 'The place you get covered in mud?'

The singer replied with a laugh, 'You've got to bring good wellies.'

Her next destination was the third floor where Fran Unsworth, acting director of news, introduced her to several Radio 4 staff, including *Today* presenter John Humphrys. She joined another *Today* presenter, James Naughtie, and Sian Williams live on Radio 4 where she gave an address to declare the BBC's new home open, saying, 'I hope this new building will serve you well for the future and I am delighted to declare it open today.' Afterwards, she met TV presenters Huw Edwards and Sophie Raworth at the start of a tour of the BBC newsroom, followed by other big names including David Dimbleby and Sir Bruce Forsyth.

When veteran BBC radio presenter John Humphrys 'ambushed' her with a question about her husband's condition, she responded, 'I've no idea, he's only just gone in.'

He added, 'He looked on awfully good form yesterday.'

She was giving nothing away. 'Did he?' she replied. 'That's because he's not ill.' It was a consummate performance by the consummate professional.

On his 92nd birthday, 10 June, the Queen arrived clutching a birthday card, with HRH The Duke of Edinburgh, written on the envelope. He had been too tired to accept any visitors since he had had an exploratory operation, but nothing was keeping his wife of 65 years away. In the next few days, the rest of his close family went to see him. The Prince of Wales left smiling and, when asked about his father's health, replied, 'Much better.' Perhaps, quietly, and without an insistence on drama, the family would have attempted to counsel the Duke that now was an appropriate moment for him to follow his own advice and 'wind down'. There could, after all, be no doubt that he had 'done his bit'.

Any transition that there may be will, of course, be seamless. But this does signal a dramatic change for the younger royals. Both Prince William and Prince Harry – serving officers seconded to the RAF and Army Air Corps respectively – will be expected to share the workload of their grandparents. Prince William, who loves his work as a search and rescue pilot, will now have to focus more on royal duty, and is expected to end his military career in September this year, or at least to switch duties that will free him to take on more royal commitments. Prince Harry too, who has completed two tours of duty in Afghanistan, may need a posting in the future that frees him up to do more royal engagements. The Duchess of Cambridge herself is now experienced and ready to serve, at both joint and solo engagements. All three of them will need to shoulder some of the burden.

Finally, after almost nine months of speculation and reports, Kate performed her last official engagements just a few weeks shy of her baby's birth. In the preceding months, she treated us all to a rainbow selection of charming outfits, always smiling, always focused on the job in hand and on the people who had turned out to see her. At a Buckingham Palace garden party, she admitted one benefit of the dreadful spring was that it had kept her temperature down, and she was grateful to be cool. Even so, throughout the pregnancy, she always looked the picture of health.

On 13 June, her final engagement was at the Southampton docks. She was there to officially name a new Princess cruise liner, *Royal Princess*. As the ship's godmother, she was central to the ceremony; a blessing and the celebratory tradition of smashing with a £1,250 Nebuchadnezzar of Moët et Chandon over the hull of the ship as she named it. Sporting a £169 Dalmatian print coat from high-street retailer Hobbs, which she accessorised with classic black court shoes and a neat black fascinator, the Duchess had arrived to find a royal-blue carpet laid out for her, and enjoyed a rousing musical welcome courtesy of the Band of Her Majesty's Royal Marines Portsmouth and The Pipe Band of 1st Battalion Irish Guards.

The Duchess looked relaxed as she stepped from her chauffeur-driven vehicle to the quayside in Southampton, after making the journey from London by helicopter.

Smiling broadly, the eight-months pregnant Duchess shook hands with officials and representatives from the cruise operator watched by guests and a celebrity contingent that included veteran TV presenter Sir Bruce Forsyth, actor Christopher Biggins and former Atomic Kitten singer Liz McClarnon.

She took her place on a stage in blustery conditions that threatened rain and was seated opposite the liner in a large grandstand, which contained the guests associated with charities that have the Duke and Duchess of Cambridge or Prince Harry as their patron. Among the spectators were representatives from East Anglia's Children's Hospices, the Duchess's charity, SkillForce – which has the Duke of Cambridge as its figurehead – and Prince Harry's organisation WellChild.

A beaming Kate was given a tour and met the crew of the spectacular cruise ship. She was shown around the *Royal Princess* by its captain, Tony Draper, and enjoyed views across the Solent, before being shown the ship's bell from the previous *Royal Princess*, which was christened by William's mother Princess Diana in 1984 in the same spot. Captain Draper gestured to a button on a console and asked Kate if she would like to sound the liner's whistle. After a window was opened, the Duchess pressed the control and a long low sound reverberated around the dock. She laughed and smiled and described the experience as 'brilliant' adding, 'I was expecting something high pitched.'

Two children, Isobel Rowbotham, 14, and her 8-year-old brother, Charles, handed the Duchess a pair of scissors to cut the rope and release the huge bottle of champagne. The children were chosen after their brother had died from a brain tumour as a toddler at the East Anglia's Children's Hospice.

Before cutting the rope, the Duchess chatted to the siblings and then completed the ceremony with the words: 'I name this ship *Royal Princess*, may God bless her and all who sail in her.'

Finally, it was time to wave goodbye to royal duty for a while. On her final public appearance, Kate wowed the crowds at Trooping the Colour; pretty in a pale-pink Alexander McQueen coat and matching hat, she was cheered by thousands as she travelled to the pageant in a carriage with Camilla and Prince Harry for the traditional parade to mark the Queen's official birthday. She later joined the rest of the royals on Buckingham Palace balcony to watch the traditional RAF fly-past – featuring 32 aircraft, including a World War II Hurricane and the Red Arrows.

As ever, she added the 'X factor' to traditional royal events. The crowds packed along The Mall cheered loudly, of course, for Her Majesty as she rode past in the Glass Coach, especially this year as she was still without hospitalised Prince Philip at her side. But the cheers for Kate's open carriage – with Camilla and Prince Harry alongside her – were deafening. Kate was blooming. Once again, she rose to the occasion; stunning, she performed her royal role with aplomb. After that, it was time for her to put her feet up and go on 'maternity leave'. The next time we would see her – officially at least – would be on the hospital steps with her new baby in her arms and proud husband at her side.

There is no doubt the birth of her baby would be her biggest test to date, and, indeed, it would be a crowning moment. Princess Diana, who was of course much younger when she had William, had found raising royal children tough. Often, she blamed the royals, saying they did not support her. Like Diana, Kate will have to balance motherhood and public duty. It will not be easy, but there is no reason to doubt her. She has risen to every other occasion. I am sure the Royal Family and especially loving husband Prince William will do everything to support her. They should – she is, after all, clearly the brightest jewel in the Crown.

Kate's engagement diary has been left open until the New Year, although she will no doubt be out and about sooner. Royal mothers retreat and reappear at different times, depending on how they adapt to pregnancy and motherhood. Diana was pretty visible during her pregnancy and insisted on doing things her way. The Princess was concerned at the idea of having her first baby, William, at Buckingham Palace, telling friends she couldn't imagine anything worse than giving birth among the ornate grandeur. Instead, she gave birth in the Lindo Wing of St Mary's Paddington, where her gynaecologist, George Pinker, was the senior consultant. It was the first time an Heir Presumptive was born in a public hospital, albeit in a private ward. It was also the first time an heir to the throne had sat at his wife's bedside while she gave birth.

Prince Charles was considered progressive to want to be at his wife's side. Like his father, William has followed modern convention by taking two weeks' paternity leave from the RAF to bond with the baby they have nicknamed 'our little grape'.

As the birth day approached, Kate threw herself into preparing her royal nest. She spent time getting the temporary nursery at Nottingham Cottage, in the grounds of Kensington Palace, ready. The discovery of asbestos delayed the building works in apartment 1A, which is in fact a four-storey house that forms half the Clock Tower Wing. For Kate, one of the main attractions of the house, designed by Christopher Wren in the 17th century, is the beautiful walled garden, perfect for pushing the baby around and indulging in some gardening. With the help of her mother, Kate had been choosing furnishings and fabric for the house in very much the same way Diana did 30 years before. William and Kate, throughout the pregnancy, have been royal trendsetters, introducing far greater informality to the process. As parents, too, those close to them are confident they will at least try to do the same.

CHAPTER 18

PRINCE THE YOUNGER

'I look forward enormously to that relationship.'

HRH THE PRINCE OF WALES, WHEN ASKED ABOUT THE PROSPECT
OF BECOMING A GRANDFATHER

The Prince of Wales is a serious, thinking man. A tireless campaigner on environmental issues, he believes it is his duty to raise a debate so that real action is taken now to stop the human race destroying the natural world for future generations. It is a responsibility he feels all the more acutely now that he is a grandfather. Before the birth of the royal baby, he spoke of it time and time again. He said he did not want to 'hand on an increasingly dysfunctional world' to his grandchild.

In an interview with ITV *This Morning* presenters Phillip Schofield and Holly Willoughby, he went further. He told them, 'I've gone on for years about the importance of thinking about the long term in relation to the environmental damage, climate change and everything else. We don't, in a sensible world, want to hand on an increasingly dysfunctional world to our grandchildren, to leave them with the real problem. I don't want to be confronted by my future grandchild and them saying, "Why didn't you do something?" So clearly now that we will have a grandchild, it makes it even more obvious to try and make sure we leave them something that isn't a total poisoned chalice.'

Already the longest-serving heir to the throne, with a wealth of experience, he will play a pivotal role in the raising of Prince George who will one day reign, like him. He received a bad press as a father when his sons were small, mainly because Princess Diana was briefing against him. Actually, despite his having a very busy life of duty, packed with engagements, he was a surprisingly hands-on father.

Prince Charles often turned up at bath-time, and loved reading to the children just before they went to bed. A favourite tale was the enormously successful children's book *The Old Man of Lochnagar*, which he himself had penned years earlier to entertain younger brothers. Privately, those close to him say he is thrilled at becoming a grandfather. When asked about it on air, publicly, he only replied, 'It's a lovely thought,' one of his stalling catch-phrases when confronted by personal questions; he said the same when quizzed about getting married to Camilla. Further into the interview, though, his demeanour changed – there is a lighter more open side to our next king in his later years – he added, with a natural smile, 'I look forward enormously to that relationship.' He joked too that he felt 'a bit old'.

It is clearly a relationship he will enjoy. He is totally natural around young children and they warm to him. Perhaps it is his whimsical sense of humour, or just a natural affinity. Sadly, he himself barely knew his own royal grandfather, King George VI, who died at just 56. There are a few enchanting photographs of the young Charles sitting next to his proud grandfather; it is one of his most cherished images. Of course, he had an extremely close relationship with his own grandmother. She played a pivotal role in his upbringing, always there for him when his mother was, understandably, occupied with matters of state. The Queen Mother, as she became, cared for him often when duty meant his mother and father had to travel the globe.

He will, of course, not be Prince George's sole grandparent. The Middletons, Kate's parents Mike and Carole, will have a significant role too. But he will be the future sovereign's leading light in understanding the complex world of royalty. After all, he is not only our longest ever heir to the throne, but he has raised a future heir himself too, much of the time as a single father after the death of his first wife Princess Diana.

Fortunately, Charles has the perfect supporter in his role as a grandfather. Camilla, the Duchess of Cornwall – having declared she loves her role as a grandmother – will be there for him to turn to for advice. She spends hours with her own grandchildren, often away from the glare of royal life, at her private residence, Ray Mill House. She is a down-to-earth woman who appreciates the importance of family. She loves the country life and country pursuits. Charles, too, loves nothing more than stomping around the countryside – it helps him think. There is no doubt it is something that they will both encourage their grandchild to do when older.

Camilla will not interfere too much, however. She knows she has a semi-detached role as a 'step-granny', and would not want to try to fill the role that William's late mother, Diana, would have held. Her hands-off approach has helped her relationship with both William and Harry as a stepmother. She has never overplayed it, but she has always been an ear to listen if they want her. She is a trusted lynchpin between the young and old.

Diana of course won't be there for William, but his father and Camilla won't be alone – the Middletons will be there too, especially Carole, whom he loves dearly. Carole is well aware of the demands that the palace will make on her daughter and son-in-law. She will defend and shield them with a healthy dose of normality and, in return, William will ensure that Kate's mum and dad are not frozen out, however unintentionally, by the palace and the royal bonds.

William will almost certainly look to learn from how he was raised by his own father. Charles was always relaxed about his sons' special status as royals. He knew they had special responsibilities and would have to grow up to shoulder them. While Diana battled against royal tradition, Charles – who after all was born to it – wanted his sons to embrace it. The result of this conflict was William and Harry, despite all the distractions and complications of their parents' dysfunctional relationship, grew into remarkably well-balanced young men. William and his middle-class-raised wife Kate will have a similar dilemma. They will want their son to be raised in private as normally as possible. But, the problem is, what is normal for a baby born to reign?

So, no matter how hard Prince William and Kate try to give their first baby an ordinary upbringing, he will be special. After all, this baby will one day reign. It will also be a royal Prince – as the Queen has issued a special royal decree to ensure 'Baby Wales' will be made an HRH.

Fortunately, Prince William and Kate are not bothered by stuffy protocol – but they understand that, because their baby will one day be King Regnant, they have to be less protective over his privacy. However, as best they can, despite all the pressures from the media, the public, and, indeed, their very own family, the new parents will strive to give their first-born as normal a childhood as possible.

CHAPTER 19

THE GREAT KATE WAIT – #ROYALBABYWATCH

'They're going to be amazing parents – because they are so loving towards children. William has grown from that young boy into an unbelievable gentleman. And that's a great quality for a father.'

DAVID BECKHAM, JULY 2013 FORMER ENGLAND FOOTBALLER
AND FRIEND OF WILLIAM AND KATE.

Britain was in the grip of a heat wave by mid-July. Temperatures soared into the high 80 degrees Fahrenheit, and, on a couple of days, hit 90 (32 degrees Celsius). British tennis ace Andy Murray won the men's singles title at Wimbledon, England had beaten the Australians in the first couple of matches of the Ashes tests and the country eagerly awaited the birth of a future King or Queen. It was sticky and uncomfortable in London. Understandably, Kate flitted between her parents' Berkshire mansion and Kensington Palace while Prince William packed in the hours in his day job as an RAF search and rescue pilot in north Wales. She didn't, it seemed, want him hovering around her. Instead, when he did have free time at the weekend, he played charity polo matches with his brother Prince Harry.

The first photographer's ladder – used to stake a position – had already gone down outside the Lindo Wing, St Mary's Hospital,

Paddington in west London, where the royal baby would be born, at the end of June. No official due date had ever been given; all William and Kate's private office at Kensington Palace had said about a due date was to repeat what the duchess herself had let slip during a public walkabout earlier in the year – that the baby was expected in 'mid-July'. The story now began to get a life of its own. It was reported in several newspapers that the public had been misled and the new third-in-line to the throne had in fact been due earlier, even though it had been vehemently denied by Ed Perkins, the Duke and Duchess of Cambridge's official spokesman.

For the press, the starter pistol had now been fired as far as photographers were concerned after a matter-of-fact operational note from officials at Kensington Palace had been issued. It was an innocuous enough memo, laying out the media arrangements once the Duchess of Cambridge has been admitted to hospital. However, as far as some photographers were concerned it was a sign; the baby was imminent. Like lemmings, more and more photographers arrived with their ladders, to give them the elevation they desired to get the best shot available when the long-awaited moment came. Within hours it was like a decorators' convention with around 80 ladders with the name of the owner marked on them placed on the pavement outside. A steel press pen was erected and police barriers placed along the route. Outside the Lindo Wing, eight police officers were working 12-hour shifts. Even members of the public, complete with Union Jack outfits, sleeping bags and tents pitched up outside the hospital.

The great 'Kate Wait', as it became known, had started in earnest.

*

Teams of television crews were by now arriving from all over the world. Tape was placed on the ground with the names of their television networks on them, marking their spots too. My colleagues from Australia's Channel 7 – *Sunrise* anchor Melissa Doyle and US bureau chief Mike Amor – were among them. Outside Canada Gate, Buckingham Palace camera positions for satellite feeds, complete with white canopies to shield the broadcasters from the sun, were erected and marked as off limits to the public. Nobody could be in any doubt how seriously the world was taking the birth of this royal baby. With so many journalists in town, and with very little to actually report until Kate was inside the hospital, false alarms and wayward stories became the order of the day. Some TV broadcasters became so bored that they all started interviewing each other. Natalie Morales, the American news anchor, was filmed knitting a pink bootie live on NBC's flagship Today Show.

Inevitably, the Lindo Wing was dubbed the 'Limbo Wing'. Tourists even started making detours just to look at the mountain range of aluminium stepladders outside the street entrance to the private hospital wing. It had become a bit of a circus. The more overdue the baby, the more desperate things became in the area dubbed 'ladder land'.

Kensington Palace officials had been clear from the outset: they would only issue a comment once Kate had been admitted to hospital. At that point we could assume she had gone into labour. That didn't, of course, stop the William and Kate press team, led by the affable Ed Perkins and his number two Nick Loughran, being bombarded with calls on a minute-by-minute basis every time a helicopter landed at Kensington Palace, despite the fact that other royals live there, such as the Duke of Kent, the Queen's cousin, causing royal helicopters to land there on a regular basis.

Stories ranging from William's plans to hold Kate's hand while she was in labour, to the couple already planning for a second baby began to appear in the tabloids. The reporters quoted 'well-placed' sources, but it was clear that no such sources existed. How could they possibly know such intimate details? The palace was prepared to let these stories go. They were speculative and difficult to deny anyway. What would be the point of correcting them? It was what Fleet Street calls 'the silly season' after all.

Polls became the order of the day for newspapers desperate to fill their pages with royal baby stories with very little to actually report. The *Mail on Sunday* – middle England's staple newspaper diet for the weekend – proclaimed the public believed Kate should be a stay-at-home mother and not rely on a nanny to help bring up her baby. Their 'Survation' poll of 1,000 people found that more than half supported the couple's plan to bring up their baby themselves, and that nearly six out of ten believe Kate should 'significantly' cut back her royal duties, though she is thought likely to return to work in some capacity by the autumn. Fifty-three percent thought that the Middleton in-laws should be given a greater role in the baby's formative years than Prince Charles and Camilla should. The reality was, of course, that in time they would need all the support available, because by autumn Kate would be expected to be back alongside William and Harry; secretly, behind the scenes, a major tour to Australia and New Zealand next spring was being planned too.

It was reported, too, that wagers on the name, sex and date of birth of Kate and William's first child had reached fever pitch. Punters had staked more than £1,000,000 on the royal baby. Bookmakers said betting on the royal baby had smashed the all-time record for a 'non-sports' market. One of them, Coral, has reportedly taken more than £500,000 in bets on the royal arrival and William Hill had received £100,000 in bets from around the world. One unnamed Austrian had placed a wager of £1,000 on the baby being a boy and a second £5,000 on it being a girl. Coral was even forced to suspend betting on the baby's name after a flurry of wagers in central London ended with it odds on to being called Alexandra if the baby was a girl.

One newspaper tale, however, did rankle enough to get a reaction from the palace. In several newspapers, including the usually reliable establishment *Daily Telegraph*, published an 'authoritative' story on 8 July that the royal baby would become the first HRH The Prince or Princess of Cambridge. It was sloppy and incorrect.

The palace stepped in the next day and issued a memo for guidance. It read, 'For the avoidance of doubt since several newspapers have published advice to the contrary, the new baby will be either His Royal Highness Prince (name) of Cambridge or Her Royal Highness Princess (name) of Cambridge ... "NOT" HRH The Prince or Princess of Cambridge.' It went on, 'Incidentally there has been at least one "HRH Prince (name) of Cambridge" before: Prince George of Cambridge, born 1819, grandson of King George III.'

Prince Adolphus, 7th son and 10th child of King George III and Queen Charlotte, like William, was created Duke of Cambridge by the monarch. He married Princess Augusta of Hesse-Cassel in 1818 and they had three children: George (1819–1904), Augusta (1822–1916) and Mary Adelaide (1833–1897). Mary Adelaide was in fact the Queen's great-grandmother. The Duke of Cambridge died in 1850 and was succeeded by his son, George, who became the Duke of Cambridge. His marriage was in contravention of the Royal Marriages Act, so his three sons and their male line descendants used the surname FitzGeorge. The second Duke died in 1904, and his title reverted to the Crown. Therefore not only was the royal baby not the first to be styled as 'of Cambridge', he is a direct descendant of Prince Adolphus,

Duke of Cambridge, through his youngest child, Princess Mary Adelaide of Cambridge.

It also emerged that when Prince Charles succeeds to the throne, William will become the Duke of Cornwall and be styled HRH Duke of Cornwall and Cambridge until he is named as HRH The Prince of Wales. This means William's children will be HRH Prince or Princess 'Christian name' of Cornwall and Cambridge until the Prince of Wales title is bestowed. After that, they will be HRH Prince or Princess 'Christian name' of Wales.

Given the changes in the law of royal succession, the Queen had already made provision for this by issuing what are called new Letters Patent to ensure that her future great-granddaughter would have a title suitable for a future monarch.

Letters Patent are simply a way that the Sovereign signifies making an alteration or proclamation that doesn't go through Parliament. When Prince William was made Duke of Cambridge, for example, there, was a new Letters Patent under the Great Seal of the Realm.

For the change in the law, a notice was published in the *London Gazette* announcing her decision. It read: 'The Queen has been pleased by Letters Patent under the Great Seal of the Realm dated 31 December 2012 to declare that all the children of the eldest son of the Prince of Wales should have and enjoy the style, title and attribute of royal highness with the titular dignity of Prince or Princess prefixed to their Christian names or with such other titles of honour.'

No matter how much William and Kate wanted their unborn child to have as ordinary an early life as possible, it was clear this baby was going to be special.

With the Royal Family and their officials still remaining tight-lipped, the Duchess of Cornwall, down to earth and not stifled by protocol, let the cat out of the bag and gave what the newspapers dubbed 'The first big clue'. By now the world's press corps had been camped outside the Lindo Wing of St Mary's Hospital for a fortnight. So when Camilla, who already has five young grandchildren of her own, gave the strongest hint that a new royal baby was imminent, telling well-wishers to expect a bundle of joy by the 'end of the week', it made headlines around the world.

The Duchess, perhaps cleverly wanting to draw some attention to a cause close to her heart, let slip the royal secret during a visit to Little Harbour children's hospice at Porthpean, near St Austell, Cornwall. Camilla and expectant grandfather Prince Charles had been in the West Country for their annual 'Cornwall Week', meeting locals and highlighting the work of worthy causes. They had started off in Bude Town, where many mothers brought their babies to meet them. One of them, Trudi Lindsay, holding her three-week-old daughter Ellie-Mae, told Charles, 'You have got one of these coming soon', to which the prince replied, 'Hopefully!'

Camilla was much more forthcoming as she unveiled a plaque to mark her visit to the hospice, aided by 13-year-old Alex Smith, who suffered from spinal muscular atrophy: as she gave an impromptu speech to the assembled guests, she said, 'We are all just waiting by the telephone. We are hopeful that by the end of the week he or she will be here.'

Even the usually tight-lipped monarch joined in the public debate. She too had become as impatient as any excited great-grandmother-to-be. During a walkabout on 17 July she met ten-year-old schoolgirl Fay Batey, who summoned up the courage to ask her, 'Do you want Kate's baby to be a boy or a girl?'

The Queen replied instantly, 'I don't think I mind.' Then, after a short pause, she said, 'I would very much like it to arrive because I'm going on holiday soon... I wish it would hurry up.' Turning to move on, she added with a laugh, 'No sign yet!' Her comment to Fay, a pupil at Wiggonby Church of England School, near Wigton, Cumbria, drew laughter from the watching crowds.

Kate was clearly now overdue, although it would not have bothered her doctors who would not consider inducing labour until any patient is at least a week overdue. In the meantime, Kate and William, temporarily off-duty from his day job in the RAF, were staying outside London with her parents, Michael and Carole Middleton, at their mansion in Berkshire in order to escape the city heat. Royal aides confided that they were confident that even if the duchess's contractions start while she was in the country, they could get her into London with a police escort in less than an hour. Nobody could really blame this baby – who after all would spend his or her entire life governed by royal timetables and on-the-dot punctuality – for keeping everyone waiting for just a little bit longer.

But it was clear that the long wait was nearly over.

CHAPTER 20

'IT'S A BOY'

BABY CAMBRIDGE'S FIRST
PRESS CONFERENCE

'He's got a good pair of lungs on him, that's for sure.
He's a big boy, he's quite heavy.'

HRH PRINCE WILLIAM, DUKE OF CAMBRIDGE, OUTSIDE THE
LINDO WING, ST MARY'S HOSPITAL, PADDINGTON, COMMENTING ON HIS
BABY SON HRH PRINCE GEORGE ALEXANDER LOUIS OF CAMBRIDGE

It was a truly extraordinary and historic evening in west London. Packed in like sardines behind the steel barriers of the specially erected media pen, I, like hundreds of broadcasters, camera crews, photographers and reporters from media organisations from around the world, had been waiting outside the Lindo Wing, the private maternity unit of St Mary's Hospital, Paddington, for days. Then in a flash all the waiting was over. At 7.14 p.m. on 23 July 2013, 27 hours after the birth, an exhausted but beaming Duchess of Cambridge emerged through the door with her proud husband, Prince William, who could hardly keep his eyes off his son and heir as he stood at her side. In her arms Kate showed off their 8lb 6oz bundle of joy amid tumultuous cheers from hundreds of well-wishers and hospital staff crammed into every vantage point. Simultaneously, television transmitted the picture-perfect image of our 'New Royal Family' to hundreds of millions of people watching live around the globe. Nothing could trump that moment. For me, after nearly 25 years chronicling the royal story, this capped everything.

At this moment the baby born to be King was still only known as 'Baby Cambridge', for His Royal Highness Prince George of Cambridge's name had yet to be made public. Barely visible, a wisp of dark hair peeping from the £45 merino shawl made by Nottinghamshire firm G. H. Hurt and Son Ltd, he underwent his baptism into the mayhem of the demanding modern media world that will chronicle his life from the cradle to the grave. After just a few seconds, smiling as the cameras whirred, Kate, wearing a bespoke cornflower-blue crêpe de Chine dress by Jenny Packham, carefully passed their baby boy to her husband, looking relaxed in an open-necked blue shirt with two buttons undone and casual trousers, before they walked forward to speak to a waiting press hungry for more information about the little day-old prince. At this moment the baby, hardly awake, managed to free his hands. The auto-drive cameras clicked and clattered in unison. It was, the newspapers would record the following day on their front pages, as though he had perfected his first royal wave.

Prince William, calm and confident, stood tall. For so long described in the media as 'Diana's boy' he was now very much a man, a loving husband and proud father. He had spent much of the previous 24 hours tending to the baby, sleeping in the same hospital suite. Kate, radiant, her hair perfectly coiffed, was also confident as she spoke: 'It's the first time we have seen him really, so we are having a proper chance to catch up. It's very emotional; it's such a special time. I think any parent will know what this feeling feels like.' William, standing protectively close to his wife and baby, added: 'It's very special.' Then, seeming to confirm that their son had been born after his due date – the topic of much media hype – the Prince joked: 'I'll remind him of his tardiness when he's a bit older. I know how long you've all been standing here [to the press] so hopefully the hospital and you guys can all go back to normal now and we can go and look after him.'

William, who confirmed that he had had a chance to read the newspapers and watch the news reports about his son on the television from inside his private hospital suite, then gave the newsmen the perfect sound bite: 'He's got a good pair of lungs, that's for sure. He's a big boy, he's quite heavy.' He added, 'We are still working on a name so we will have that as soon as we can. He's got her looks, thankfully,' he said in his typically self-deprecating way. 'No, no, I'm not sure about that,' Kate chipped in. Asked what colour the boy's hair was, the Prince gazed adoringly at his firstborn, and the smattering of fine hair on the boy's head, before joking: 'He's got way more than me, thank God.' Kate revealed, too, that her husband was a hands-on father: 'He's done his first nappy already,' she said. When asked how he had got on, William said 'Good' and his wife added, 'Very, very good.'

The couple then returned to the hospital briefly before re-emerging with their son strapped into his first 'throne' – a £99.99 Britax baby car seat. As the Duchess got into the back of their black Range Rover, Prince William put the baby seat containing his son and heir into the car for the first time. He let out a mock sigh of relief that he managed to do this without a hitch with the cameras ready to record any mistake. With only their Scotland Yard personal police protection officer accompanying them, William then drove his new family off to their temporary Kensington Palace home, the two-bedroomed Nottingham Cottage. It would be their secure sanctuary for the next couple of days, since their new home at the palace, Apartment 1A, was not yet ready. Now, safe behind the security gates, protected, and hidden away from prying eyes, they could start bonding as a family.

*

His Royal Highness Prince George Alexander Louis of Cambridge was born at 4.24 p.m. on Monday, 22 July 2013. He is third in line to the throne and for the first time in 120 years, back to the days when the Queen Empress Victoria reigned, there are three direct male heirs from three succeeding generations living while there is a reigning monarch on the throne.

It was to be days before his name would be revealed. Firstly, of course, the Queen would have to be introduced to him. But George – from the Greek meaning farmer or earth worker – was a name that had been touted as the clear favourite by bookmakers and, given the history of the monarchy – and in particular the House of Windsor as the Queen's father and grandfather had reigned under that name – it came as no surprise. The Duke and Duchess, however, insisted that the newborn is not named after the Queen's father; they chose George, they said, simply because they liked it.

He will one day be the 43rd occupant of Windsor Castle as monarch. After all the wrangling over the change in the ancient laws of primogeniture, so that a first-born may succeed to the throne regardless of his or her gender, it did not matter after all – Prince William's heir is male. Even so, he is the first sovereign-in-waiting born under the new, non-sexist, non-sectarian constitutional arrangement that was still making its way into law through the parliaments of Commonwealth countries around the world where the Queen is till head of state. The announcement of the birth was delayed to give William the chance to telephone his grandmother and his father to break the news. He and Kate also wanted time in private to get to know their baby without the world knowing their son had had been born.

When the news was released there were whoops of joy and cheers outside the Lindo Wing. Even the police officers stationed outside the hospital had beaming smiles. I was live to Australia for their top-rated morning show *Sunrise* when I got the 'five-minute' warning. Furiously, I started texting and emailing Dougie Walters at Brekky Central 'mission control', as well as anchor Melissa Doyle and US Bureau Chief Mike Amor, who had come over to London to cover the story with me for the 7 Network. With seconds before I was on air I managed to get the story filed from my iPhone and ready to break it online for the *London Evening Standard*, as I am Royal Editor for both organisations.

Then the statement dropped into the email inbox on my iPhone. It read: 'Her Royal Highness The Duchess of Cambridge was safely delivered of a son at 4.24pm. The baby weighs 8lbs 6oz. The Duke of Cambridge was present for the birth. The Queen, The Duke of Edinburgh, The Prince of Wales, The Duchess of Cornwall, Prince Harry and members of both families have been informed and are delighted with the news. Her Royal Highness and her child are both doing well and will remain in hospital overnight.' The statement had been issued at 8.29pm, four hours after the baby was born. The reason for this was that the couple 'just wanted to spend a little time together to bond as a family', and also to have time to inform members of both families privately before the news was disseminated to the world. William made those calls personally. The waiting game that had been dubbed 'The Great Kate Wait' was now well and truly over. I knew there would be little or no sleep for me for the next 48 hours.

Outside Buckingham Palace the announcement was also greeted with cheers and the honking of car horns. Earlier Her Majesty had arrived back at the palace to loud cheers after spending the weekend at Windsor. She had been due back for a reception anyway and arrived in a convoy of just two Range Rovers. As Prince Philip was still off duty convalescing she had one of her beloved dogs for company, a dorgi – a cross between a corgi and a dachshund – and the two of them were photographed as she was driven in. For her, our oldest-ever reigning monarch, it was business as usual. The Coldstream Guards got on with the sacrosanct business of Changing the Guard to a detachment of the Grenadiers, while the band of the Welsh Guards serenaded the crowds with a summer medley that included the theme tune of the James Bond movie *Skyfall*.

As soon as the news reached them an excited crowd ran forward to the gates of Buckingham Palace, where the Queen was now inside. She immediately declared herself 'delighted'. Three cheers kept ringing out long before the crowd had seen the official announcement – or even knew any of the details about the new royal baby. Press releases and Twitter were of no interest to the faithful. For them, the news was not real until they had seen it written in black and white in the traditional way, on a sheet placed on an easel by the palace railings.

The original plan had been to announce everything to the world just in the old way. But the plan was changed at the 11th hour. Palace officials did not want to chance a stray tweet spoiling the announcement. Yet in the event it did not really matter, for the theatre of the moment added to the dignity of announcing the birth of a little boy who will one day reign.

Scotland Yard sent police reinforcements to Buckingham Palace. One officer was given a rapturous reception as he escorted the easel to its position. Within minutes a blacked-out car arrived from the hospital where, earlier, the Duke and Duchess of Cambridge's Press Secretary, Dr Ed Perkins, Cambridge University Ph.D., reservist in the British Army and former ITN editor, had performed his historic duty by handing over the sheet of foolscap paper bearing all the details of the royal birth. Moments later more shrieks rang out from the spectators as Her Majesty the Queen's press secretary, Mrs Ailsa Anderson LVO, and a young palace footman, Badar Azim, emerged into public view from the Privy Purse door at the front of the palace with the framed announcement. Azim had only been in his job less than a year and just happened to be the duty footman at the door when his five minutes of fame came.

The statement on the headed Buckingham Palace paper and signed by the medical team read: 'Her Royal Highness The Duchess of Cambridge was safely delivered of a son at 4.24 p.m. today. Her Royal Highness and her child are both doing well.' The newest and hottest tourist attraction in the land had been unveiled and the crush to see it had already begun. Inside, the Queen told guests at the reception she was hosting that she was 'thrilled' at the birth of her great-grandson.

That night Prince Charles, who cleverly pretended that he had no news of the baby when questioned by well-wishers in Yorkshire while carrying out royal engagements there, issued a statement too. It said: 'Both my wife and I are overjoyed at the arrival of my first grandchild. It is an incredibly special moment for William and Catherine and we are so thrilled for them on the birth of their baby boy.' Clearly overjoyed he added: 'Grandparenthood is a unique moment in anyone's life, as countless kind people have told me in recent months, so I am enormously proud and happy to be a grandfather for the first time and we are eagerly looking forward to seeing the baby in the near future.'

Next day Charles and Camilla were met by cheering crowds of well-wishers on a visit to East Yorkshire, where villager after villager offered the couple their congratulations as they walked around the green in Bugthorpe. The Prince burst out laughing when the crowd shouted 'Morning, granddad.' He said, 'I'm thrilled and very excited.' His wife, already a grandmother five times over, was more gushing, saying her husband would make a 'brilliant' grandfather. 'I think it's wonderful news. I think mother, son and father are all well,' she told the BBC, 'and I think it's a wonderfully uplifting moment for the country. It's very exciting and it's wonderful for the grandfather – he's brilliant with children.'

Dozens of world leaders joined in the chorus of approval, immediately offering best wishes to the Cambridges and their new child. British Prime Minister David Cameron described the news as 'an historic moment in the life of our nation,' adding that 'above all, it's a wonderful moment for a warm and loving couple who have got a brand-new baby boy.' US President Barack Obama said that the new baby's birth was a 'joyous occasion'. Australian Prime Minister Kevin Rudd wished the 'royal bub' all the best on behalf of all Australians. 'This is a day of great joy,' he said. 'When a new bub comes into the world, any old day, any part of the world, it is frankly a time for rejoicing. To Prince Charles and Camilla, they have the delight of being grandparents, all I can say is, this is probably one of the best experiences of your life and I'm sure they're going to have a wonderful time with the royal baby.'

Other heads of other leading nations followed. Stephen Harper, Prime Minister of Canada – where William and Kate had carried out their first royal tour together – said Canadians were 'delighted' to learn of the birth of their son and sent 'heartfelt congratulations'. He continued, 'This new beginning reminds us of the remarkable and enduring relationship our country has enjoyed with generations of the royal family. We recall with fondness the years of unfailing service by Her Majesty Queen Elizabeth II and His Royal Highness the Duke of Edinburgh and their deep affection for and loyalty to this country.' New Zealand's Prime Minister John Key said the nation's official gift to the royal couple is a hand-spun, hand-knitted fine lace shawl, similar to the one given when Prince William was born. 'This is wonderful news for Prince William and Catherine. The birth of a child is a time of great joy and excitement, and I know they will make excellent parents. New Zealanders remember with fondness the visit of Prince William when he was just a toddler, playing on the lawn of Government House with a Buzzy Bee. It would be a great pleasure to welcome Prince William's son to New Zealand as well. On behalf of the people of New Zealand, I wish Prince William, Catherine and the royal family all the very best.'

The arrival of the royal baby was toasted by celebrities on Twitter, too, and even marked in an episode of *EastEnders* after show bosses ordered some last-minute filming to reflect the birth. A scene showing Dot Cotton (June Brown) and Abi Branning (Lorna Fitzgerald) discussing the happy news was filmed on Monday night and featured in the BBC soap. Kermit the Frog and Miss Piggy were also among the stars to offer their congratulations to the Duke and Duchess of Cambridge on the birth of their son. The Muppets stars – who are in London filming their new movie, *Muppets Most Wanted* – had sent a video message to the royal couple, and Miss Piggy confessed she was starting to feel broody. She shrieked to Kermit: 'Isn't it exciting?! Kate is a mummy, Prince William is a daddy. It kind of makes you want to have a royal child of your own, doesn't it Kermit? Can't you just hear the patter of little tadpole feet.' Kermit shrugged: 'Not really... tadpoles don't have feet.'

On the next day gun salutes sounded across London to mark the birth of the royal baby as the armed forces join in the celebrations. The King's Troop, Royal Horse Artillery and the Honourable Artillery Company carried out the ceremonial royal salutes that are fired for the birth of every prince or princess, no matter where their place is in the line of succession. The last royal salute had been for the birth of Prince William's cousin Princess Eugenie 23 years earlier. In full dress uniform the King's Troop paraded past Buckingham Palace to Green Park, where they staged a 41-gun royal salute. They went from their forward mounting base in Wellington Barracks into Green Park, where 71 horses pulled six First World War-era 13-pounder field guns into position for the royal salute at 2 p.m. Each of the six guns fired blank artillery rounds at 10-second intervals until 41 shots were fired. The Honourable Artillery Company (HAC), one of the City of London's TA regiments, also fired a salute from Gun Wharf at the Tower of London at 2 p.m. Uniquely, at the Tower of London, a royal residence, 62 rounds were fired as the salute also includes an additional 21 rounds for the citizens of the City of London, to mark their loyalty to the monarch.

At St Mary's Hospital on 23 July the excitement was palpable. Ed Perkins issued a statement on behalf of the couple by email. 'We would like to thank the staff at the Lindo Wing and the whole hospital for the tremendous care the three of us have received. We know it has been a very busy period for the hospital and we would like to thank everyone – staff, patients and visitors – for their understanding during this time.' A Kensington Palace spokesman added: 'Mother, son and father are all doing well this morning.'

The press photographers mounted their tall ladders and we all waited for the next chapter in the story to unfold. It was still unclear when the royal couple would leave the hospital but by mid-afternoon, there had been telltale signs: the arrival of the car seat, and the fact that Amanda Cook Tucker, the Duchess's hairdresser, had sneaked inside. Next came the first pair of grandparents – in a London taxi. Carole and Michael Middleton have seen a few media circuses in recent years but the scale of this one clearly took them aback. They had arrived by simple black cab at around 3 p.m. As they emerged after spending just over an hour inside Carole Middleton described her grandson – her first grandchild, and the future king – as 'absolutely beautiful,' and said that his parents are coping 'fabulously'. She added, 'They are both doing really well, and we are so thrilled.' Asked what the first cuddle with her grandson was like, Mrs Middleton, who had been ushered forward by her husband, Michael, to speak to the press, said: 'Amazing. It's all coming back.' When asked by waiting media if she and Michael had suggested any names for the third in line to the throne, she replied, laughing: 'Absolutely not!' Michael, beaming with pride, said nothing, just smiled before ushering his wife into a waiting taxi. She had been so excited she had walked straight past it.

Prince Charles and his wife, Camilla, followed them at 5.30 p.m. after being rushed to London by helicopter following two days carrying out official duties in Yorkshire. Before mounting the hospital steps, the smiling Prince of Wales asked journalists, many of whom had been standing outside St Mary's for almost three weeks: 'Have you been there long?' When he left around 10 minutes later, Charles said the baby was 'marvellous' then added, tantalizingly, when asked what his grandson was like: 'You'll see in a minute.' It was the signal that the new prince and his parents were about to leave; the cat was well and truly out of the bag.

Soon afterwards Kensington Palace confirmed: 'Her Royal Highness The Duchess of Cambridge will be discharged this evening… The Duke and Duchess of Cambridge and their son will travel home to Kensington Palace. Their Royal Highnesses would like to reiterate their thanks to the hospital for the care and treatment they have all received.' With that the couple and their tiny son left with huge cheers ringing in their ears, to spend a couple of days relaxing, bonding as a family. As they left, palace officials confirmed for the first time that they would not be engaging a nanny; instead, they will rely upon their families for help. 'They have both got families that will care hugely for this baby.' From the reaction of spectators and media alike, they have families – and an entire nation as well.

CHAPTER 21

'BOY GEORGE'
HRH PRINCE GEORGE ALEXANDER
LOUIS OF CAMBRIDGE

'To make sure he has a good upbringing, to keep him out of harm's way, and make sure he has fun. The rest of it I leave to the parents'.

PRINCE HARRY, ON HIS MISSION AS AN UNCLE IN HELPING
TO RAISE HIS NEPHEW, PRINCE GEORGE

Seven days elapsed before Prince William's name was announced after his birth in 1982. Clearly keen to stem the media circus surrounding the royal birth 31 years later, he and Kate would not keep the world's media waiting that long. As William prepared to drive his new family from the hospital, the BBC's unflappable royal correspondent, Peter Hunt, asked him whether he would name his son George in line with the bookmakers' predictions. The Duke laughed and said: 'Wait and see... We're still working on a name so we will have that as soon as we can.' First, however, the couple had to initiate an historic meeting between Her Majesty Queen Elizabeth II and her first great-grandson and third in line to the throne. It had been almost 120 years since a reigning monarch had met a future king three generations ahead, and she was 'thrilled' to meet the latest addition to her family. This time, however, there would be no cameras or television reporters shouting out questions. This after all was the sovereign, and such behaviour just would not do.

The Queen made the short journey from Buckingham Palace to Kensington Palace in a dark green Bentley to meet her great-grandson for the first time. It was just after 11 a.m. on 24 July as she arrived and was photographed sitting in the back seat by Jeremy Selwyn, a veteran staff lensman with the *London Evening Standard*. Within minutes my report under the banner headline 'Queen Drops in on Great-Grandson' was splashed with Jeremy's photograph across the front page of the respected 187-year old newspaper. Meanwhile, inside the palace, William, Kate and the baby were awaiting Her Majesty's arrival. Prince Harry, a proud uncle now pushed down the line of succession to fourth place due to the arrival of his nephew, waited too.

William and Kate already had a few names in mind. But given their little boy's status and what he represented they wanted to be sure their choice met with the monarch's approval. She would not make suggestions – it is not her style – instead leaving the choice of name to the parents. But, as many prime ministers and advisers had learned in the past, the slightest raising of an eyebrow from Her Majesty would be enough indication that the couple might like to think again. There are no formal rules when it comes to picking a royal name; like Britain's constitution, they are well understood but unwritten. Traditional names are considered good, especially for a child in the direct line of succession who will one day reign. After all, royal names come to define much more than an age, for they also stand for values – like the Victorians – or architecture, like the Georgians.

When Peter Hunt had pressed them about the name George, the royal couple had appeared to flash a knowing glance at each other and give a slight chuckle before William said that naming his son was still a 'work in progress'. Huge sums of money had been wagered at bookmakers on everything from the sex, weight and date when the royal baby would be born. Now there was only one bet left: what would he be called? George was the bookmakers' favourite at odds of 7/4, ahead of James (4/1), Alexander (8/1), Henry (12/1) and Louis (12/1). It would be, after all, a name that would be a clear and touching tribute to the Queen's father, George VI – as, indeed, would Albert, for the late King's original names had been Albert Frederick Arthur George, and he had been known to his family as Bertie. George was also one of the seven names of Edward VIII, who abdicated the throne. He had been christened Edward Albert Christian George Andrew Patrick David, but was known to his family by the last of these. William's father, the Prince of Wales, had been christened Charles Philip Arthur George. Perhaps it is not surprising that his bride, Lady Diana Spencer, mixed them up while taking her wedding vows.

The Queen, who was due to travel to Balmoral for her traditional annual holiday two days later, stayed for 34 minutes. An hour and a half after her departure the Cambridges left too. Less than 24 hours after returning to Kensington Palace from hospital they were on the move again, this time to stay with the Middletons at the family home in Berkshire. The new parents drove away in a Range Rover at 1p.m., with Prince George in the back, strapped safely into his car seat. An hour later they arrived at the £4.8 million Georgian mansion recently bought by Kate's parents in the leafy village of Bucklebury, where Carole Middleton had been busy redecorating a 'nursery-style' room for her first grandchild. According to officials, the Duke and Duchess just wanted 'private time together, like any new family', adding, 'They just want to get to know their son.'

Yellow police cones showing 'no waiting' symbols lined both sides of the road every few yards for around a mile either side of the Middletons' majestic Bucklebury Manor, a substantial estate set in 18 acres of land and boasting its own tennis court, swimming pool and library. A bright yellow notice stuck to a road sign confirmed an emergency three-week bylaw prohibiting any form of waiting in the road, while a pair of police officers stood at both entrances to the Grade II-listed Georgian mansion, and marked police cars swept past the entrances every couple of minutes. A large police horsebox marked 'Mounted Section' arrived in the picturesque village at lunchtime, and a small marquee surrounded by marked and unmarked police cars was visible in a nearby field.

But there was still no name.

Then, at 6.18 p.m. on 24 July, Kensington Palace issued its last royal baby statement. It was the final piece of the jigsaw. Under the headline 'The Duke and Duchess of Cambridge name their baby,' it read: 'The Duke and Duchess of Cambridge are delighted to announce that they have named their son George Alexander Louis. The baby will be known as His Royal Highness Prince George of Cambridge.'

It is a name synonymous with the British Crown since the German-speaking Hanoverian first King George took the throne back in 1714. Since then, five other Georges have ruled over the British Empire – the most famous, George III, went mad, leading to the era known as the Regency, and was on the throne 59 years, 96 days, making him the longest-reigning king and third longest-reigning sovereign behind his granddaughter, Queen Victoria, and our current monarch, Elizabeth II. The last King George – the Queen's father, George VI – had died aged just 56 as recently as 1952. As said, his first name was actually Albert and he was known to his family as Bertie, but he selected George – his fourth name – to use as sovereign to honour his father, George V.

As well as the monarchy, the name is also strongly associated with England, as St George, a fourth-century Christian martyr, is the country's patron saint and gives his name to the country's flag. It represents honour, bravery and gallantry. The legend of St George slaying a dragon and rescuing an innocent maiden is medieval, dating from long after the saint's time. Despite all this, however, the baby's parents declared that they simply like the name George, while aides also insisted that the couple had not named their son after the man who reigned during World War II, but had just liked the name. Whatever the truth, Her Majesty must certainly have approved, for it does, after all, continue a clear family line. The second given name, Alexander, is likely to prove particularly popular in Scotland, where Alexander III is regarded as one of the country's greatest rulers, while Louis is likely to have been chosen in honour of Lord Mountbatten, the Duke of Edinburgh's late uncle and Prince Charles's beloved mentor, who was assassinated by the IRA in 1979.

There has only been one other Prince of Cambridge and he too was called George – although it is unlikely that the Duke and Duchess of Cambridge will want their son to emulate his behaviour. The first Prince George of Cambridge was a grandson of George III and the only son of Prince Adolphus Frederick, the first Duke of Cambridge. Prince George of Cambridge had been born in 1819 and refused to undergo an arranged marriage. He wed a commoner for love after falling for the actress Sarah Louisa Fairbrother, who was said to be a classic beauty and a graceful dancer. They married in 1847, when she was already the mother of two of his children and pregnant with his third. Perhaps it was this story of the royal prince marrying for love that swayed the couple, who after all had done the same.

If they read a little deeper into his life's story, however, they may have had second thoughts. For the first Prince George of Cambridge did not seek the sovereign's approval for his marriage and it was never recognised, meaning that his children were not eligible to inherit royal titles. Miss Fairbrother, who generated much scandal including having a portrait painted in which she showed off her bare legs, was ostracised by the royal family and never given a title either, becoming known by the nickname Mrs FitzGeorge, and this was the surname adopted by Prince George's offspring by her. Yet despite his marriage, George had a wandering eye, and soon after he wed he took up with a mistress, Louisa Beauclerk, who remained his lover for more than 30 years.

He went on to become the second Duke of Cambridge after his father's death. He had been commissioned into the Army and served in the Crimean War in the 1850s. He was promoted to Commander-in-Chief in 1887, and was said to have been a disciplinarian, who believed promotions for Army officers should be based on social connections rather than ability. He died in 1904, and an equestrian statue of him stands in the middle of London's Whitehall. His father, the first Duke – who lived from 1774 to 1850 – was never a Prince of Cambridge, but had been given the title of Duke of Cambridge by his father, George III, in 1801, when he was 27. But that was in a very different age. The Hanoverian sons of George III, who despite his mental frailties, believed to be the result of the blood disease porphyria, was much loved by the people and a loyal and loving husband to his wife, Queen Charlotte, were a louche bunch. Excessive drinkers, womanisers and debtors, they were widely ridiculed for their extravagant lifestyle by cartoonists and popular newspapers of the day.

As Thursday, 25 July drew to a close, it was left to a latter-day fun-loving prince, Harry – the new Prince George's uncle – to have the final say on the royal baby. That evening, with his older brother, sister-in-law and nephew safely away from public view,

Prince Harry faced the cameras waiting outside at a private viewing of a photographic exhibition showcasing the work of his charity Sentebale, which he established in honour of his mother to help vulnerable children in Lesotho, one of the world's poorest countries. He joked that his mission as an uncle would be is to make sure baby Prince George 'has fun', and spoke for the first time about the 'fantastic' addition to the Royal Family.

The Prince, now 28, who had met his nephew at Kensington Palace that morning, said, 'When I saw him he was crying his eyes out, like all babies.' Asked if he had a cuddle, he smiled: 'Of course.' He went on: 'It's fantastic to have an addition to the family. I only hope my brother knows how expensive my baby-sitting charges are.' But what would be his mission as an uncle? 'To make sure he has a good upbringing, to keep him out of harm's way, and make sure he has fun. The rest of it I leave to the parents.' Harry said it was too early to say whether Prince George takes after any member of the family, because 'He is about four days old so I think you can judge that one for yourself. I've no idea.' And when he was asked whether Prince William was up to the job of fatherhood, he replied: 'Of course he is! Hopefully most people are.'

Sentebale, which means 'Forget Me Not' in the local language, was founded in 2006 by Prince Harry and his friend Prince Seeiso of Lesotho to help improve the lives of thousands of children in that impoverished country. It provides healthcare and education to those most in need, including children orphaned by the country's HIV/AIDS epidemic. It was Harry's way of carrying on the work of his late mother, Diana, Princess of Wales. In all the brouhaha this amazing woman – prince George's grandmother – who had died tragically in a car crash in Paris in 1997, seemed to have been lost; but not to her sons. They had embraced warmly when they first saw each other after the birth as William introduced his brother to his son.

Had she lived, Diana, a July baby herself, would have just turned 52 at the time of her grandson's birth. His arrival would have been one of the most fulfilling moments of her life, and she would have been perhaps the most glamorous granny ever. She had championed her sons' right to live their lives freely and fully, her primary ambition being to see them content, safe and happy. There is no doubt Diana would have been delighted by William's choice of bride in Kate – a woman he married for love who is his best friend, confidante and lover. The idea of a loving family meant everything to Diana. Helping Kate and William steer Prince George on the right path would have been a joy for her. Additionally, the baby prince shares one vital quality with his paternal grandmother. Like Diana, his star sign is Cancer. 'He will have the psychic imprint of Diana,' says her one-time astrologer Penny Thornton.

It was left to Diana's brother, Prince William's uncle, Charles, Earl Spencer, to speak for their family and describe his joy at the birth of the new royal baby. 'We're all so pleased – it's wonderful news,' Lord Spencer said. 'My father always told us how Diana was born on just such a blisteringly hot day, at Sandringham, in July 1961. It's another very happy summer's day, half a century on.'

If Diana had taught her elder son anything, it was to stand his ground. Yes, he had duty and obligation that came with the role; but this new father is not about to be pushed around by anyone. He has always made it clear that he will find his own path in life. Nothing demonstrated this strength of character and purpose better than the manner in which he took charge of they way the birth of his son was handled publicly. He called all the shots – and that is clearly how he intends it to continue.

As the couple gave the world its first glimpse of the future king outside the hospital it was William who dictated proceedings. He ensured Kate was ready before putting them though the ordeal of facing the world's media. He took the lead, he fielded the questions, and – by now a consummate performer in front of the cameras – he did most of the talking. When it was time to leave it was he who took the wheel of the car and drove Kate and their baby boy home to Kensington Palace. It was very much the image he wanted to portray. There was not a chauffeur in sight, a statement that he wanted to enjoy this precious moment in the way that any other family would.

Before the birth, he had also masterminded, along with his SO14 Scotland Yard protection officers, how to elude the hundreds of photographers outside the hospital and get his pregnant wife, now in labour, inside without being seen. Two photographers did give chase as they spotted the convoy at 6 a.m., but William won that battle. Despite photographers' protestations that they would not have taken a shot of Kate in labour, William knew that they would and did not want to give them the opportunity. One security official was so delighted that William's plan had come off he was seen pumping his fist in the air in apparent triumph.

It was William, too, who decided to delay the official announcement of the birth for four hours and ten minutes after the delivery. He also decided not to make what has become a traditional appearance on the hospital steps to tell the world about his new son and how happy he was. When William himself was born, in 1982, he was barely two hours old when Prince Charles, often so awkward in public, emerged happily from the hospital and informed ecstatic crowds outside that the infant had fair hair and blue eyes. But William made sure that the world had to wait until day two. He wanted to make the announcement as a family. That was the image he wanted to portray.

It was, perhaps, a marker put down by the future King that things were going to be different. He wanted to keep his baby son and wife to himself for as long as possible, knowing that little George's destiny would inevitably become, like his, public property. For him it was crucial to keep that shared intimacy for as long as he could before the world could take ownership of him, before the newspapers and the TV channels could have their say.

Royal tradition has its place and has to be respected, but Prince William clearly feels that this modern monarchy not only has to adapt with the times, but help shape them. He has a new, more inclusive way of doing things. That means openly embracing the involvement of Kate's family, whom he has grown to love as his own. In doing so he will help his son – who after all is descended from working-class and middle-class roots as well as from aristocrats, princes and kings – with a middle-class informality, too.

This crossing of traditional, if antiquated, class boundaries was something that *Time* magazine picked up on. Writer Andrew Ferguson said the royal baby's birth represents 'Almost American-style upward mobility, with a British twist: if you work hard and play by the rules, regardless of race, color or creed, you too can marry your daughter off to become the mother of a King.' He also noted: 'It's an oxymoron, this phrase commoner King – a crossing of self-canceling categories, an unnatural hybrid like a jackalope or heffalump… Yet a commoner King is the very thing that burst upon us, and upon Kate Middleton… The future King of England and Defender of the Faith had emerged from a mother who is without a drop of peerage blood. My guess is the boy, quite apart from his personal qualities, will prove an inconvenience to anti-royalists and monarchists alike.' Perhaps that will turn out to be true. But as for William, he seems to have one clear aim: to love and honour his wife and ensure she is happy, something that perhaps also explains why Kate's first visitors, after himself, were her parents, with whom she stayed for weeks before the birth. He was not demoting the Royal Family in doing this – they would understand his reasoning – but in doing so William demonstrated once again that he is his own man.

Certainly, the loss of his precious mother, Diana, when he was just 15, and his determination afterwards to protect Prince Harry gave William a steely independence. He has hand-picked his team of officials – straight-talking Private Secretary Miguel Head and Press Secretary Ed Perkins – and neither would presume to dictate to him in the way the powerful courtiers in the past did to his family and ancestors. He was not about to allow royal duty to overwhelm his family life. Neither will he allow the prying media and outside world to get too close. He will give them what they want on the understanding that when he and his family are off limits, that really does mean off limits. Over-familiarity from members of the press is something he is also keen to eradicate. He knows they have a job to do, but so does he – preparing to be King. That is something he has learned from his grandmother, the Queen.

He knows that if he has an issue he can go straight to the top. The way he handled the problem of guests at his wedding showed that. He made an appointment with the Queen, discussed his concerns and resolved it. It shows his single-mindedness. To some the Queen appeared to be a passive observer in the royal baby story, but she is far more than that. More than anyone, Her Majesty knows that the birth of Prince George has secured her dynasty, up to three generations into the future – perhaps into the 22nd century.

Only a few decades ago in Britain, the public was in republican mood. The press could be blamed for some of the bad taste with which it reported stories, but it could not be blamed for the stories themselves – of royal marriages breaking up, publicly damaging the reputation of the institution itself. Monarchy looked questionable then. Not for the first time the Queen, 87 at the time of this book going to print, steered the monarchy out of the troubled waters. But she cannot be expected to go on indefinitely. Her husband, Prince Philip, suffered repeated bouts of ill health and had exploratory surgery just before the birth of Prince George. It meant he was unable to meet his great-grandchild as he was recuperating at Sandringham, the Queen's Norfolk estate.

She and Prince William have a close, warm relationship. She knew, too, that the best hope for the future of the Crown was for Prince William to marry for love. She encouraged him to do what he wanted to do. Wise after serving in the 'top job' longer than all but one of her predecessors, she could see that, in the modern world, for the monarchy to survive it had to ditch its dated, class-obsessed sense of hierarchy.

She is a woman of her time, an old-fashioned person, a devout Christian – which is the source of her inner strength. She is dutiful to her core, too. But in her own quiet way she has transformed the 'ship' of monarchy and helped steer it into calmer waters. Thousands flocked to Buckingham Palace this week for news of the royal birth, just as millions swarmed into the Mall during the two Royal Jubilees in 2002 and 2012 to thank the Queen for getting it so very right.

My ringside seat in the arena of recent royal history has given me the opportunity to cover all these events up close. In my capacity as a journalist I have met all the key players from Her Majesty to the late Diana, Princess of Wales to Prince William. In time, God willing, I may meet young Prince George, too, as I continue to chronicle the fascinating and fluctuating story of the House of Windsor, as I have done for nearly a quarter of a century.

In that time I have covered the Queen's Golden and Diamond Jubilees, as well as royal marriages – including breaking the news that Prince Charles was to marry Camilla Parker Bowles – and travelled the world reporting on royal tours overseas from Borneo to Sydney, from Fiji to New York. Sadly, I have covered deaths too – including the funerals of Princess Margaret, Queen Elizabeth, the Queen Mother and, of course, when the world stopped with the tragic loss of Diana, Princess of Wales. But for me the birth of a future monarch, Prince George, edges them all. There was a real buzz of excitement. The world's modern media went into overdrive. Within minutes of the birth I appeared on top-rated TV shows across the globe from NBC's *Today Show* to *Sunrise*, the top morning show in Australia, where this little boy may one day be king – unless there is a change in the constitution Down Under. The scenes outside the Lindo Wing as the news came were truly memorable and historic. Loud cheers and smiles – not just from royal fans but from hardened newsmen and seen-it-all police officers too.

Yet what does all this mean for the Royal Family – already at its most popular for a generation? What kind of monarchy will this young prince one day inherit as King George VII? It is a global institution that has far-reaching influence over almost a third of the world, as the Queen is currently Head of the Commonwealth. Her Majesty is not only Queen of Great Britain but of 15 other realms too, including nations such as Australia, Canada and New Zealand who, to greater or lesser degrees, have flirted with republicanism for some time. William and Kate are expected to travel to Australia and New Zealand at the earliest opportunity – 2014 has been pencilled in. Just as Prince Charles and his Princess, Diana, did, William and Kate are expected to take their little boy with them too. There they will be enthusiastically received by huge cheering crowds. But it is unlikely to stem republican sentiment for long Down Under. Like Britain, Australia and New Zealand are now multicultural countries. Monarchy might seem out of step as the years pass.

It follows, therefore, that Prince George of Cambridge will be raised to be a monarch who will have much less influence on a world stage. It will then be up to him to redefine his reign and role. Unlike our Queen – the daughter and heir of the last Emperor of India, George VI –William and Kate's son will have to content himself as sovereign probably of Britain alone, by the time he ascends to the throne in perhaps more than 50 years time. This little royal baby is descended from coalminers as well as kings. He will need to be adaptable, someone who like his truly 'great' great-grandmother, Queen Elizabeth II, has learned to change with the times.

But for William and Kate, the prince and the commoner who fell for each other as undergraduates at St Andrews University, this was not just about baby Prince George's destiny or duty to come. It was simply about their love for him and the joy of becoming parents. They are a natural couple, clearly in love. As William proudly held his son in his arms with his beautiful wife at his side, they were the perfect picture of happiness – the 'New Royal Family' for a new generation.

CHAPTER 22

THE NEW ROYAL FAMILY
PRINCE GEORGE:
'THE REPUBLICAN SLAYER'

*'I think he is a republican slayer. He is just so cute
and William and Kate are such a lovely couple.'*

TV HOST AND REPUBLICAN SHELLY HORTON ON
AUSTRALIA'S TOP BREAKFAST SHOW, *SUNRISE*

It was to be the most significant royal tour for a generation.
Even in the frenetic days of the late Princess Diana, the media
interest was not this intense. The accredited media contingent
from across the world for the New Zealand leg of the two-
country tour Down Under in April 2014 alone was 450-strong.
The numbers would swell even greater when they reached
Australia. The sense of anticipation and the enormity of the tour
seemed to have got to the couple themselves. Privately, they
admitted they were unnerved by what lay ahead. Even their key
staff at Kensington Palace, who had helped to prepare the
schedule, had consciously downplayed the expected size of the
crowds that would greet them when they stepped off the plane.

New Zealand's Prime Minister John Key, a savvy former
banker, privately revealed that, although the cost of the visit
could be more than NZ$500,000, the exposure his country
would get in terms of branding and tourism while the royals were

there would be worth every penny. His prediction was to prove spot on. Television crews from US programmes such as ABC's *Good Morning America* and NBC's *The Today Show*, as well as teams from Japan, Germany and of course Australia, would be beaming images and reports of William and Kate back home. They were clearly a global phenomenon.

As we'll see, Prince William, Kate and baby George would be the stars of this show, and in the weeks that followed all three would demonstrate what, when deployed appropriately, an incredible asset they could be if the monarchal system was to survive and maintain its relevance in the Commonwealth realms. They would prove in their three-and-a-half-week tour – more of which later – to be a symbolic embodiment of what is good about Great Britain PLC and, of course, the wider Commonwealth.

The anticipation had been more intense because the wider public had hardly seen anything of Prince George since the moment his mother had carried him from the hospital. Apart from a few officially released photographs, one taken by Kate's father Michael, the new third in line to the throne had been kept under wraps. While William served out the reminder of his service as a search and rescue pilot before eventually bowing to the inevitable and quitting operational military service for good in September 2013, Kate divided her days between her parents' Berkshire home and Kensington Palace. A nursery was established at the Middletons' 18-acre estate so their daughter could focus on the early days of motherhood cushioned by her family.

William said publicly that he wanted to be a 'hands-on' father and he would not take a job that required him to be away from his young family. His 'transitional year' – as the palace described it – would give the future King a chance to develop his role, to work out what causes he wanted to throw his considerable celebrity and influence behind. Kate, as far as the palace was concerned, did not have to overcomplicate her role. She, courtiers said, was on maternity leave for the foreseeable future. With their London home, Apartment 1A Kensington Palace, now complete, she could focus on being a wife and mother; royal duties could wait.

The first significant moment in the Cambridges' diary was their son's Christening on 23 October 2013. It would be the first time the wider public would get a glimpse of the elusive George. Even then, it was a very low-key event. Everything ran to Prince William's timetable. The guest list, too, had his stamp all over it for what was arguably the most private christening of a future king or queen in memory. Just five senior members of the Royal Family had been invited. William's uncles the Duke of York and the Earl of Wessex and aunt Princess Anne were among those who had been left off the list. This meant the Cambridges could invite close friends instead. Zara Phillips, William's cousin, however, did attend, as she was chosen as a godparent.

The couple's choice of the Chapel Royal at St James's Palace as the venue for the ceremony meant the guest list had to be kept down to fewer than 50, meaning there would not have been room for close friends if the couple's various aunts, uncles and cousins had all attended.

The only senior members of the Royal Family who were there, apart from Prince George and his parents, were the Queen, the Duke of Edinburgh, the Prince of Wales, the Duchess of Cornwall and Prince Harry. They were joined by the Duchess's parents, Carole and Michael Middleton, and her siblings, Pippa and James.

It was in stark contrast with William's own christening at Buckingham Palace in 1982, on the day of the Queen Mother's

82nd birthday. Then, a large crowd had gathered outside the Palace and the Queen Mother appeared on the balcony before the ceremony. This time it was a closed event.

Show-business photographer Jason Bell was selected to take the historic photographs at Clarence House, including one of the three direct heirs, Princes Charles, William and George, the first time such a picture had been taken since 1899, when an 80-year-old Queen Victoria posed with her direct successors, Edward VII, George V and Edward VIII. This time, the Queen, then 87, is pictured with her son the Prince of Wales, then 64, grandson the Duke of Cambridge, then 31, and three-month-old great-grandson Prince George.

Once again, William had demonstrated he was his own man, not afraid to stick to his guns on matters concerning his immediate family, just as he had over the organisation of his wedding. He showed he was not afraid to let his hair down when on royal duty – singing on stage at a charity bash with Taylor Swift and Bryan Adams and high-fiveing the rapper Tinie Tempah at the 2014 BAFTAs. His critics have claimed this type of behaviour cheapens the royal brand. But he clearly does not see it like that. Stuffy protocol and enforced formality are anathema to William. If people don't bow or use his correct title, it does not worry him as it would other members of his family.

But it's a fine balance – and on occasion his image took a battering. When he spoke out against elephant poaching and said he would like to destroy all the ivory housed in Buckingham Palace, it ruffled feathers. Even his father, Prince Charles, thought it was naïve and told him so privately. The exchange was not heated but the point was made firmly by Charles. Art critics, too, warned against destroying historic pieces, of which there are more than 1,000 items in the royal collection, including an 1851 ivory throne gifted to Queen Victoria from India.

William was also accused of inconsistency by the media in February 2014 as a result of his decision to go wild-boar hunting in Spain, the weekend before he joined his father at a London symposium to speak out against the illegal wildlife trade.

His mother's former royal protection officer, Ken Wharfe, who watched over the Princess for eight years, said the timing of his hunting trip was unfortunate. 'From my experience, royal courtiers would have had prior knowledge of the Spanish visit,' he says. 'Failing to advise against the boar shoot is symptomatic of the sycophantic culture that surrounds the royal princes.' William did not seem particularly bothered by the criticism – just as he did not seem unduly concerned that some people are surprised he is not paying the full amount for a specially tailored agriculture crash course at Cambridge University, despite possessing a huge personal fortune.

Then, just weeks after Kate had returned from a lavish break on the Caribbean island of Mustique with her parents, with George but without her husband, she and William were off on another luxurious jaunt, this time to the Maldives. The couple arrived at Cheval Blanc Randheli on Noonu Atoll for a seven-night holiday, while Prince George stayed at home with a Spanish nanny. Packages there, including flights, can cost £6,799 per person. Social media lit up. Was Kate being elfish and uncaring for leaving her baby at home? One mother posted on Mumsnet: 'Seriously? . . . seems it's just one long holiday for the D and D of Cambridge.'

Being your own man is one thing; being immune to criticism is another. Certainly, the Queen would not dream of doing such a thing on the eve of a major tour. For her, one of the most travelled people in the world, holidays have been mainly on British soil. That means Easter at Windsor Castle, Christmas at Sandringham in Norfolk and summers spent at Balmoral,

Scotland. Even Prince Charles stopped taking his annual ski holiday after he started speaking out about the perils of excessive flying and the impact on climate change.

All this made the April tour of New Zealand and Australia even more significant. The palace knew it, and so did the principals. Ahead of the tour, I was among a select group of correspondents invited to Kensington Palace for a drinks reception. It was an upbeat occasion attended by Prince William, Kate and Prince Harry. But, as a taster of things to come, and to the surprise of all the guests, we also met Prince George. His mother carried him around the room. He was in good form and even grabbed my wine glass. He had the room in raptures. The Prince of Cuteness had clearly arrived.

The tour had been planned with military precision. Prince William's fingerprints were clearly all over it. The limited number of evening jobs, the rest days – two in New Zealand – and the use of Wellington as a hub while they were there all showed he was in control. He knew the power of this new Royal Family brand, but, showing his credentials as a future King, he refused to let it be overexposed. Every step had been carefully planned. He also knew that his son and heir, Prince George, would be the focus of the ensuing media circus. That worried him. But he was prepared to make only a few concessions over the little boy's privacy. William was resolute. He was conscious of what the media wanted, but was prepared to play the game only so much. It was a sign of his confidence in his role as second in line to the throne, as well as his role as a father and husband.

CHAPTER 23

GEORGE DOWN UNDER
BABY PRINCE'S
ANTIPODEAN ADVENTURE

*Catherine and I were very grateful for the many kind messages and gifts from
across the country that we received when George was born.*

PRINCE WILLIAM, DUKE OF CAMBRIDGE, DURING HIS, CATHERINE'S
AND PRINCE GEORGE'S TOUR OF AUSTRALIA, 2014.

The baby Prince George began his official royal career on a
chilly, rain-swept military airport tarmac in Wellington. The
eight-month-old future King's first ever official duty was to be
welcomed by Prime Minister John Key. With his bare legs
showing, his mother carried the little Prince from a Royal New
Zealand Air Force flight. Not to be outdone by her son, Kate
showed more than hint of Jackie Kennedy's 1960s style in a
scarlet Catherine Walker coat and matching pillbox hat by Gina
Foster. The Duchess accessorised the outfit with a diamond
brooch in the shape of New Zealand's national symbol, the silver
fern, which was loaned to her by the Queen.

The photo lenses in a crammed media pen for once focused not
on her but the star of this royal roadshow – George. It was his
first public appearance since his christening in October and he
looked relaxed at the attention he was receiving despite his long
flight from the UK. As a future King, he faces a lifetime of official

243

royal engagements, so perhaps having a play date with babies of his own age isn't a bad place to start.

Within days he was to carry out his next official gig – and did his first public crawl – at a baby group held in his honour at the official residence of his great-grandmother the Queen in New Zealand. His mother and father looked on as the little prince played with ten other children at the Governor-General's Wellington home, Government House, organised by a parent support group, Plunket. The Royal New Zealand Plunket Society, known to all as Plunket, was founded in 1907 by the paediatrician Sir Frederic Truby King. He wanted to help babies and mothers dying of malnutrition and disease, and in 1908 the influential Victoria Plunket, wife of the then Governor-General, became its patron, giving the organisation her name.

The babies who met Prince George were born within a few weeks of the new prince's birthday, 22 July. It was the first time he had undertaken a 'public duty', of sorts. Yet again, George was the star attraction. A limited pool of reporters, camera crews and photographers were invited in to record the historic moment. The ten families – who included a single mother and a gay couple – were chosen to meet the young Prince, and William and Kate spoke of their excitement. George, whose first two bottom teeth had recently popped through, showed confidence at interacting with the other babies.

He crawled on the blue, patterned carpet of the Blandor Room, which was full of toys, including building bricks and a xylophone. Gorgeous George – as the local papers in New Zealand dubbed him – was one of the biggest babies there. 'Quite a bruiser,' one onlooker remarked. Dressed in blue dungaree shorts with a ship on the front, a white blouse and soft blue pre-walking shoes, he did not seem worried about taking toys from other children. Mother Kate, wearing a Tory Burch dress, occasionally wiped dribble from George's chin, as Prince William chatted to some of the other parents.

'It's madness – there are babies everywhere!' William said. At one point Kate pulled George to his feet and bounced him up and down.

The idea behind the event was to give William and Kate the opportunity to introduce George to the world in a less formal way than usual. Kate Bainbridge, 29, a tax accountant whose daughter Sophie was born 11 July, said in advance of the meeting, 'I've had a few jealous looks from other parents when they found out we were meeting the Duke and Duchess. We're all first-time parents, like them, so it should be quite easy to chat to them.'

Also meeting the royal visitors were gay couple Jared Mullen and Ryan McRae and their daughter Isabella. Jared, from Oregon in the United States, and Ryan, from Australia, were chosen to represent the growing numbers of same-sex couples in New Zealand who use Plunket's parental-support services.

As the media were invited in, the Duchess was holding George on her hip as the teething prince pulled at her hair and put it in his mouth. He was a lively youngster, waving his arms and kicking his legs in excitement as he spotted the other children with their toys. Kate frequently shifted him from hip to hip, distributing his not inconsiderable weight on her slight frame. The future King then turned to a little girl called Paige, who was with her parents, Jenny Stevens, 34, who is British, and New Zealand dad Mark, 43. George waved his arms to get her attention and touched Paige's face – before grabbing her toy wooden doll. Mother Jenny told the Duchess, 'Paige grabs toys; she's just started teething.' Kate replied, 'George too.' Paige started crying after losing her doll to George and turned to her mother to be comforted, burying her face in her arms.

Kate then stroked Paige's hair in an attempt to comfort her, as

George looked around, bored, waving his arms and indicating he wanted to be put down. Then she gave him a blue plastic block, which George put in his mouth but then threw to the floor. She eventually put him on the carpet and immediately George took off, taking a particular liking to a toy tambourine. Baby Eden, dressed in floral dress and headband, got in George's way and he reached out to stroke her face. Then he reached a little too far and boffed Eden in the face with a flailing arm. She lost her headband in the mêlée but seemed unperturbed. He grabbed at several other toys being held by other youngsters before Kate encouraged him to crawl to her and then pulled him to his feet.

Grant Collinge, 38, and Magda Gurbowicz, 35, met the royals with baby Lucas. Grant said, 'We chatted to the Duke first and asked about how they and George coped with the jetlag. William said sleeping and distracting [the baby] was the best thing to get over jetlag and that's what they'd done with George. The Duchess said George was sleeping well through the night and that he's on solid food now, so that has really helped his sleeping.'

Some enthusiastically compared the charming photographs of baby Prince George crawling to those taken of his father 31 years before. Both sets of photos are touching in their own way. But there is a distinct difference. The shots of William as a baby – nicknamed Wombat by his mother and father – were exclusive. There was no interaction with other children. It was very much an 'us and them' scene back in 1983. Access was restricted and there was not a member of the public in sight. It was lovely, too, but George will be a monarch of a very different time. He will have to be a prince of the people if the monarchy is to have a global influence in the wider realms. And if the monarchal system is going to be relevant to a modern generation – particularly in Commonwealth countries such as New Zealand and Australia, where there are strong Republican movements –

the principal players will have to adapt to modern times and modern demands.

I think the photo call was a brave and bold statement by William and Kate. There was nothing precious about them as a couple. They were confident enough to share George in a public situation – albeit with parents and babies vetted in advance. The images show how Kate's face lit up like any new mother's when she played with her son. They really do paint a picture of happiness. But what I believe is significant about this event is that – as Princess Diana did – Kate and William were clearly showing that they want their son to mix with other people from all walks of life. That can only be a good thing.

It will, in time, prove to have given this special baby – born to a life of duty and privilege – something of the grounding he will need for a life of royal engagements and encounters with the public. George seemed a cheerful little baby, happy to interact and play. He was not fazed by the media attention he received.

The royal aides organising the tour Down Under also deserve some credit for that. This tour had to be handled with care. They, like William and Kate, knew this visit – initially at least – would be all about George.

Then it was on to Australia, and the little prince's next cameo role came in Sydney at the city's famous Taronga Zoo, where the Cambridges had gone to open a new exhibit named in honour of their son: the Prince George Bilby Exhibit. George also got to meet the bilby – a rabbit-like marsupial – that was named after him. But they had to warn keeper Paul Davies about their son's ironlike grip when he threatened to grab one of the ears of the creature, affectionately known as Australia's Easter bunny.

George clearly enjoyed his trip to the zoo and, when he had arrived, carried by his mother, he'd looked on in wonder at the crowd surrounding the enclosure and wriggled his arms and legs in excitement, squealing and gurgling when he spotted his namesake. His parents took turns to hold him in their arms and then to support him as he stood up and held onto a low, clear-plastic fence that surrounded the marsupial's pen. And it seems the young prince was interested only in the real thing, because, when Kate handed him a stuffed-toy replica of a bilby, he threw it to the floor – much to the delight of the crowd and embarrassment of his parents.

'He loves it really,' William said apologetically as his wife bent down to pick up the discarded toy.

Timing is everything, they say. And there is no doubt that, on this royal tour of Australia, the starring role of Prince George had come right on cue. The TV networks and commentators could not get enough of him; even the republicans were impressed. One, Shelly Horton, on Australia's top breakfast show, *Sunrise*, said live on air, 'I think he's a republican slayer. He's just so cute and William and Kate are such a lovely couple.' She certainly hit the mood of the country on the button, as Prince George seemed to put the case for ditching the monarchy in Australia back years.

All the talk was about the impact of the 'Prince of Cuteness' – as they were calling the future king – after photos of him and George the bilby went around the world. Even Geoff Gallop, of the Australian Republican Movement, admitted, albeit grudgingly, live on air on the country's biggest television network that the Royal Family have a 'pretty good' PR machine.

However able the Kensington Palace communications secretary Dr Ed Perkins and his team were in bringing together this one-in-a-generation tour, arranging picture-perfect photo opportunities, this royal renaissance had nothing to do with spin. It was the principals, particularly Prince William, who were driving this unique, new-style royal roadshow. The New Zealand

and Australia visits gave Prince William's 'New Royal Family' a chance to show *his* brand of royalty – a new style for a new generation. The large crowds Down Under were testament to that, providing a warm, genuine and vocal reception for the three royals.

Their tour put clear water between them and the past. All the talk before they went to New Zealand and Australia had been by way comparisons with the Charles and Di tour of 1983. Would Catherine live up to Diana's style? Would the crowds compare? In truth, as soon as they had arrived at Sydney Airport, babe in arms, and wowed the significant guests at the Sydney Opera House, the comparisons just stopped. For me it was a watershed moment.

The young Prince was again the star of the royal roadshow as he was carried down the steps from an Australian Royal Air Force jet by his mother. This time his dad William also got a chance to carry the little prince in his arms, as the Duchess, in a stunning yellow dress – a nod to Australia's national colours – was presented with some flowers.

After a brief welcome at the airport, the royal couple – minus George – went to the Sydney Opera House to be given a rapturous welcome by a huge crowd. The only tricky moment came as the Premier of New South Wales – who was scheduled in the official programme to greet the royal couple there –decided to resign after accusations of being close to a corruption scandal. After stepping out of their four-by-four Jeep, William and Kate walked up the steps to the Opera House admiring the view of Sydney Harbour Bridge. The crowds were screaming to Kate to turn towards them for a picture, which prompted William to touch her hand to usher her to turn around. At that moment she turned and gave one of her winning smiles and the crowds went wild.

Inside, William also spoke about his late mother Princess Diana's love for Australia. He said, 'My mother's deep affection for Australia – which you were so kind to reciprocate – needs no reminder.' He also spoke about his son: 'I don't think I could finish these brief words to you without mentioning one other family member, George, who is now busy forging his own link with Australia. Catherine and I were very grateful for the many kind messages and gifts from across the country that we received when George was born. I suspect George's first word might be "bilby" – only because "koala" is harder to say. We really look forward to our time here together as a family.

'Australia is an inspiring place, as this amazing opera house shows so vividly, and I know that a truly unforgettable few days lie ahead.' The Prince also spoke of the importance of the visit to the Queen. He said, 'The affection that my grandmother the Queen has for this nation is infectious. Her Majesty spoke recently of how, since her first visit here sixty years ago, she has been privileged to witness Australia's growing economy and flowering self-confidence.'

William added, 'For Catherine, Harry and me, born in the early eighties, we've never known anything else – Australia and Australians have always been for us a beacon of confidence, creativity in the arts and sporting ability.'

Almost from the outset, it was clear that this was a different type of tour. The crowds were packed with youngsters, enthusiastically greeting this new royal family. A new younger generation of Australians clearly wants to keep the monarchy. Figures showed that more than 60 per cent of younger Australians – the 18- to 24-year-olds, who were just children when Diana died in Paris in 1997 – wanted William and Catherine as a future King and Queen.

The unsubtle Diana–Catherine comparisons obviously and understandably rankled the principals, just a little. For clearly on this and future 'Cambridge' tours, William, supported by Catherine, will do it his way. The Cambridge brand is a curious hybrid of formality and more populist, photo-led events. The Duke wants to carve out his own style, a distinct style unlike that of his grandmother the Queen and unlike that of the Prince of Wales and his brother Harry, too, and certainly different from the Diana days.

The nature of events on this two-country tour showed William's passion for conservation and his devotion to supporting the military at home and in Commonwealth realms. Evident, too, was support for the couple's own charitable patronages – such as Catherine's for children's hospices. So, while comparisons with the 'Diana days' may irritate, as media push more for similar shots, this couple will continue on their path – and with the blessing of the Queen.

It is all, I was told, part of a considered development by Prince William as he tries to find his style and develop his character and own role. In many ways there is a lot of the 'old-fashioned' in the way they do things, a back-to-the-future monarchy – less Charles and Diana, more the Queen and Prince Philip on their grand Commonwealth tour of 1953–4. Like the Queen – and unlike Charles and even Prince Harry – William did not give any TV interviews on this trip. His words and views were in his speeches, which had become more smoothly delivered, more interesting, more personal in their content.

Grand, formal, 'tiara moment', glamorous events while meeting the 'great and the good' of a country were also subtly avoided. A trip to Royal Randwick racecourse, where the Queen's horse Carlton House was running in the second biggest race in the Australian calendar, was sidestepped, too.

Instead, on a night off, the royal couple took their team for downtime at an evening rugby match. That is not to say that there won't be 'tiara moments' – more formal moments – for Catherine on future tours.

Geoff Gallop, a respectful and erudite man, acknowledged that the republican movement would have to restate its argument. He said that it, too, had to get mainstream political support, something that was not currently on the agenda.

Australian Prime Minister Tony Abbott, a Liberal and staunch monarchist, made great hay during the sunshine this royal visit brought to his country. He was one step behind the royal couple on many of the engagements – introducing them to his favoured Manly Beach in Sydney's northern coastal suburbs, where he still surfs, and joining them for an Anglican Easter Sunday service, despite being a Catholic himself.

But the monarchy should not be complacent. Gallop is right when he says opinions polls are fickle, that they often depend on what questions are asked. Republicans in Australia and New Zealand believe that, if the electorate were asked the question, 'Should we have an elected head of state when the next British monarch comes to the throne?' they would win the argument. The Charles-and-Camilla factor is still an issue. I reported on the royal tour to Australia when Prince Charles and Camilla visited in 2012. The welcome was warm, but much more subdued than this visit.

William, Kate and George inspired the leading TV networks to broadcast live coverage for two hours in the afternoon and it was wall-to-wall coverage on the popular morning shows such as *Sunrise*. I have never in 24 years of covering the royal story experienced anything like it. But, if the monarchy is to remain relevant in a modern, vibrant, cosmopolitan country like Australia, the royals need to be a constant presence – not just a glamorous roadshow every seven or so years. I would argue that the royal players need to spend more time than they do in the Commonwealth countries. Prince Harry's weekend in Australia in 2013 was not long enough. He should spend more time here.

I understand that there is a policy for the star royals to go back to the leading Commonwealth realms every three years or so, although nothing is planned at the time of writing. Supporting the Commonwealth – which the Queen has supported tirelessly since its inception – is clearly the big policy, too, for these new royals. Whether that will be enough for Prince George to be King in Australia and New Zealand one day is doubtful. But, for the moment, those wonderful images of him playing with the endangered bilby at Taronga Zoo with a proud and relaxed mum and dad looking on did the monarchist cause no harm at all. It also established William, Kate and George as the most famous family unit in the world.

There could be no doubt in 2014 that this was a monarchy in transition. The place of Prince William, the Duchess of Cambridge and Prince George in that transition is paramount. But it is important not get ahead of ourselves. The next in line to the throne is the Prince of Wales. His wife Camilla, not Kate, is still in line to become the first commoner, non-aristocrat Queen Consort since Anne Hyde. As we stand almost a century on from the creation of the House of Windsor in 1917, seismic shifts are happening. There has been much talk about Prince Charles effectively becoming King in all but name as his mother takes a step closer to an unofficial retirement.

But a move by Sir Christopher Geidt, the Queen's principal adviser (who, in an announcement that went largely unnoticed, received his second knighthood in the 2014 New Year Honours for 'a new approach to constitutional matters . . . [and] the preparation for the transition to a change of reign') towards a more formal transition, with Prince Charles becoming a King in all but name, has not quite gone to plan. The prince at first went along with plans to merge the royal publicity machine under a new Royal Communications Department, but they encountered problems. Charles, always a deep thinker, went cold on the idea, as some courtiers openly talked of their role as 'kingmaker'. Charles felt the advisers were getting ahead of themselves and he told them so.

Monarchy is all about order and timing. Prince Charles believes that he still has an important role to play as heir to the throne. He believes he is heir until the moment he becomes King, with all the limitations that brings. He made it clear to courtiers in 2014 that he is not prepared to compromise on that relative freedom – spearheading his charities and speaking out on issues he cares about – until his moment to take the top job comes. That said, he will of course support his mother and monarch wherever and whenever she needs his support.

She enters her 90th year in 2015, and there can be no doubt that the level of her work load will be reduced in the coming years and, in compensation, the workload of her son and heir and her grandsons will increase. One senior figure told me it is not beyond the realms of possibility that, should it be needed, the Regency Act, effectively making Prince Charles the King in all be name, could be used. 'Yes, we have dusted off the Regency Act and taken a look at it,' one told me. It is not anticipated it will be needed, as it was in the case of the reign of 'mad' King George III, but it is significant that senior Palace figures have acknowledged that it is a possibility.

That, after all, is the nature of monarchy. Nothing is left to chance.

As for Prince William, he is still developing his role. He is, in effect, the understudy's understudy. Insiders say he is even considering options other than becoming a full-time royal devoted to engagements that his birthright demands. That may prove a step too far, as the need for him to take on more public duties increases with his grandmother's age. He knows more than anyone that the passing of his grandmother will catapult him and his family further into that role – but, as it stands, that day has not arrived. However, it is clear that, when his time comes, Prince William will wish to preside over a modern monarchy, in tune with its time, and he believes that, in the years until that time arrives, he will use his influence to shape it.

The Queen appreciates that William has to find his own path. She is a traditionalist, dutiful to her core, too. But she knows that, for monarchy to survive and be relevant in a modern society, it must be in harmony with the people. She knows that Prince William will transform the institution, too, just as she did in her way.